The Crusades

By the same author

Theodora: Portrait in a Byzantine Landscape

Antony Bridge

The
Crusades

GRANADA
London Toronto Sydney New York

Granada Publishing Limited
Frogmore, St Albans, Herts AL2 2NF
and
3 Upper James Street, London WIR 4BP
866 United Nations Plaza, New York, NY 10017, USA
117 York Street, Sydney, NSW 2000, Australia
100 Skyway Avenue, Rexdale, Ontario M9W 3A6, Canada
PO Box 84165, Greenside, 2034 Johannesburg, South Africa
CML Centre, Queen & Wyndham Streets, Auckland 1, New Zealand

Published by Granada Publishing 1980

Copyright © Antony Bridge 1980

ISBN 0 246 11080 5

Printed in Great Britain by
Ebenezer Baylis & Son Limited, The Trinity Press, Worcester, and London

Granada (R)
Granada Publishing (R,

Contents

List of Illustrations

Maps

Preface

The men and women of the First Crusade set out from Europe to conquer the Holy Land in 1096; the last citizens of the Crusader kingdoms and principalities, which they founded there, were driven into the sea by the armies of Islam in 1291. For just under two hundred years the armed struggle for control of the holy places of the Christian faith, many of which were also sacred to the Moslems, involved men from every nation in Europe as well as citizens of the Byzantine Empire, Armenians, Jews, Turks, Arabs, Egyptians, and Mongols, let alone the native populations of the countries of the Middle East over whose lands the various armies fought each other. Old empires fell into decay, new ones rose over their ruins, and the way of life of everyone involved in the vast struggle was slowly but inexorably changed.

It was truly a war of the worlds: the world of western Christendom, which was emerging painfully from the barbarism of the Dark Ages, came into collision with the immensely civilised world of Byzantium, which had passed its political prime; and both were opposed by the world of Islam in which Arabs, whose culture was built on Hellenistic and Roman foundations, were at variance with Turks from the steppes of Asia with no pretentions at first to civilised manners or standards. These two momentous centuries were also notable for internal religious divisions on both the Christian and the Moslem sides, for as the years passed the Christian participants in the events of the time were divided into two bitterly hostile camps; western Catholics distrusted and despised the Byzantine Christians of the Orthodox Church, and were heartily detested in return by their Greek-speaking brothers and sisters in Christ; while the world of Islam was also split between Sunnites, who acknowledged the authority of the Abbasid Caliphs in Baghdad, and Shi'ites, who gave their allegiance to the Fatimid Caliphs in Cairo.

All this sounds immensely complicated, and indeed it was: so much so that it would be impossible to write a detailed history of it all in one comparatively small volume. But there are many scholarly, comprehensive, and detailed histories of the period, foremost among them being the great three volume *History of the Crusades* by Sir Steven Runciman, and I can see no point in trying to write another. However, apart from an excellent and moderately concise history by Hans Eberhard Mayer, which has been translated from the German, I know of no good short history in English. It has been my aim to tell the story of the Crusades as simply and as graphically as possible in the hope that such a work may prove of interest to the general reader, who has neither the time nor perhaps the taste for weightier and more scholarly studies. The source of material is abundant and readily available, and my greatest difficulty has been to decide what to leave out; but I have had to be ruthless or I should have found myself writing too long a book. I have also had to resist the temptation to analyse the *zeitgeist* of the Crusades. Were they the last barbarian invasion of the civilised Graeco-Roman world? Or the first movements in the vast expansion of western Europe, which culminated in the nineteenth century? Or were they economically determined, as orthodox Marxists would doubtless assert? Perhaps they were all these things, but I have not tried to decide; such speculations lie outside the scope of this book.

Only one thing remains to be said: if the general reader is horrified by the brutality of the times, and if the Christian reader is appalled by what some of the Christians of the day did in the name of Christ, perhaps the horror of the one and the dismay of the other are signs that, despite the wars and barbarities of our own sombre age, people have been changed a little by Christian faith and teaching over the centuries: not changed enough of course, but at least changed a little bit.

Chronology

1154   Nur ed-Din takes Damascus

1155   Baldwin III makes an alliance with the Emperor Manuel Comnenus

1156   Earthquake in Syria

1162   Death of Baldwin III and accession of his brother, Amalric I

1163-9   War against Egypt
   Rise of Saladin

1169   Saladin occupies Cairo as Nur ed-Din's lieutenant

1174   Death of Amalric and accession of Baldwin IV, a leper
   Death of Nur ed-Din: Saladin becomes ruler of Damascus as well
    as ruler of Egypt

1176   Battle of Myriocephalum: destruction of the Byzantine army by
   the Turks

1180   Baldwin IV's sister Sibylla marries Guy of Lusignan
   Death of the Emperor Manuel Comnenus

1182   Reynald of Châtillon's expedition to the Red Sea

1183   Guy of Lusignan becomes Regent during Baldwin IV's illness

1187   Saladin's victory at Hattin, 4 July
   Conrad of Montferrat arrives at Tyre, 14 July
   Saladin captures Jerusalem, 2 October

1189   Guy of Lusignan begins siege of Acre

1190   Death of Frederick Barbarossa in Cilicia

1191   Third Crusade: arrival of Philip Augustus of France and Richard
   Coeur-de-Lion at Acre
   Recapture of Acre by the Crusaders

1192   Assassination of Conrad of Montferrat
   Departure of Richard

1193   Death of Saladin

1200   Saladin's brother, al-Adil, becomes Sultan of Syria and Egypt

1204   Constantinople taken by the men of the Fourth Crusade

1212   Children's Crusade

1218   Death of al-Adil and accession of al-Kamil in Egypt

1219   Capture of Damietta by the Crusaders

1221   Crusaders lose Damietta

1229   Emperor Frederick II of Hohenstaufen regains Jerusalem

1244   Jerusalem lost to the Turks

1249   King Louis IX of France lands in Egypt and captures Damietta

1250 Defeat of the Crusaders at Mansourah: capture of King Louis and his army; ransomed by surrender of Damietta

1254 King Louis returns to France

1258 Mongols capture Baghdad and massacre the inhabitants

1260 Defeat of the Mongols by the Mameluks: Baibars becomes Sultan of Egypt

1261 The Emperor Michael Palaeologus reconquers Constantinople

1268 Baibars captures Antioch

1271–2 Crusade of Edward of England
Krak des Chevaliers submits to Baibars

1277 Death of Baibars: two years of disputes for the succession end with the triumph of Qalawun, commander of the Syrian troops

1281 Mongols defeated by Qalawun near Homs

1290 Death of Qalawun: accession of his son, al-Ashraf Khalil

1291 Acre captured by Khalil, 18 May

I

♣♣♣

The Blanket of the Dark

> Come, thick night,
> And pall thee in the dunnest smoke of hell...
> Nor heaven peep through the blanket of the dark.
> Shakespeare, *Macbeth*

The dark ages in Europe were very dark indeed. They followed the slow destruction of the Roman Empire by barbarians; but Europe was not plunged into darkness all at once. For as Rome had not been built in a day, so it was not destroyed in a day either. However, as wave upon wave of nomadic barbarians from beyond the Rhine and the Danube swept across the Roman world again and again, the fabric of civilisation in the West gradually broke up. By the latter half of the sixth century the blanket of the dark had fallen so completely over the old heartlands of Rome that Pope Gregory the Great actually welcomed a virulent epidemic, which was devastating Italy at the time, as a merciful deliverer from the horrors of everyday life. 'When we consider the way in which other men have died,' he cried in despair, 'we may take comfort from the kind of death which threatens us. What mutilations, what cruelties have we seen inflicted on men, from which death was the only escape, and under which life was sheer torture...All the pomp of the dignities of this world is gone... The Senate is no more, and the People has died, yet sorrow and sighing are multiplied daily among the few that are left. Rome is, as it were, already empty and burning.'

During the centuries which followed, little was done to arrest the process of destruction and decay, except in Charlemagne's time, and much hastened it. Cities were allowed to fall into ruin, fires devastated them, they were damaged by wars, their inhabitants were massacred or wiped out by disease, and they became the haunt of owls; people avoided them for fear of the robbers who sometimes hid in the wreckage of their houses. Other places survived but with reduced populations of a few thousand people where ten times that number had lived in Roman days. At the same time, the great network of Roman roads, which had once bound the world together in prosperity, was neglected; and although the roads themselves proved to be virtually indestructible, they were not proof for ever against pot-holes or the ravages of time and the weather; dust drifted over them in summer and turned to mud in winter, grass and weeds spread over them, and sapling trees sprang up between their paving stones and eventually blocked the way.

In low-lying country, which the Romans had drained and protected from floods behind great artificial dykes, nature reasserted itself; the old earthworks crumbled, and the waters returned to drown thousands of acres of good agricultural land; whole villages disappeared, and a few fen dwellers were left to eke out a precarious and primitive existence by fishing and eating frogs and eels. Elsewhere great tracts of rich farmland, which had been worked in Roman days, were abandoned because there was no one left to till the soil, so drastically had the population been reduced by war and disease. In other parts of the country, remote from any town or village, farms were left to grow thistles and thorn bushes, because in the murderously disturbed state of the country it was too dangerous to live there.

Meanwhile, it is easy to forget that, even in Roman days before the coming of the dark ages, Europe was still a place of vast forests, swamps and open grass land, rather as Canada is today. Packs of wolves roamed the hills and woods of Germany, France and northern Italy; the European bear was commonplace; wild boar rooted for truffles in the outskirts of Paris and on the hills around Florence; while huge herds of deer were to be seen everywhere. As civilisation collapsed, these stretches of wild country encroached more and more upon the old areas of cultivation, pressing man and his works back into pockets of farmland around the remaining towns and villages and the large country houses which had escaped the destruction of the times. Things reached their worst about the year 800 with the advent of the Normans, who were the last of the northern barbarians to sweep down in a great wave of arson, pillage and murder over the already shattered lands of Europe, and thereafter, for the next two hundred years, life became so chaotic and anarchical that it was as much as anyone could do to stay alive.

Towns everywhere were fortified, and those who could do so withdrew at night into the safety of their surrounding walls. Villages clustered around a castle or some other strongpoint for protection, while the owners of country houses turned them into miniature fortresses, digging moats and building wooden stockades around them so that men and women could take refuge with their children and cattle in an emergency; for during this terrible time there was neither law nor order anywhere. Trade had died except for a precarious commerce, carried on mostly by Jews and Levantines, in luxuries such as jewellery, carved ivory, works of art for the nobility and incense for the Church, and each little clustered community was forced to become self-supporting and self-reliant.

Life under such conditions was acutely uncomfortable. Even the local lords owned little but their land, and the castles or fortified houses in which they lived had few if any amenities to alleviate their damp and gloomy discomfort in summer or the freezing misery of their stony halls in winter. The clergy and the monks fared no better, and the peasants lived in squalid and ill-thatched hovels built either of turf or of wattle and daub, which they shared with their domestic animals and any cattle which they were lucky enough to own. Personal hygiene was unknown, and washing was regarded by most people as both unnecessary and effeminate, while some regarded it as positively sinful. One of the things which the civilised Romans had found most offensive in their barbarian conquerors had been their smell, and many of their descendants had not changed their personal habits much since the time of the first barbarian invasions.

Food was nearly always in short supply, for the pressure of population, even though it had been greatly reduced since Roman days, on the small areas of land still under cultivation was incessant, and the poor seldom had enough to eat. Even the nobility had to be content with a rather monotonous diet although, since they hunted over their own estates, they always had plenty of meat, game and fish. There is a description of a meal taken by St Louis, who was an ascetic man and a frugal eater, but apparently did not think it inappropriate on a fast day to dine on eels, crayfish, crabs, beans and bread. Vegetables and fruit were summer luxuries, and potatoes were unknown. In bad years, when drought or floods ruined the crops, there were few reserves with which to stave off famine, and people died; and such years were common. In the century preceding the Crusades there was famine in Europe in forty-eight years out of a hundred.

By this time, new waves of barbarians were no longer the main danger to society, for society itself had become barbarous. War was endemic; every petty lord fought every other petty lord in the district, and there was no central authority strong enough to control them, let alone put an end to their eternal and murderous feuds. War was their business, their pleasure, and their sole occupation except for hunting. A warrior class directly descended from the various barbarians who had conquered the Empire, now dominated its shattered fragments; they owned most of the land, they were masters of the peasants who tilled it for them, and in return they protected them as well as they could from the hazards of the times. They had the virtues of their kind, courage, loyalty to their comrades in arms, and a kind of lyrical appetite for life which made them live their appalling lives with immense gusto; but they were also thugs without much honour, betraying each other without a qualm, lying, cheating, torturing, and killing in a nightmare world of greed and ambition.

If this warrior class of landed nobility dominated the dark ages at their darkest, making life hideous with its perpetual wars, its dominance was challenged by the Church; for collectively the Church was almost as large a landowner as all the secular lords put together, and it also wielded an immense spiritual authority. On the whole, it used its power and exercised its authority wisely, for with all its faults it tried to promote a way of life which it believed would be more Christian than that forced on everyone by the anarchy and brutality of the ninth and tenth centuries. Indeed, by the end of the latter some churchmen were so sickened by war that they started a movement to enforce peace by threatening to excommunicate people who resorted to arms without good cause. Leagues of Peace were formed, massively backed by the clergy, and they became so popular that the castles of some local lords, who refused to join them, were violently attacked by bands of armed pacifists in a splendid paradox of belligerence in the cause of peace.

The attempt to banish war altogether failed, but less ambitious and more realistic endeavours to limit its horrors were more successful; hostilities were forbidden on Sundays and Holy Days, and later still the Archbishop of Rouen proclaimed a Truce of God, which limited private war to three days a week. However, there still remained one outlet for men's natural bellicosity: the Moslems of Spain could be killed by anyone who took the trouble to cross the Pyrenees, not only with impunity, but also with the blessing of the Church and the warm approval of God. Since the slaughter of infidels was regarded as a devout pastime, and since churchmen, although they genuinely tried to promote peace between Christians, were children of their time and products of their society, it was by no means unusual to find bishops and archbishops in full armour fighting side by side with their fellow Christians in holy wars against the enemies of Christ, their episcopal swords red with the blood of unbelievers; if they themselves were killed in battle, they died in the comfortable knowledge that the Pope had guaranteed them absolution and remission of all their sins as a reward for their pious pugnacity.

This was enormously important to them. It has been said that it is in the nature of men to suffer from certain intrinsic anxieties which, if they are not coped with, become the cause of neurosis and make them ill; one such anxiety is that arising from the knowledge of one's own guilt, and another is that resulting from the certainty that one day all men must die. Medieval men were obsessed by guilt, which is perhaps not surprising when the contrast between their deeds and their Christian ideals is remembered, and nothing meant more to them than to be absolved of their sins; for such a prize men would go to astonishing lengths of self-denial and put up with almost any kind of hardship; for the alternative was the certainty that, if they died suddenly and unshriven, they would have to suffer all the torments of hell as conceived in the terrible crucible of the medieval imagination.

They were almost equally obsessed with death, and this too is not surprising; for death was an ever present possibility, not only as a result of the chronic violence of the time, but also from natural causes. In our day the medical profession has banished early death so successfully that, if a child or a young adult dies, everyone is deeply shocked, and even when a man in his early fifties succumbs to a heart attack or a stroke, his death is regarded as tragically premature. In medieval days, however, death was an everyday occurrence, and most people died young; infant mortality was enormous, and the gauntlet of lethal diseases and other hazards run by growing children on their way to maturity was only too effective in thinning their ranks. One Pope, born into a family of twenty-two children, was one of only two to survive to the age of twenty: the rest died; and this kind of thing, far from being unusual or shocking, was completely normal. To cite only a few examples from families which later ruled one or other of the Crusader kingdoms, Baldwin V of

Jerusalem died at the age of nine, Hugh II of Cyprus at fourteen, and Queen Maria of Jerusalem at twenty-one. Even the Holy Roman Emperor Henry VI of Hohenstaufen died as an experienced, much feared, and deeply respected elder statesman at the age of thirty-two.

Everything was a potential killer; a mild infection might take a turn for the worse; a fever, a quinsy, a colic, a burst appendix, or one of a dozen different kinds of growths could carry a man off after a few days' illness; such diseases as leprosy and the plague were scourges which killed millions in their different ways from time to time, and famine took a huge toll with monotonous regularity. Even minor accidents were often the cause of death; men died as a result of falling, from a hunting wound, or were drowned while fishing. Frederick Barbarossa died when he fell from his horse into a stream, although whether he was killed by the fall or by drowning was never determined. Other people managed to kill themselves in a variety of unlikely ways, as when King Amalric II of Jerusalem died as a result of eating too much fish; they were white mullet.

The effect on men's minds of the ever present possibility of sudden death, combined with their obsession with sin and guilt, was to create an atmosphere of radical insecurity, in which they had to live their lives whether they liked it or not; and this had far-reaching effects on the way in which they lived them. The Prophet Isaiah might have condemned such sayings as, 'Let us eat and drink, for tomorrow we shall die,' but they had a very sharp edge to them for people to whom the word 'tomorrow' might mean the very next day instead of some vague and distant date in the geriatric future, as it does to us; nor was feasting the only thing which men enjoyed while they could; they married young, bred families, grasped power, killed their rivals, and acted upon the spur of every passing moment for fear that their moments might be few. In fact, medieval men followed Brutus' advice and took every tide which came their way at the flood, in the hope that it would lead on to fortune before the grave claimed them; and this released great fountains of energy in them, driving them through life in a way which looks at once marvellously vigorous and enterprising and yet incredibly restless and reckless, when viewed from the more leisurely vantage point of our own assurance of longevity. It also made them bewilderingly volatile; at one moment they were loving, chivalrous, noble and filled with the loftiest of lofty ideals, while at the next they behaved with callous and murderous brutality, shrinking from no violence and respecting neither old age nor women and children.

The physical world inhabited by the men of the dark ages was conceived by them in a way so different from our own conception of the world that it is hard for us to recreate it in imagination. Their notional model of the universe, which formed the unchanging background to the landscape of their minds, bore no relationship at all to the mental image of the universe which we carry around in our heads. It is hardly necessary to point out that none of the phenomena revealed to us by the telescopes of modern astronomy were known to them; but, obvious as that may be, it is easy to forget how completely this separated their mental world from ours. First and foremost, they lived in a world which was flat: a world which stretched out around them like some infinitely extended plain towards edges which no man had seen, but which every sane man knew must exist somewhere vastly remote and hidden in the mists of unknown lands. It was both a far bigger and a far more mysterious world than ours: bigger because its distances were measured by the length of time it took a man to cover them, and more mysterious because so much of it was uncharted. Journeys were unthinkably long. A pilgrim to the Holy Land from, say, St Albans or Coutances or Frankfurt might take anything from three to seven years to complete the round trip; we fly from London to Lydda in five hours. That same pilgrim had probably never travelled more than twenty miles from his birthplace before setting out on his marathon journey, and even the next county would have been a mystery to him; he might never have seen the sea, and people speaking a different language from his own would have been almost as strange to him as visitors from outer space would be to us.

But, of course, he would have heard of foreign countries, and he would have soon grown accustomed to the wonders of travel; what never lost its mystery was the huge unexplored portion of the earth beyond the confines of the known world. Rumours of strange beasts and exotic people beyond the eastern borders of Persia, of Indians, Chinese and Mongolians filtered through, mixed with fables of giants and centaurs, one-eyed monsters and people who ate their own children; tales reached him of kingdoms to the south of the dust and heat of the north African deserts, where ivory, gold and precious stones were as common as dirt, and where the land was filled with strange animals, unicorns and camelopards and the biblical behemoth as described in the book of Job, which was probably a garbled account of a crocodile, whose 'strength is in his loins, and his force is in the muscles of his belly; who moves his tail like a cedar tree; the sinews of his thighs are knit together. His bones are as tubes of brass; his limbs are like bars of iron.' But what lay beyond even these unimaginably remote and extraordinary places was wholly unknown, and almost anything was possible. What lay beyond the Atlantic Ocean? Did the rumoured land of perpetual cold and darkness north of the icy mists from which the barbarians had come hold even fiercer races? No one knew. And where did it all end? It was a great mystery, and no one could resolve it.

In fact, the everyday world in which medieval man lived was in some ways more mysterious to him than the next world, to which he knew that he would inevitably go after death, for the main outlines of that future world were perfectly clear in his head and were doubted by no one. Above him was the vault of heaven, where God dwelt in glory surrounded by angels and archangels and all the company of heaven: God who neither slumbered nor slept, and whose ever-watchful eye missed no detail of a man's performance in the mortal race for immortal stakes; his sins, great and small, were inexorably entered in the judgement book of heaven, as were his acts of penitence and virtue. If, when he died, his celestial balance sheet was in credit, he would join the great company of saints and martyrs in heaven; if it was in debit because of an accumulation of venial sins, he would have a chance to put things right by years of pain and penitence in purgatory; but if it was loaded with a great weight of mortal sins, he would undoubtedly go to hell to be tortured by devils, roasted in eternal fire, and subjected to the everlasting suffering reserved for the damned.

This description of the worlds which respectively over-arched and under-girded the great flat plain of the natural world was regarded by no one as an attempt to describe the indescribable in picture language, let alone as a mythological way of speaking of God, man, destiny and choice; heaven and hell were material realities, and every man would go to one or the other of them in the future. Indeed, perhaps the most difficult thing for anyone living in the twentieth century to grasp is that for medieval man the primary reality was not that of everyday affairs, economics and politics, with religion thrown in as an optional extra for the spiritually minded on Sundays and perhaps for a short time each day during the rest of the week; on the contrary, for medieval man the primary reality was that depicted in the mural paintings and stained glass windows of his churches and cathedrals, and his everyday life was lived in the perspective of judgement and eternity.

Only those who, when they were children, were terrified of the dark, or of passing a particular corner on the stairs which had something frightening about it, or of stepping on the junctions of paving stones for fear of some terrible disaster befalling them as a result, only someone with such memories can have any idea, and that only a pale and distant one, of what it must have felt like to be a medieval man. His world was a profoundly frightening and numinous place, transparent to the supernatural; it was a place of miracles, where material things were obedient to the power of spirits, and where a battle between the powers of heaven and hell was in constant progress; evil spirits lurked in wait for the unwary at cross-roads, near the graves of suicides, on the fringes of forests, by standing stones, and in the gaping mouths of great limestone pot-holes and caverns, which obviously led down to the mouth of hell. Changelings, elf-children, werewolves, witches, warlocks and the ghosts of the unquiet dead were feared by everyone; they were the disguised shock-troops of the devil, and they could be resisted only by those who recognised them in time to ward them off by uttering the name of Christ or by making the sign of the Cross, from which they fled in terror.

Fortunately, however, men were not left without heavenly allies in this incessant spiritual warfare going on around and in them; there were guardian angels upon whom they might call in an emergency, and the prayers of the saints worked wonders. Older gods, too, were enlisted on the side of the angels in the cosmic battle; thinly disguised as miracle-working Christian saints, they had sanctuaries in churches built over their old sacrificial altars or beside the sacred streams, wells or ancient trees where they had been worshipped for centuries in pre-Christian times. Young brides who did not become pregnant quickly enough to stifle the fear that they might be barren made little offerings at the shrine of some local saint, or paid their humble respects to a particularly holy image of the Mother of God, upon whom the mantle of some old fertility goddess or that of an even older Earth Mother had fallen; sufferers from chronic diseases travelled miles to seek cures in places where perhaps once Aesculapius or Amphiaraos had been consulted by Romans or Greeks; and at places where there are now wishing wells or fountains into which tourists throw a coin or two, medieval men and women came to pray for help to some ancient indigenous god or *genius loci* who had been worshipped or feared there since stone age days.

This close association of spiritual powers with particular places had its counterpart in their even closer association with particular things. The cult of relics was universal, and although today it is regarded at best with

A king and a bishop on a pilgrimage. One of the main reasons for mounting the First Crusade was to protect the pilgrim routes to the Holy Land. When the Turks conquered Palestine, access to the holy places of the Christian faith became much more difficult than it had been hitherto. The illustration is of a detail from a stained glass window in Chartres Cathedral.

Scala

The Church of the Holy Wisdom, Santa Sofia, in Constantinople. It was built during the reign of the Emperor Justinian and completed two days after Christmas in 537. The minarets are Turkish additions.

Sonia Halliday

Part of the interior of the Church of the Holy Wisdom, in Constantinople. The roundels with the Arabic lettering and the hanging chandeliers are Turkish additions. No photograph, however good, can give any idea of its immensity and its splendour.

Sonia Halliday

suspicion and at worst with derision and contempt, it had its own logic; for if a man today may treasure a lock of hair from the head of his wife who has died, but in whose arms he once knew the creative miracle of love, how much more reasonable was it for a man of the middle ages to treasure a splinter of wood from the Cross upon which the miracle of God's love had once worked the redemption of the whole world? By the same token, he revered the bodies of dead saints, through whom God had once both spoken and acted, the tongue of St Mark, Veronica's miraculous handkerchief, or the robe worn by Polycarp when he was martyred at Smyrna. Indeed, not only were such objects highly prized but, wherever they were to be found, often enclosed in superb and marvellously worked reliquaries of gold encrusted with precious stones, they too became the objects of pilgrimage. Many places owned them. Rome was full of relics, but even Rome could not compete with Constantinople, and thousands of pilgrims to the Holy Land went by way of that greatest of all the great cities of the world (it was ten times larger than any other city of the day) in order to gaze in awe at its unrivalled collection of holy objects. They ranged from the Wood of the Cross, the Crown of Thorns, the Seamless Garment and the Nails of Christ's passion, through such things as the Girdle once worn by the Blessed Virgin and a hair from the severed head of John the Baptist to an abundance of relics of other saints and holy men. Daniel's body had been brought to the city by Constantine's sainted mother, Helena; the bodies of St Timothy, St Andrew, and St Luke had arrived a little later; they had soon been joined by those of Samuel and Isaiah, and in Justinian's day the mortal remains of St Anne had been acquired to swell this stiff and silent company of august corpses.

In a world thus crowded with holy things and holy places, inevitably people came to consider some holier than others; and naturally enough the places where Christ had once worked his miracles and trodden the same ground as that still trodden by sinful man came to be rated as the holiest of all. To visit them, to stand where Christ and his apostles had once stood, and to gaze with reverence and awe on the hills and olive groves, the lakes and little streams, cities and villages which they had known in their lifetime was to enter into a mystical contact with them which had a quality of immediacy about it that nothing else provided. So a kind of geographical hierarchy of sacred places slowly developed. Compostela in Spain, where the body of James the Great, brother of John and son of Zebedee, was treasured, ranked next to Rome where St Peter and St Paul had lived and died, and Rome ranked second only to Jerusalem and the other holy places of Palestine; to make a pilgrimage to such places was everyone's deepest desire, and to satisfy it a man was willing to put up with almost any degree of hardship and danger.

But there were limits. There came a point, even in the ages of faith, beyond which many men were not prepared to go in order to travel to Jerusalem, however much eternal merit such a pilgrimage might earn them on the day of judgement. It had been a terrible shock to the whole of Christendom when Jerusalem had fallen to the armies of Islam in 638, but in the event its Moslem conquerors had proved to be surprisingly tolerant of their Christian subjects. In fact, some Christians there greatly preferred life under their new rulers to that which they had had to endure for centuries under the Byzantine Emperors, who had not only taxed them heavily, but had often persecuted them for their heretical beliefs: heretical, that is to say, according to criteria accepted in Constantinople but disputed in Palestine, Syria and Egypt. At least the Moslems allowed them to believe what they believed and to worship as they thought fit. They also allowed pilgrims from the West to visit the great shrines of their faith without let or hindrance, and the number of Christians coming to pray in the Holy Sepulchre, on the Mount of Olives, or in Justinian's Church of the Nativity in Bethlehem increased steadily as the years went by. Sometimes the journey proved difficult and hazardous, as when an Englishman named Willibald took seven years to do the round trip in the early years of the eighth century, and sometimes the eastward flow of pilgrims was interrupted; pirates infested the Mediterranean at the height of the dark ages in the ninth century, and a mad Caliph made life hideous for everyone at the end of the tenth; but for the most part the Moslem authorities encouraged pilgrims and protected them.

This comparatively happy state of affairs came to a sudden end on 19 August 1071. The Seljuk Turks, a race of nomadic shepherds from the steppes of central Asia, who had been converted to the faith of Islam during the course of the great westward migration forced on them by pressure of population upon the limited resources of their old Asiatic pasture lands, had been growing in power for many years. In 1055 they had entered Baghdad by invitation of the Caliph there, and from that time they had become masters of an empire which stretched from central Asia and southern Russia to the northern borders of Syria. Here they came into contact with the Byzantine Empire; there were skirmishes on the frontier in which people on both sides were killed; little unofficial wars blazed up when tribes of Turkish nomads wandered with their flocks and tents over the border into the uplands of Anatolia in search of pasture, and came into conflict with the Byzantine farmers and land owners whose homes they thus invaded; and with the inevitability of a Greek tragedy the two powers were drawn along a collision course which could only lead to the destruction of one or the other. It was the Byzantine army which was destroyed, in August 1071, in a battle at a place named Manzikert near Lake Van in what is now eastern Turkey; and after its destruction there was nothing to stop the Turkish shepherds from pouring across Anatolia.

It was a shattering disaster for the Byzantine Empire, and it closed the roads across Asia Minor to western pilgrims to the Holy Land. If Christians in the West still wanted to visit the land where Christ had lived and died, they would either have to travel by sea, or help their fellow Christians in the East recover the lands they had lost. They were well accustomed to fighting the Moslems in Spain, both in order to rescue Christian lands from infidel rule, and also in order to gain credit with God for defending the Christian faith against its enemies; it was inevitable that the idea of a holy war against the Turks to rescue the holiest of all the holy places of Christendom from their evil domination would soon occur to someone, and indeed it did. The Crusades were the outcome.

II

♣♣♣

The Invincible City

I dream'd in a dream I saw a city invincible to the attacks of the whole of the rest of the earth.

Whitman

Constantinople was built by the Emperor Constantine on the site of the ancient city of Byzantium, and renamed after its founder. It was dedicated as the new capital of the Roman world on 11 May 330, and it was destined to stand there, invincible in a dark and hostile world, for over a thousand years until 29 May 1453, when eighty thousand Turks under Mehmet the Conqueror poured through a breach in its walls, defended by no more than seven thousand exhausted men. Again and again during its long history, while the West went down into chaos and darkness, it had been attacked by enemies of all kinds, both barbarous and civilised; but although Huns, Goths, Slavs, Bulgars, Arabs, Russians, Saracens and Seljuk Turks might wash against its huge and forbidding walls in a black tide of men and horses, invariably they broke upon them; and it was not until Mehmet and his Ottomans blew a hole in them with a new invention called gunpowder that at last Constantinople fell to an enemy attacking the city by land. It is no wonder that the Byzantines themselves called it 'the city defended by God'.

Edward Gibbon, the greatest and for a long time almost the only English historian of the Byzantine Empire, said that its history was 'a tedious and uniform tale of weakness and misery'. There has seldom been a more monumentally mistaken or prejudiced historical judgement; it deserves to take its place in any collection of the world's great lies. The truth is more complex. Byzantine history, far from being tedious or uniform, is a fascinating and varied tale of glory and humiliation, of great strength interspersed by periods of weakness, of deep and genuine religious faith mixed with a peculiarly Byzantine brand of urbane cynicism, and of high intelligence shot through with elements of gross superstition; through all of which the Byzantines remained a profoundly civilised people.

After Constantine's day the eastern half of the Empire, with its new capital on the Bosphorus, managed to withstand the attacks of the barbarians who destroyed the West; it lost much European and north African territory in the process, and its own lands were invaded and devastated from time to time, but it managed to throw the various invaders out again and kept most of the eastern Balkans under its control. Syria, Palestine and Egypt also remained firmly Roman, as did a small and important outpost in the Crimea. Two hundred years later, during the reign of Justinian, a great counter-attack was launched against the barbarian conquerors of the West; Italy and Sicily were taken back, and so was most of north Africa and some of Spain, but these victories were won at so great a cost in blood and treasure that, when Justinian died, the Empire was overstretched, and most of the territory which had been regained was lost again. There followed a period of great danger and difficulty; Slavs and Bulgars poured across the Danube, over-running the central Balkans and Greece, while the fanatical and apparently invincible armies of the new religion of Islam swept everything before them in the East; Egypt, Palestine, Syria and Mesopotamia were lost, and twice Constantinople itself was completely invested by the Arabs, while much of Asia Minor fell to their arms. But incredible as it must have seemed at the time, both to their enemies and to the Byzantines themselves, the Empire was nowhere near its last gasp. Its citizens could still draw on great reserves of strength, both moral and military, in their determination to resist the attacks of their Moslem enemies, 'godless spawn of Hagar', as the Emperor Nicephorus Phocas once described them, 'sons of dogs, slanderers of the *Logos* of God, disciples of the false prophet, who eat the unclean flesh of camels,' and their greatest period was yet to come. About a hundred and fifty years after the last abortive Arab attempt to take Constantinople by force, in the mid-ninth century when western Europe was beginning to experience its darkest and most anarchical time of brutal hopelessness, Byzantium, led by a series of great warrior Emperors, launched a triumphant counter-attack against the Moslem world in the East and the Bulgars and Slavs in the West. The Empire expanded again, and for the next two hundred years Byzantine civilisation flowered as it had never flowered before; once again it was universally recognised as a world power second to none, and it was only the insidious growth of certain internal weaknesses, combined with the coming of the Seljuk Turks, which eventually reduced its power again in the period immediately preceding the Crusades.

Even this thumb-nail sketch of a thousand years of Byzantine history reveals how important a role was played by the city of Constantinople itself in Byzantine civilisation and its survival, and this is proof enough of Constantine's genius in choosing the place as the site of his New Rome. Built on a triangle of land bordered by the Sea of Marmara on one side and the Golden Horn (the world's most perfect harbour) on the other, once the great wall which ran from sea to sea at the landward end of the triangle was completed by the Emperor Theodosius II in 413 and further strengthened after an earthquake in 447, Constantinople became the strongest place on earth. But it was not only from the military aspect that Constantine's choice of Byzantium was inspired; it was a stroke of genius from the point of view of trade and economics too, for the city lay at that point where Europe was separated from Asia only by the narrow waters of the Bosphorus, and whoever held Constantinople controlled all movement both along and across that waterway. Thus the city was the mistress of the great east-west caravan routes along which the silks, spices and jewellery of China, India, and Persia reached the western world, and it also lay across the north-south trade routes along which furs, salt-fish, and slaves from the steppes of Russia travelled down through the Black Sea to reach the Roman world. Inevitably, as the centuries went by the city became vastly rich.

It was a cosmopolitan place, and by the standards of the day it was enormous. At the height of its power and prosperity in the ninth and tenth centuries, the population of the city was probably about three-quarters of a million, and perhaps more if people living in the suburbs are added to that number. Later, at the time of the First Crusade, its inhabitants may have been fewer, but probably more people still lived in Constantinople at that time than lived in the whole of England during the same period.

The Byzantines were a multi-racial lot. Indeed, almost every race on earth was represented there from pure Greeks and Romans who could trace their ancestry back a thousand years through illustrious lines of Senators and Patricians, to people whose racial origins may have been Armenian, Syrian, Cypriot, Jewish, Gothic, Slavonic, Turkish or Arabic, but who all spoke the same language, and who all regarded themselves as good Byzantines; for the Byzantines had much the same genius for making people of different racial origins into good Byzantines as the Americans have shown in making people of Polish, Russian, Italian, German, Hungarian, Jewish, English and Irish stock into good Americans. Only once for a short time was there a colour-bar in Byzantine society, and that was in the fourth century, when the safety of the state seemed to be menaced by a racially distinct, under-privileged minority of Goths, who were used as household slaves, and who were employed in the dirtier and least lucrative civic jobs; for a while the ordinary Byzantines were so frightened of a Gothic uprising that anyone with fair hair, a pink and white skin and blue eyes was regarded as being not only a political menace to the fabric of society but also a racially inferior type of human being. But this ethnic xenophobia did not last long, and the Goths were eventually accepted and absorbed into the body politic like all the other minority groups which went to make up the Empire.

Three things welded them all together, and made them primarily and proudly Byzantine; they all spoke Greek, they were intensely conscious of being citizens of the Roman Empire, and they shared a deep and passionate Christian faith. It may seem odd that a race of people speaking nothing but Greek should have thought of themselves as Roman citizens, but the Roman Empire had been a melting pot for the races of mankind from its earliest days, and Greek had been the *lingua franca* of the eastern half of the Empire since before Roman days; not only had Greeks colonised that part of the world for centuries, but Alexander of Macedon had adopted a deliberate policy of Hellenisation throughout the enormous realm he conquered; so Greek had become everyone's second language in the cities of the Near East, rather as English became everyone's second language throughout the sub-continent of India in Anglo-Indian days. It was inevitable, therefore, once the centre of gravity of the Roman world moved eastwards from the banks of the Tiber to the shores of the Bosphorus, that eventually Greek would replace Latin as the language of the Empire.

But the fact that they spoke Greek did not diminish the Byzantines'

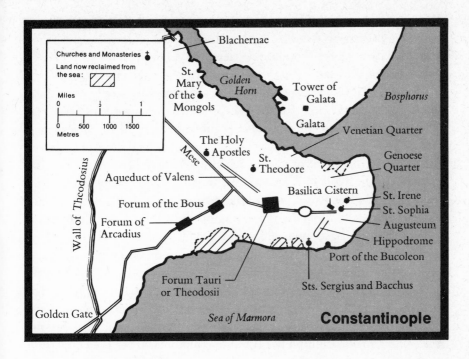

Constantinople

Map labels:

Churches and Monasteries
Land now reclaimed from the sea:
Miles
0   ½   1
0 500 1000 1500
Metres

Blachernae
St. Mary of the Mongols
Golden Horn
Tower of Galata
Bosphorus
Galata
Venetian Quarter
The Holy Apostles
Mese
St. Theodore
Genoese Quarter
Wall of Theodosius
Aqueduct of Valens
Basilica Cistern
St. Irene
St. Sophia
Forum of the Bous
Augusteum
Forum of Arcadius
Hippodrome
Port of the Bucoleon
Forum Tauri or Theodosii
Sts. Sergius and Bacchus
Golden Gate
Sea of Marmora

awareness that they were the heirs of Rome, and this was a source of enormous pride. Indeed, it is difficult for us to imagine what it must have felt like to know oneself to be a Roman in the world of the day. Some of us are proud to be English or French or American or what-have-you, but few of us would claim an exclusive right to patriotic pride: we recognise the right of other people to be proud of being German, Spanish or Russian. But to be Roman in Byzantine days was to be a citizen of the one great and eternal nation, which had become synonymous with civilisation itself; Rome was civilisation, and civilisation was Rome; the two were coterminous; outside the frontiers of Rome there was darkness and barbarism, while inside for nearly two thousand years the heritage of Greece with its arts and its literature had been lovingly preserved, law and order had been brought to a multitude of races of mankind, and the treasures of Christ and the Christian Gospel had been saved from destruction by the powers of darkness, which reigned supreme in the non-Roman world. To be Roman was not only to be civilised in a quite unique way, it was also to be a defender of everything civilised in a world where civilisation itself was increasingly threatened by black tides of chaos and disorder.

3

In most respects, the Byzantines could not have been more different from the people of western Europe, but in their Christian faith they resembled their western contemporaries closely. For them too the primary reality was not the everyday world of secular living but the world of religion; in fact, to be a Byzantine was to be passionately religious almost to the point of obsession. Religion was their favourite topic of conversation, an endless cause of enjoyable argument, the stuff of their hopes, dreams and perspectives, the heart of their politics, and even the concern of their foreign policy; for very much as Moscow today assumes that if a country can be won to Communism it will automatically become an ally and a friend of Russia, so the Byzantines assumed that if they could convert the pagan Bulgars, the Avars or the Russians to Christianity, they too would have won allies and friends. Indeed, such mass conversions of entire peoples were sometimes the subject of diplomatic treaty, as when the Grand Duke Vladimir of Kiev in Russia promised to become a Christian himself and to convert his people to Christianity in return for the hand in marriage of a Byzantine Princess named Anna, who was the sister of the then Emperor, Basil II. From a political point of view, the result was a major triumph for Byzantine diplomacy, for the conversion of the largest Slavonic state in the world to Christianity brought it permanently within the sphere of Constantinople's influence; indeed, it had even more far-reaching consequences, for as the peasants of Kiev were driven into the dark waters of the Dniepr to be baptised, whether they liked it or not, Holy Mother Russia was born in its own peculiar and inimitably Russian way. What poor Princess Anna thought of the bargain is not recorded, but it is unlikely that she was very pleased; Vladimir, her husband, was an uncouth barbarian who had already accumulated such a prodigious number of concubines that his contemporaries described him as a *fornicator immensus et crudelis*, which could hardly have encouraged her to look forward to a life of marital bliss.

But despite the depth and sincerity of their Christian faith (or perhaps because of it), the Byzantines generally took a pessimistic view of mundane affairs and prospects. They were far too conscious of their own civilised isolation in a sea of barbarism to be anything but urbanely cynical about their long-term chances of escaping the fate which had already overtaken the western Empire. Like some of our own contemporary intellectuals, who do not rate very highly the chances of our civilisation surviving the threats to which it is exposed, the Byzantines were fairly sure in their well-mannered way that one day even the city defended by

God would succumb to the surrounding darkness; for they did not reckon that it was God's way to bolster up the kingdoms of this world for ever, even though their own was ruled by the vicegerent of Christ on earth, the Emperor, head of both Church and State.

The term 'Caesaro-papism', which was coined to describe the role of the Byzantine Emperors, exactly defines their unique position; they were in the fullest sense both Caesars and Popes, and no one questioned their right to such a dual autocracy. They lived in the Sacred Palace in Constantinople. This was a great complex of buildings which had been built by various Emperors over the years; it was more like the Kremlin in Moscow than Buckingham Palace or the White House, for as well as residential quarters of great magnificence for the Emperor and his court, banqueting halls, throne rooms, halls of State, and the *gynaeceum*, where the Empress alone reigned supreme over her ladies in waiting and personal maids, there were also churches, administrative buildings in which the business of government was conducted by members of the vast Byzantine bureaucracy, and quarters for the Palace Guard. The whole was built around gardens and fountains on hilly ground overlooking the Sea of Marmara and the Bosphorus, where the Sultan Ahmet Mosque now stands; and the world had been ransacked for its beautification. Inside, the main buildings were of extraordinary magnificence, with mosaic floors, inlaid marble walls, painted and gilded ceilings, hangings of tapestry or silk carpets from Persia, ceramics from China and furniture of ivory, silver and even gold. The Emperor and his court were dressed with equal splendour. The old days of the loose Roman toga had gone long ago; the men wore straight, long-sleeved tunics originally copied from the robes of Chinese Mandarins, stiff as boards with embroidery and encrusted with precious stones, while the women wore silk, were painted to the nines, and glittered with every kind of superb jewellery.

The effect of all this magnificence on visitors was stupendous, as of course it was intended to be. There is an account of an audience granted by the Emperor Constantine VII Porphyrogenitus in the tenth century to the ambassador of the German Emperor, Otto I. The ambassador's name was Liudprand, and later in life he became Bishop of Cremona. He was received in audience in one of the great halls of the Palace, where a choir was singing as he was ushered into the imperial presence by two eunuchs; the floor was strewn with ivy, laurel, rosemary and rose petals, which scented the air as they were crushed under the feet of the courtiers, and the Emperor was seated on a great golden chair known as the Throne of Solomon. It was, in effect, a highly ingenious mechanical toy. As Liudprand approached and prostrated himself before the Emperor, as he had been instructed, the machinery of the throne went into action; a pair of golden lions roared, some little golden birds sang, and Constantine was slowly and majestically lifted up on high as the seat upon which he was sitting propelled him towards the ceiling. The effect upon the future Bishop of Cremona is not recorded, but similar performances are known to have deeply impressed visiting barbarians to the Byzantine court; and later, when the first Crusaders arrived in Constantinople, even though they were shocked by what they chose to consider the effeminate luxury and manners of their civilised hosts, they too were overwhelmed by their magnificence.

Another aspect of life in Constantinople which shocked the Crusaders was the ubiquity of eunuchs. They were everywhere, but they were to be found especially in the enormous civil service by which the Emperors governed the Empire; indeed, some of the most senior and powerful posts were by long established custom open only to eunuchs, who had one great advantage over other men from the Emperors' point of view: they could have no dynastic ambitions. Other men in positions of great power might be tempted to plot on behalf of their children; eunuchs by their nature could not do so, and so they were safer than other people as Ministers of the Crown. Moreover, they were often very able men. The widespread idea in the West that a eunuch is invariably a fat, sly, lazy, scheming, untrustworthy, cowardly, epicene and unmanly monstrosity is wholly untrue; in Byzantine days, they often proved themselves to be highly intelligent, brave, hard working, and as open and honest as any other human being. Eunuchs became generals of distinction, admirals of the Byzantine fleet, and statesman of the highest calibre. Indeed, they were so highly respected that it was not unusual for parents to have one or more of their sons castrated in infancy in order to better their chances of attaining high office when they grew to maturity.

If Byzantine society gave eunuchs a good chance in life, few societies have given women a better chance of making their mark, and few societies have produced more remarkable women than those to be found in the annals of Byzantine history. This was at least in part a result of the way in which the heirs to the Byzantine throne sometimes chose their future brides by organising an Empire-wide beauty competition, and then marrying Miss Byzantium 771 or whatever, although on one occasion

the winner lost her chance of becoming Empress by returning too pert
an answer to a question put to her by the Emperor; but it was also a
result of the way in which their rights were protected by law. As
Christians, the Byzantines had every theological reason to treat women
with as much respect as men, and when they failed to do so, as inevitably
sometimes occurred, Byzantine women seldom lacked a champion in
high places to fight their battles for them. The Empress Theodora,
Justinian's wife, who could scarcely have begun life in humbler circumstances, and who made a living for a short time as a strip-tease dancer and
a part-time courtesan, nevertheless after her marriage became one of the
most remarkable Empresses in Byzantine history, and a staunch defender
and champion of other members of her own sex.

Other Empresses were little less remarkable as people, although not
always as attractive as Theodora. An Athenian girl of great beauty and
unlimited ambition, Irene by name, who married the Emperor Leo IV in
the eighth century and long outlived her husband, ruled the Empire with
such an unquestioning and unquestioned authority that she insisted upon
being referred to as Emperor rather than Empress. There was talk at one
time of the possibility of her marrying Charlemagne, and it was said that,
even though she was fifty years old at the time, when his ambassadors
came to Constantinople to discuss the matter she greeted them in her bath;
but the story is – alas – unlikely to be true. Yet another girl of the humblest
possible origins, a certain Anastasia who changed her name to the more
aristocratic Theophano upon marrying Romanus II in the tenth century,
was quite as remarkable as any former Empress, but remarkable for the
depth of her infamy rather than for any virtue, of which she showed not
the slightest trace. She was suspected of poisoning both her father-in-law,
the Emperor Constantine VII Porphyrogenitus, and her husband, but
probably she was innocent of their deaths. There is, however, no doubt
at all that she murdered her next husband, the Emperor Nicephorus, with
the help and connivance of her lover, who succeeded his victim and
became the Emperor John Tzimisces. Meanwhile, she had had two sons
by her first husband, and they eventually grew up to become Emperors
in their turn; so that, at the end of her life, this lethal female could claim
to have been the daughter-in-law of one Emperor, the wife of two more
(one of whom she murdered in the coldest of cold blood), the mistress of
another, and the mother of yet two more. It is a remarkable record even
by Byzantine standards, especially since at least four of the Emperors in
her life were as great as any in Byzantine history.

But, of course, not all Byzantines lived in court circles or in circumstances of great splendour; outside the Sacred Palace nearly three-quarters of a million people pursued their daily lives in circumstances as varied as in any other city at any other time in history. Some were rich, and lived in luxurious houses built around central courtyards, where there were little gardens ornamented with statues of pagan gods and nymphs and cooled by fountains, while others lived in small crowded houses with balconies overlooking narrow streets in the older districts of the city. But Constantinople was a spacious place, and everywhere there were public squares, gardens, parks, orchards, and even fields and olive groves. Around the main square of the city, which had been named the Augusteum by Constantine in memory of his mother, the Augusta Helena, were built the Sacred Palace, the Hippodrome, the Senate House and the great Cathedral Church of the Holy Wisdom, Santa Sophia, and from it the main street of the city, the Mesê, ran its splendid marbled way three miles or more to the Golden Gate in the great wall of Theodosius. It was a great shopping street; goldsmiths, perfumers, silk merchants, furniture makers and other craftsmen selling goods of all kinds had their shops in colonnades on either side, and the life of the city could always be seen there, for the Byzantines spent more of their time out of doors than we do. The *beau monde* mingled with peasants in from the country for the day to sell their wares; civil servants, soldiers off duty, children playing in groups, workmen cleaning the streets of animal dung, lawyers, tourists on holiday and, above all, monks and priests were always to be seen in the streets, gossiping with their friends or going about their business. The clergy were ubiquitous, for Constantinople was supremely a city of churches and monasteries, and the monastic ideals of poverty, chastity and obedience to the will of God were seen by many Byzantines as great and necessary counter-balances to the imperial splendour of the Court. A popular monk or hermit sometimes became as much an idol of the people as any pop star or football favourite of today, and the throne of an unpopular Emperor could be shaken by the words of a half-naked ascetic living a life of extreme austerity in a cave in the hills of Cappadocia far more effectively than it was usually disturbed by the more conventional plots of ordinary political opponents nearer home. In fact, the Church was very much a power in the land.

But not all Byzantines lived in Constantinople. In the provincial cities life was much the same as that in the capital, although it was less exciting; but in the country it was so much duller that the owners of the great landed estates spent as much time in Constantinople as they could, leaving the country to the peasants who had no choice but to stay there. Since land was the best investment throughout Roman history and during the whole of the Byzantine period, there was a permanent tendency for these large estates to grow larger, and this was a dangerous process; not only did the power of the great landowners grow at the expense of the government in Constantinople, which they very often threatened, but they also progressively expropriated the small independent freeholders, who had always produced much of the Empire's basic wealth, and who had always filled the ranks of the Byzantine army when called upon to defend the Empire from its enemies. This was especially true of the sturdy peasants and countrymen of Anatolia, that great expanse of fertile country and rolling steppe, which seems to stretch for ever and ever from the Aegean coast in the West to the borders of Syria and Mesopotamia in the East. So Emperor after Emperor did his best to curb the power of the big landowners and protect the interests of the peasants and small-holders of Asia Minor, but it was uphill work, and small independent farmers became rarer and rarer; their children emigrated to the towns, a few lacklustre serfs worked the land for absentee landlords, and the Emperors were forced to fill the army with mercenaries.

It was a process which increasingly weakened the Empire, but it was nothing to the weakness which resulted from the disaster that overcame the Byzantine army at Manzikert, when the soldiers of the Emperor, nearly all of them mercenaries, were routed by the Seljuk Turks, who then swarmed across Anatolia with their tents and their cattle and their families and occupied the very heartland of Byzantine power. It had happened before, and always the invaders had been expelled, and the Empire had eventually recovered its old strength and glory. The Byzantines had no doubt that by the grace of God the Seljuks would be expelled in due course too; but in the meantime the Empire needed military help to reinforce the grace of God and, with the armies of Islam triumphant again throughout the East, the only place to which the Emperor could turn was the West.

The Emperor whose unenviable task it was to try to restore the fortunes of Byzantium after the catastrophe of Manzikert was Alexius I Comnenus, who was both an able man and a brilliant diplomat. He did not appeal to the Christians of the West to help him restore the fortunes of his own Empire, nor did he ask them directly to help him turn the Turks out of Asia Minor, which was almost certainly his true concern; instead

Captions for following pages

The walls of Constantinople. They were built by the Byzantine Emperor Theodosius II in 413, and remained unbreached for over a thousand years until 1453 when the Turks captured the city. The men of the Fourth Crusade attacked the much less formidable sea wall from the Golden Horn. Over the years these walls have been extensively damaged by earthquakes, and neglected by the Turks.

Sonia Halliday

St Mark's in Venice was a copy (though not an exact or slavish one) of the Church of the Holy Apostles in Constantinople, which had been rebuilt on the site of an earlier church by the Empress Theodora in the sixth century. It is a splendid example of Byzantine architecture at its best.

Picturepoint

This is almost certainly a portrait of the Byzantine Emperor Alexius I Comnenus, who welcomed the leaders of the First Crusade to Constantinople. He needed all his reserves of diplomacy, which were great, to deal with them, and to send them on their way before they could cause too much trouble. This mosaic is in the Church of the Holy Wisdom in Constantinople.

Sonia Halliday

he appealed to the Pope in Rome to help him rescue the Christians of the East and their churches from the tyranny of their Moslem conquerors. It was intolerable that they and the holy places of their faith, to which so many pilgrims had travelled in the past, should now be crushed under the oppressive heel of infidel Turks, he said, and his words were destined to evoke such a response in the hearts and minds of ordinary men and women throughout western Europe that its history and that of the world was to be changed by them. But it was to be changed in a way very different from that envisaged and hoped for by the Emperor Alexius.

III

♣♣♣

When Beggars Die

When beggars die, there are no comets seen;
The heavens themselves blaze forth the death of princes.
                                        Shakespeare, *Julius Caesar*

The Pope to whom the Byzantine Emperor appealed for help was Pope
Urban II. He was an impressive man, who had been born in Châtillon-
sur-Marne of a noble French family. He had become a monk at Cluny
before he was thirty years old and Cardinal Bishop of Ostia before he was
forty; then, in March 1088, when he was about forty-six, he had been
made Pope.

He could not have ascended the throne of St Peter at a more difficult
time; the Papacy and the German Emperor had been locked in a power
struggle for years, and at the time of Urban's election the Emperor
Henry IV was having very much the better of it. There had been a
celebrated incident, in the days of one of Urban's predecessors when the
Emperor had been forced to wait humbly, bare-foot and dressed in the
clothes of a penitent, in the courtyard of the Castle at Canossa in order to
receive absolution from Pope Gregory VII, who had excommunicated
him; but those days were gone, and the tables had been turned with a
vengeance. Henry was triumphant everywhere; he was supported by an
anti-Pope (a failed candidate in the papal elections) who reigned supreme
in the city of Rome itself, and he had no patience with Urban, whom

he regarded as an obstinate man. Indeed, it had not been long since he had imprisoned him in Germany for his stubborn support of Pope Gregory.

Now Gregory was dead, and Urban brought to the task of reasserting the power of the Papacy a formidable array of talents which were destined to redress the balance between himself and the German Emperor. He was gentle, firm, courteous and peace loving; he hated bloodshed, avoided controversy, and won people's hearts by a combination of forbearance and innate authority, so that he had not been Pope for five years before he was acknowledged by everyone to be the spiritual leader of western Christendom. Having won the western Church, he turned eastwards in an attempt to improve the strained relations which existed with the Byzantines. Alexius responded warmly, and it was not long before the two men were, at least by correspondence, firm friends. As a result, Byzantine ambassadors were despatched by Alexius to Urban's first great Council, which was held at Cremona in March 1095, and there they explained on the Emperor's behalf the plight of Christians in the East under Turkish domination. The assembled bishops were deeply shocked, and so was Urban. It is almost certain that it was at Cremona that he first began to think of calling upon the Christians of the West to rally to the aid of their eastern brothers and sisters in Christ, but for the moment he did nothing. He was a cautious man, and he needed time to develop the idea which had occurred to him.

By November of the same year, he had made up his mind. He travelled in a leisurely way through France, occupying himself with various affairs of the Church which needed his attention, and eventually he summoned the bishops of France and its neighbouring countries to a Council at Clermont. Over three hundred bishops assembled there on the eighteenth of the month, and for the first few days they concerned themselves with routine business of one kind or another: King Philip of France was excommunicated for adultery and the Bishop of Cambrai for simony, the Truce of God was reaffirmed and urged on everyone, and the seniority of the See of Lyons over two rival Sees was established. Then, just before the Council was about to end, Urban let it be known that he wanted to make an important announcement before everyone went home, and that he would do so in public session on Tuesday, 27 November.

The crowds which assembled that day to hear what the Pope might have to say were so great that room could not be found for them in the

Cathedral where the Council had met hitherto, and a platform for the Pope to stand on was erected in a field outside the eastern gate of the city. Amongst his many talents, Urban had a gift for oratory, and on this occasion he used it to the full; his audience listened to him spellbound. Christians in the East had appealed to him for help, he told them; the Turks were advancing into Christian lands, maltreating innocent men and women and desecrating their churches. This was bad enough, but the desecration of Jerusalem with its multitude of holy places and the appalling indignities and brutalities to which pilgrims to the Holy Land were being subjected, was even worse. It was time for Christians in the West to rise up in righteous wrath and march to the rescue; let them stop making war on each other at home and wage a holy war against God's enemies instead. God himself would lead them, and give them the victory, and to all who died in battle he, Pope Urban, promised there and then absolution and remission of all their sins. Why were they wasting their lives in sin and misery here, when they could be finding happiness in this world and salvation in the next as soldiers of Christ in the land where Christ had lived and died? There must be no delay; the time was ripe for action, and when the summer came, the armies of Christ must be mobilised and ready to move.

It was heady stuff, and the response was immediate and overwhelming. There were cries of '*Dieu le volt*'–'God wills it'–as people gave vent to the emotions which Urban had aroused in them The Bishop of Le Puy, a man named Adhemar, fell on his knees before the Pope and begged to be allowed to join the expedition to the Holy Land; a Cardinal began to say the *Confiteor* in a loud voice and thousands joined in, and when it was over Urban gave them absolution, and told them to go home and pray about what he had told them, dismissing them with his blessing. Nor was their departure the signal for a return to normal life and the end of their enthusiasm; on the contrary, the Pope had started something even greater than he could have expected, and great waves of enthusiasm spread out from Clermont across the whole of France to spill over into all the western European countries and set their people alight. Everywhere, bishops, priests and monks began to preach a holy war against the Turks in order to liberate the Holy Land, and no one did so with greater effect than a little monk on a donkey.

Peter the Hermit, as he came to be called, was a small, middle-aged man with a dark, unsmiling face almost as long and lugubrious as that of the donkey which he always rode. He wore nothing but an ancient and indescribably dirty monk's habit and a hermit's cloak, and his bare feet had not been washed for years. He would eat neither bread nor meat, but lived on a diet of fish washed down by wine. Apparently, he had tried to make a pilgrimage to Jerusalem in the past but he had been ill-treated and turned back by the Turks, whom he had hated ever since. He had the demagogue's power to move men by his words, and those who heard him said that he seemed to speak with an almost divine authority, so that wherever he went men and women followed him. During the first months of the year 1096 he travelled through northern France, preaching as he went, and thence through Lorraine down the Meuse valley to Aachen and Cologne, which he reached in Holy Week before Easter with about fifteen thousand followers. A few were unemployed or impoverished knights, including a man named Walter Sansavoir who was to play a leading part in subsequent events, but most of them were either poor peasants or the drop-outs and riff-raff of medieval society, of whom there were many. In Germany, Peter's preaching attracted several thousand more people, until he probably had between twenty and thirty thousand followers, although exact numbers are difficult to determine for contemporary records are invariably greatly exaggerated.

His success was extraordinary, but it was at least in part due to the hardness of the times. Plague had stalked Europe since 1083, floods had swept through France and Germany in 1094, ruining the crops, and the next year had brought drought; famine had been the result. During periods of famine in medieval days, men and women were sometimes driven to terrible lengths in order to survive. Glaber of Cluny, writing earlier in the century, described how, in a time of famine, sometimes travellers, putting up for the night at some local inn, would have their throats cut, while they were sleeping, by their hosts who would eat them the next day. A recluse living by a church in the Forest of Chatenay had buried the remains of forty-eight people, whom he had killed and eaten, before his crimes were discovered. Even in years when the crops did not fail, the pressure of population on resources was so great that in the country there were always hungry, landless peasants who were out of work, while most towns had large populations of beggars with no means of supporting themselves and nowhere to live. Even the Truce of God had made life more difficult for some people, for not only were the knights, whose one occupation had always been making war on each other, out of a job, but the men who had been their mercenaries in the old days of unlimited killing now tried to keep alive by roaming the countryside in bands, pillaging and robbing everyone in their desperation. They were so common in the country round Brabant that they became known as Brabaçons, although they were by no means confined to the Rhineland. Peter the Hermit's appeal to join the armies of Christ and to march with him to the conquest of Jerusalem was irresistible to such people, many of whom in their simplicity probably thought that they were marching towards the promised New Jerusalem of Christian hope, that city of gold and jasper where men 'shall hunger no more, neither thirst any more; neither shall the sun light on them, nor any heat; for the Lamb which is in the midst of the throne shall feed them, and shall lead them unto living fountains of waters; and God shall wipe away all tears from their eyes.'

No medieval city was equipped to feed or house twenty thousand visitors, and Cologne was no exception. In any case, many of Peter's followers were impatient to be on their way to Jerusalem, and so a few days after Easter Walter Sansavoir and several thousand Frenchmen decided to move on. They took the road up the Rhine and thence down the Danube to Hungary, which they reached early in May. The ruler of Hungary, a certain King Coloman, did not regard them as an army to be feared but rather as a crowd of armed pilgrims to be helped wherever it was possible, and he allowed them to pass through his country and did his best to provide for them on the way. All went well until they crossed the frontier into Byzantine territory near Belgrade, where the local military governor was taken by surprise by their arrival; the harvests were not ripe so early in the year, the markets had few provisions for sale, and as the pilgrims began to get hungry tempers became frayed. Some stragglers robbed a bazaar in the small Hungarian frontier town, through which the main body had already passed, and were caught by the authorities, who stripped them of their arms and clothing and sent them naked to join the others at Belgrade. These had already begun to pillage the countryside for food, and when the military governor sent troops to restore order several of the Frenchmen were killed, while others were burned alive in a church where they had gone for safety. The resulting situation was explosive, but order was restored, and Walter had the sense to move his men on towards Nish as quickly as he could; there, food was at last found for them, and the anger of the Crusaders subsided. After that, all went well; the newcomers were discreetly escorted by Byzantine troops when they continued their journey, and they reached Constantinople without further trouble in July.

Meanwhile Peter the Hermit had left Cologne with a far larger number of armed pilgrims in his train, including a number of German knights and younger sons of noble families, and was marching towards the Hungarian frontier along the same road as that taken by Walter and his men, while some of his disciples stayed behind to recruit yet more Germans for the armies of Christ; foremost among these was a certain priest named Gottschalk, as was a man named Emmich, Count of Leisingen, of whom much was to be heard in the near future. Peter was also greeted with kindness by King Coloman of Hungary, and all went well until he reached the little frontier town where Walter's men had fallen foul of the authorities and been stripped of their arms These were still hanging on the town wall for everyone to see, and it was not long before wild rumours about how cruelly their owners had been treated began to spread through the great unwieldy crowd; hostility towards the Hungarians flared up, and a quarrel over the sale of a pair of shoes turned into a riot, which soon became a pitched battle. The town was attacked by Peter's men, the shops and markets were looted, and four thousand Hungarians were killed. Then, and only then, frightened of King Coloman's reaction to the events of the day, they began to try to cross the River Save into Byzantine territory.

The local military governor, who had failed to cope with the arrival of Walter's men a few weeks earlier, was at an even greater loss to know how to deal with Peter's much larger army of angry followers. They were too numerous for him to bar their way, so he decided to retire to Nish and there summon as many reinforcements as possible; meanwhile he left some Turkish mercenaries behind with orders to try to delay them as they began to cross the river. It was a hopeless task, and when the wretched Turks tried to intervene they were captured and killed. News of the fighting caused a panic in Belgrade, where everyone fled to the mountains leaving the city open to Peter's men, who entered it without opposition, sacked it and set it on fire; then, loaded with provisions looted from the city's markets, they marched for a week through the huge oak forests of Serbia until they reached Nish.

On arrival, they asked permission to buy some more food, and the governor agreed willingly enough, only demanding hostages for their good behaviour in return. These were given by Peter, and once again all went well for a time; but at the very last minute, when the army was marching away from the city, some Germans who had fallen out with some of the local people set fire to some mills by the river. The military governor immediately sent troops to attack the departing Crusaders, and a pitched battle began. Peter hurried back to restore peace, but before he could do so his whole army turned in fury and attacked the town. They were beaten off by the garrison, but they returned to the charge, and this time the Byzantine governor ordered his whole force to engage them. The Crusaders were more of a mob than an army, and they were no match for professional soldiers; they were completely routed. Many of them were killed, many more with their women and children were captured, and Peter, who lost his money-chest in the battle, fled in a panic with about five hundred other people up a mountain, where he and his companions believed themselves to be the only survivors of the disaster. But the next day several thousand others joined them and, as the days passed and they marched to Sofia, more and more stragglers caught up with them, until it became evident that they had lost only about a quarter of their men. It was bad enough, but it could have been much worse.

After that, their journey went quietly enough, and they passed through Sofia without trouble. The Greeks were friendly and kind to them, and the Emperor Alexius sent Peter a message of welcome; they had suffered enough. Peter was overwhelmed with gratitude, and the rest of the journey to Constantinople was finished without any trouble. On arrival, however, Peter's men made such a nuisance of themselves, thieving like magpies, breaking into houses and palaces alike and even stealing the lead from the roofs of churches, that Alexius was constrained to move them across the Bosphorus into Asia as soon as possible. He did not think much of them as a fighting force, and he advised them to await reinforcements from Europe before engaging the Turks; having done his best to warn them of the dangers ahead of them, he moved them to a large military camp named Cibotos on the Asiatic shore of the Sea of Marmara not far from Nicomedia. There they were joined by Walter Sansavoir and his men as well as by some Italians who had arrived independently. On the way to this camp, for some reason the Germans quarrelled with the French and renounced the leadership of Peter the Hermit. In his stead they chose an Italian nobleman named Rainald, and when they arrived at Cibotos they were not on speaking terms with their fellow Christians from France. It was not an auspicious beginning to the campaign against their enemies.

Alexius had been wise to move them away from Constantinople; they were both undisciplined and ungovernable, and as soon as they reached their destination, ignoring the Emperor's good advice not to take any

4

aggressive action until they had been reinforced, they began to raid the countryside. At first they did not venture very far into Turkish held territory, contenting themselves with robbing and pillaging the nearby villages, which were easy prey; it did not seem to occur to them that the unfortunate villagers were all Greek Christians, whom they had ostensibly come to help, and worse was to come. In September a large force of several thousand Frenchmen took more decisive action, marching inland as far as Nicaea, which was the capital of the local Turkish Sultan, although he happened to be away at the time. They did not dare attack the city itself, but they attacked the villages in its suburbs, stealing all the cattle they could find and killing and torturing the Christian villagers with almost incredible savagery, and roasting their babies on spits. A small force of Turks which sallied out of the city was easily driven back again, and the Frenchmen then returned to Cibotos loaded with booty and immensely pleased with themselves.

The Germans and Italians were not to be outdone, and at the end of the month they planned an expedition of their own. Six thousand of them set out under the leadership of Rainald in the general direction of Nicaea, plundering and looting as they went but, unlike the French, sparing any Christians whom they met on the way. They succeeded in capturing an unoccupied castle called Xerigordon, and decided to use it as a base from which they could raid the surrounding countryside; but they had been there only a very short time when a large Turkish force appeared, and the Crusaders were forced to take refuge in the castle, which the Turks immediately surrounded. Unfortunately for the beleaguered men inside, the only water supply in the area was from a spring in a little valley outside the castle walls, and they were soon driven mad by thirst. A contemporary chronicler described how they 'were so tormented by thirst that they drew blood from the veins of their horses and asses, and drank it. Some pissed into the hands of others, who drank it. Many dug into moist ground and lay down, spreading the earth over them to allay their parching thirst. This lasted eight days.' At the end of those eight days, Rainald decided to sue for terms of surrender, but the Turks would promise nothing except to spare the lives of those who abjured their Christian faith. Rainald had little option but to accept, and he and a few others who renounced their Christianity were sold into slavery; everyone else was killed.

News of the disaster, when it reached Cibotos, created something very like panic. Peter the Hermit was away in Constantinople, and in his absence the remaining leaders hurriedly met to take stock of the situation; they included Walter Sansavoir and two German noblemen who had not accompanied Rainald to Xerigordon. The wiser heads among them were in favour of caution; there was no point, they argued, in rushing out headlong to attack the Turks; it would be better to wait in a strong position which could be easily defended and to let the Turks come to them. For the time being, they prevailed, but a few days later news came that the Turks were advancing on the camp in strength, and the hot-heads in the army, of whom there were many, led by a young Frenchman named Geoffrey Burel, insisted that it was sheer cowardice to sit idly in camp while the enemy approached at his leisure. Cries of 'Cowardice!' always arouse strong and irrational emotions, and Burel and the other fire-eaters had their way; towards the end of October the whole army moved out of Cibotos to march against the Turks, leaving only the women and children and a few monks and priests behind.

Three miles outside the camp, the road ran through a narrow valley; there was a wood by its side, and here the Turks, who had been told of the approach of the Christians, hid themselves in ambush. The Crusaders took no precautions; they marched noisily along in a great undisciplined mob, laughing and shouting to one another, with the knights on horseback in the van, and they were taken completely by surprise. A sudden volley of arrows cut them down in swathes; many of the knights' horses were killed under them, while others reared up in terror throwing their heavily armoured riders to the ground and plunging back into the ranks of the infantry behind them, who were thrown into confusion and panic. Before anyone could restore any kind of order, the Turks broke cover and charged in lethal, disciplined ranks into the struggling mass of Christian soldiers, already falling over one another in their haste to escape. The knights who had not been killed by the first salvo of arrows fought with their accustomed bravery, but it was to no avail; the vast majority of the Crusaders were in uncontrolled flight back along the road to Cibotos.

In the camp, the day was just beginning. Women were cooking a meal for their children, priests were beginning to say Mass, and a few people were still asleep, when a great cloud of dust along the road and the confused noise of men shouting and screaming in battle sent a ripple of fear through the place. The fighting drew nearer with the terrible inevitability of an avalanche or of death itself; the defeated army stampeded into camp, men stumbling and falling over one another in their desperate haste to avoid the pursuing Turks. No resistance was possible, and there was a massacre; soldiers, knights, priests, women and children were all cut down as they ran screaming for safety or as they stood out of breath and unable to run any farther. A few girls and young boys, to whom the Turks took a fancy, were spared; a handful of others were made prisoner when the soldiers of Islam became so sated with blood that they could not be bothered to kill any more; and somehow about three thousand people managed to escape the holocaust and take refuge in an old castle by the sea-shore, where, spurred on by desperation, they barricaded themselves against attack. The battle was over.

By some miracle, the castle managed to withstand the assault of the Turks. A local Greek succeeded in making his way to Constantinople with news of the disaster, and Alexius immediately sent a squadron of warships to Cibotos to rescue the survivors. When the Turks saw them sailing in towards the land, they lifted their siege of the castle, and retired inland. The remnants of Peter's people were taken back to the capital, where they were disarmed and lodged in the suburbs. They left behind them a desolation of corpses; from the little wooded valley where the Turks had laid their ambush down to the shores of the Sea of Marmara, the country-side was littered with the bodies of the dead, including those of Walter Sansavoir and most of the German knights. Geoffrey Burel, who had done more than anyone to bring about the disaster, escaped.

IV

♣♣♣

A Basket of Summer Fruit

Thus hath the Lord God shewed unto me: and behold a basket of summer fruit. And he said, Amos, what seest thou? And I said, A basket of summer fruit. Then said the Lord unto me, The end is come upon my people of Israel.

Amos, 8, 1–2

The first news of Peter the Hermit's expedition to reach France and Germany was of its successful arrival in Constantinople; news of the disaster came only much later, and in the meantime his various lieutenants were busily recruiting reinforcements. Gottschalk, the priest, raised a small army of men in Lorraine and Bavaria; in Bohemia a fellow priest, of whom nothing is known but his name, Volkmar, did the same, while Count Emmich of Leisingen gathered yet another and even larger army in the Rhineland. Before any of these groups of armed men set out to join Peter in Asia Minor to fight the enemies of Christ, someone asked a question. Were there not enemies of Christ nearer home, who should be dealt with first? Why march two thousand miles to fight the Turks while there were members of the race which had crucified Christ living in every great European city? The Jews had never been popular in Europe. Indeed, they had not courted popularity; instead, they had always lived apart from other people as a racial and religious minority group, keeping themselves to themselves and avoiding contact with their gentile neighbours while they led their own lives in their own way. They also practised usury, which was forbidden by the Church to Christians, and money lenders are seldom popular; but the Jews were useful as bankers and traders, especially to the nobility, and everyone acknowledged that they knew more about the art of medicine than anyone else. So they were tolerated, and the storm which broke on them at this time was wholly unexpected.

It is difficult to say what gave rise to it. Peter the Hermit had somehow persuaded the Jews of France to give him letters of introduction to the Jews of eastern Europe, from whom he had hoped to extract financial assistance on his way, and the idea of bullying the Jews into supporting the Crusades may have been based on his example. In much the same way, Godfrey of Bouillon, the Duke of Lower Lorraine, who was preparing to go on the coming Crusade, was given a thousand pieces of silver by the Jews of Mainz and Cologne in order to speed him on his way and also, it was said, to induce him to leave them in peace. He assured them that he had never had any intention of disturbing them; but nevertheless he took their money, and it is possible that other people may have seen their own opportunity in his example. But whoever it may have been who, wittingly or unwittingly, sowed the idea of persecuting the Jews in men's minds at this time, in the early summer of 1096 it sprouted in a murderous outburst of anti-Semitic violence. Emmich of Leisingen made the first move. On 3 May, he and some of his men attacked the Jews of Spier, killing a dozen of them and forcing a young Jewess to take her own life rather than be raped. As a military exercise it was unimpressive, but it was a beginning.

A fortnight later, the Count of Leisingen marched on Worms, where for some reason the Jews were more unpopular than in other places, and when his intention became known his army was immediately swollen by a mob of grinning peasants and townsfolk who joined in his attack on the Jewish quarter. The Bishop of Worms opened his palace to the Jews as a sanctuary, but Emmich and his mob were after blood, and they forced their way into the episcopal palace and murdered five hundred men, women and children despite the protests of the horrified Bishop. Five days later, on 25 May, it was the turn of Mainz, where the Archbishop had ordered the gates of the city to be locked against Emmich and his men; but news of their arrival spread, there were anti-Jewish riots in the city, and on the following day, 26 May, someone opened the gates to them. They moved into the place with the silent ferocity of a pack of wolves entering a sheepfold and with about as little mercy in their hearts for their intended victims. Terrified, the Jews tried to buy Emmich's mercy with gold; they presented him with seven pounds of it to persuade him to spare their lives. He accepted it, and on the next day he gave orders to his men to kill every Jew in the city. The Archbishop's palace, where many had taken refuge, was the first place to be attacked, whereupon the Archbishop fled, leaving the Jews to their fate; he was a good man, but he was not a hero. His guests were soon killed, but the massacre in the town took longer; for two days the killing continued, and very few Jews escaped. A few abandoned their faith in order to save their lives, but they were not many, and when the blood stopped flowing a thousand Jews lay dead.

While Emmich was killing the Jews of the Rhineland, Volkmar was already marching eastwards with his recruits, but this did not prevent him from joining in the godly work of murdering the people who had crucified Christ. News of the pogrom in Germany reached him as he and his men arrived in Prague, where they began at once to massacre all the Jews they could find. The authorities and the Bishop were appalled, but they were helpless to intervene, and it was only when there were no more Jews to kill that Volkmar marched on to Hungary. King Coloman had no intention of allowing anyone to kill any of his subjects, whether they happened to be Jews or Gentiles, and when Volkmar's men began hunting the Jews of Hungary, he gave orders that the Crusaders should be dispersed. In the attack which followed, many of Volkmar's men were killed, more were captured, but the fate of Volkmar himself and any others who may have survived is unknown; they simply disappeared to be heard of no more.

Gottschalk and his men were infected by the prevailing anti-Semitism, and as they began their long march to the Holy Land they stopped at Ratisbon long enough to murder the Jews there. They then moved on towards Hungary, where the infinitely patient King Coloman, despite all that he had suffered at the hands of itinerant western Crusaders, offered them every assistance in crossing his country, as long as they remained of good behaviour. But Gottschalk's men proved no different from their predecessors; they began to plunder the countryside as soon as they crossed the frontier. Understandably enough, the Hungarian peasants, who were the principal sufferers, proved to be less patient than King Coloman, and there was fighting between them and the Crusaders, who reacted with their usual brutality; at one village they impaled a young Hungarian boy on a sharpened wooden stake in the market place. Such behaviour eventually tried the patience even of King Coloman, and

Captions for following pages

Godfrey of Bouillon and his knights on their way to the Holy Land. The painting is an illustration to William of Tyre's *History of Outremer*, which was probably produced in Acre just before the city fell to the Moslems in 1291.

Cooper–Bridgeman

Mount Erciyas, an extinct volcano, just outside the city of Kayseri, the ancient Caesarea Mazacha, through which the main body of the First Crusade marched in early September 1097.

Sonia Halliday

Norman knights attacking English foot soldiers on a hill. Servants preparing a meal and a bishop blessing the food and drink before eating. Both from the Bayeux tapestry.

Michael Holford

exhausted it; he sent his army against these unwelcome murderers of his people. Gottschalk was the first to flee, but he did not get far, and he and all his men were destroyed.

There remained only the infamous Emmich of Leisingen, who approached the Hungarian frontier with a much more formidable force than either Volkmar's or Gottschalk's. His reputation preceded him, and King Coloman refused to allow him to enter the country. Emmich immediately gave orders that his men should fight their way across the river which formed the frontier, into the town of Wiesselburg on the Hungarian side. There was only one bridge and it was hotly defended by the Hungarians. For six weeks there was sporadic fighting, while the Germans set about building another bridge; and when it was complete they landed on the Hungarian side and drove the defenders back inside the walls of Wiesselburg, which they promptly besieged. They had brought the necessary siege weapons with them, and for a time it looked as though the city would succumb to their superior strength and numbers; then, quite suddenly, a rumour of some kind spread through the ranks of Emmich's men, and threw them into a panic. No one knows what it was, but it caused such obvious disorder that the Hungarian garrison seized their opportunity and sallied from the city in strength to attack their enemies. The Germans were caught off balance, and after a short battle King Coloman's men destroyed them; most of them were killed, some were captured, and a handful who were lucky enough to have faster horses than those of their pursuers escaped. Emmich of Leisingen was one of them.

The news of the destruction of Emmich's entire force reached the West soon after the fate of the armies raised by Gottschalk and Volkmar had become known; and when people also heard that Peter the Hermit's men had been virtually wiped out by the Turks, their gloom and bewilderment knew no bounds. God seemed to have deserted his people. Many concluded that the disasters which had fallen upon the first Crusaders were a divine punishment for the crimes which had been committed against the Jews. But although they were genuinely and deeply sorry that they had thus offended God, they did not stop preparing for a new Crusade or praying that He would lead them to victory next time. They had been chastened for their sins, but to the question posed by Psalm 79, 'Lord, how long wilt thou be angry: shall thy jealousy burn like fire for ever?' there could be only one answer: God would not be angry with his people for ever. The very idea was unthinkable. Next time things would be different.

V

♣♣♣

The Gathering of the Princes

God reigneth over the heathen; God sitteth upon the throne of
his holiness. The princes of the people are gathered together.

Psalm 47

During the summer of 1096, while disaster was overtaking Peter the
Hermit and his men, and while the Jews of Germany and central Europe
were being murdered in the name of Christ, the various princes and
nobles who had responded to Pope Urban's appeal to take the Cross were
making ready to leave. Less impetuous than Peter and less bloodthirsty
than Emmich of Leisingen, they knew that no military expedition, let
alone such a vast undertaking as an expedition against the Turks, could
possibly succeed unless it was carefully prepared. However, it is misleading
to speak of the Crusade for which the chivalry of western Christendom
was now preparing as if it were a single expedition, for it was not; what
was being prepared was a series of semi-independent expeditions under
the command of their own lords, who were bound together by a shared
Christian faith and a common goal, but not by any allegiance to a supreme
commander. Their armies varied in size as much as their commanders
differed from one another in character, temperament and motive for
taking the Cross, and each made his own way east in his own time. It is
important to understand what sort of men they were, for they were the
people who were to shape and form the first Crusader kingdoms in the

Holy Land, although some made greater contributions than others.

The first prince to go was Hugh of Vermandois, the younger son of Henry I of France. He was distinguished more by good looks and a golden tongue than by strength of character or practical ability, but having mustered a small army of followers from his modest estates in northern France, he set out for Italy in August. No one knows what were his motives for going; perhaps he had inherited a *wanderlust* from his Scandinavian mother, Anne of Kiev, but whatever his reasons, he was determined to be greeted on arrival in Constantinople with the respect due to someone in whose veins ran the blood royal of France. He despatched a letter to the Emperor Alexius in which he demanded a fitting welcome, and his letter was followed by a small group of messengers who demanded much the same of the Byzantine governor of Dyrrhachium, the small port on the eastern shore of the Adriatic to which he meant to sail with his men from Bari. His message was duly passed on to Constantinople, where it highly amused the Emperor's fourteen-year-old daughter, Anna Comnena, who could not get over the absurd effrontery of this barbarian from the West and his presumptuous insolence in making such demands upon her father; but in fact Hugh's initiative in taking the Cross was important, for his brother, King Philip, was debarred from doing so as a result of being recently excommunicated. He may have been a barbarian in Anna's Byzantine eyes, as indeed all Westerners were in the eyes of all Byzantines, but by becoming a Crusader he set the approval of the royal house of France upon the enterprise called for by Pope Urban.

On his way through France, Hugh collected some of the men who had followed Emmich of Leisingen on his ill-starred expedition. Then, crossing into Italy, he marched south to Bari in Apulia, which was a Norman kingdom at the time and was full of Normans preparing to go on their own Crusade. So far all had gone well, but soon after his small armada had sailed out of Bari harbour in early October, things began to go disastrously wrong. The year was past its prime, and no one liked setting out on a sea passage after the summer was over, for the storms of winter were dreaded by everyone; late September and early October were notorious for their gales, and everyone who could do so avoided them. But Hugh could not afford to do so, if he was to reach Constantinople before winter set in, and so he duly put to sea. A storm caught him and his men in mid-Adriatic, where some of his ships were sunk with all hands and the rest were driven onto the inhospitable rocks of the

Illyrian coast. Hugh himself was ignominiously wrecked not far north of Dyrrhachium, where, battered, bewildered, soaked to the skin, and in no mood to boast of his royal blood, he was found by some men despatched by the governor of the place, who knew from long experience that equinoctial gales were no respecters of princes.

Undignified as his arrival had been, he was treated with the greatest respect by his Byzantine host, who wined him and dined him as befitted a guest of his high social standing, while at the same time keeping a careful eye on his movements; and when eventually he was taken to Constantinople, the Emperor Alexius adopted the same policy towards him. He was greeted with respect and warmth, and showered with presents, but his freedom of movement was carefully if unobtrusively controlled: a fact which annoyed some of his followers, who privately accused the Emperor of treating him as a prisoner.

While this was not strictly true, there was some justification for the accusation, for Alexius was worried. Hugh was the first of many western princes to come to Constantinople at the head of his own private army, and the Emperor was understandably anxious to discover what they meant to do. When he had appealed to the West for help against the Turks, he had neither asked nor bargained for the invasion of his Empire by a whole series of independent armies; he had hoped for volunteers to fight as mercenaries in his own army and under his own command; and he was not going to let Hugh of Vermandois out of his sight until he had discovered his intentions, and whether he was willing to take an oath of allegiance to himself or not. He did not trust the Franks, as all the western Christians came to be called, further than he could see them; for his experience of them in the past – especially of the Normans – had not been encouraging; but he was prepared to flatter them and dazzle them with the prospect of great riches, if he could win their loyalty, and it was not long before he had completely conquered Hugh, who took the oath of allegiance with very little demur. Those who followed Hugh, however, did not prove to be so easily won.

Godfrey of Bouillon, the Duke of Lower Lorraine, was the next to march eastwards under the banner of the Cross. He has often been painted in rosy and romantic colours as the epitome of Chaucer's 'verray parfit gentil knight' of the Canterbury Tales. Indeed, one historian, Harold Lamb, writing about fifty years ago described how, when Godfrey and his two brothers, Eustace and Baldwin, set out on the Crusade, 'many eyes followed them, on their heavy chargers, pacing behind the blue gonfalon of Lorraine–three gray-eyed youths, laughing for the gladness in them, mighty of bone, and erect in their pride. The red cross was embroidered on their leather tunics to the right of the heart. Amber rosaries circled their white throats, and their gold hair hung upon their shoulders.' It is a romantic picture, but it is highly misleading. It is true that Godfrey himself was a handsome man, tall and fair-haired, but by no stretch of the imagination could he have been described as a 'gray-eyed youth' at this time; he was thirty-six years old. Moreover, despite his gracious manners and innate charm, he had in fact raised much of the money which he needed to finance the Crusade by something very like blackmailing the Jews in his duchy, even if this had been done urbanely and without Emmich's vulgar resort to violence. Baldwin, the youngest of the three brothers, fits the picture even less well than Godfrey. He was the tallest of the three, as dark as his eldest brother was fair; and where Godfrey was graceful and charming to meet, Baldwin was cold, supercilious and proud. Being the youngest brother, he had been destined for the Church, and indeed had been trained for the priesthood; but an ecclesiastical career was not to his taste, and after a short time he abandoned it. He had too great an affection for the luxuries of this life to settle down in holy orders; for the pleasures of the flesh, which did not greatly attract Godfrey, appealed strongly to Baldwin. Able, ruthless and single-minded, he was by far the most dangerous of the early crusading princes, and he embraced the opportunities for self-advancement provided by the Crusade with open arms. Being a younger son of a noble family, he had no prospects of inheriting estates in the West, and he went east to repair that deficiency. Whether he was interested in coming to the aid of his fellow Christians in need of liberation from the Turks or not, it is difficult to say; but that he was determined to make his own fortune in the East is certain, for he took his Norman wife and their little children with him, thus demonstrating as clearly as possible that he had no intention of returning.

Although the three brothers led an army of thousands of northern Frenchmen, Lorrainers and Germans through Hungary, their passage was peaceful enough. After his experience of Peter the Hermit and Emmich of Leisingen and their men, King Coloman was taking no chances, and he demanded that Baldwin should be surrendered as a hostage for the good behaviour of these new Crusaders; rather reluctantly, Baldwin agreed, and Godfrey for his part announced that any act of violence by his men would be punished by death. As a result, all went well until the army left Hungary and crossed into Byzantine territory, where the Crusaders were greeted with rumours, which lost nothing in the telling, of the virtual imprisonment of Hugh of Vermandois. They became so angry that they went on a rampage of pillage and violence, which devastated the country round a little town called Selymbria fifty miles west of Constantinople. Alexius sent messengers to Godfrey to protest about the behaviour of his men, and belatedly Godfrey restored order before moving on. He arrived under the walls of Constantinople two days before Christmas, and made camp by the waters of the Golden Horn.

If it had been important to the Emperor to persuade Hugh of Vermandois to take an oath of allegiance to himself, it was even more important to induce Godfrey and his brothers and the train of attendant knights at the head of their much larger army to do the same. But although Hugh pressed his fellow countrymen to agree to the Emperor's request, Godfrey was both puzzled by it and unwilling to agree. He already owed allegiance to the western Emperor, Henry IV, and he saw no reason to swear fealty to another man, whom he did not even know; so he refused. Alexius was both alarmed and angry; all his worst fears seemed to be confirmed, and he decided to shut off supplies to the Franks; if they would not co-operate, they should not eat. But such cavalier treatment failed to intimidate Baldwin, who led his men on foraging parties through the suburbs of the city, taking whatever he wanted without waiting for anyone's permission to do so, until Alexius relented. It was not an auspicious beginning to the Emperor's relationship with the newcomers, and peace between them did not last long.

Alexius waited until after Christmas before renewing his attempt to persuade Godfrey to take an oath of allegiance, but time was not on his side, for he knew that further armies of Crusaders were on their way to his country, and he was determined to succeed before these western reinforcements arrived to strengthen Alexius' hand. But Godfrey and his brothers remained obstinate, and once again Alexius reluctantly reduced supplies to the army, although he did not cut them off entirely. The Crusaders responded yet again by raiding the countryside and the nearby villages, where eventually they came into contact with some mercenary Pecheneg troops, who were acting as police in the area. The Pechenegs were a Turkish tribe who supplied the Byzantine Emperor with some of his best soldiers, in much the same way as the Gurkhas used to furnish the Indian army with some of its most celebrated fighters in the days of British rule in India; but when the Crusaders discovered that many of them were Moslems, their resentment and their distrust of Alexius knew no bounds. Baldwin was so angry that he laid an ambush for the Pechenegs, and captured sixty of them, many of whom he killed, although what good their deaths could possibly have done to the Frankish cause it is difficult to imagine; all they achieved in fact was to make any idea of a truce between the two sides impossible for the time being.

Realising this, Godfrey, possibly egged on by Baldwin, moved his army up to the walls of the city, where he launched a full-scale attack on one of its gates. It was Thursday in Holy Week, and the Byzantines, who were completely unprepared for such an assault, were shocked to the core of their being that people claiming to be Christians could even contemplate attacking their fellow Christians on such a day, let alone actually do so. For a time there was something like panic in the city, but its walls were immensely strong, and once the Byzantines had managed to close the gate under attack there was nothing much the Crusaders could do but retire to a safe distance after killing seven of the defenders. On the following day, Good Friday, Alexius sent envoys to speak with Godfrey, but despite the sanctity of the day the Crusaders attacked them without even waiting to hear what they had to say. This was too much for the Emperor, who was appalled as a Christian, and whose patience was exhausted; he ordered some imperial troops to attack Godfrey's men in earnest to teach them a lesson. While Byzantine archers on the city walls poured arrows at the discomfited Franks, purposely slaughtering their horses rather than trying to kill fellow Christians on such a day, a squadron of Byzantine cavalry was launched upon them from a neighbouring gate; they charged with such professional dash and assurance that the Franks were routed immediately.

This decisive defeat at last brought Godfrey to his senses and to a realisation of his weakness against the Emperor, who could still command a greatly superior force to that at the disposal of the Crusaders. He did not come to terms at once, but it was not long before he accepted the inevitable, letting Alexius know that he would come to see him in the city if the Emperor would first give him hostages for his own safety. It was probably on Easter Day that the two men met; Godfrey, his brothers and the most important nobles in his train, including a cousin named Baldwin of le Bourg, all took an oath of allegiance to Alexius, who immediately greeted each of them with a kiss of peace as his adopted son, showered them with presents, and entertained them with great magnificence at an imperial banquet. A few days later, to his immense relief, he ferried them and their army across the Bosphorus to a camp on the Asiatic shore before the arrival of the next contingent of Crusaders could increase their strength.

He was only just in time. A large but very mixed and ill-organised bunch of assorted Crusaders, most of whom had straggled in small groups across the Balkans hoping to catch up with Godfrey, began to arrive in the suburbs of Constantinople almost as soon as he had left, and they proved to be as unco-operative and belligerent as their forerunners. To deal with them Alexius needed all the tact and forbearance at his disposal – and no one has ever had more. Once again he tried to persuade their leaders to take an oath of allegiance to himself, and once again he was met by fierce resistance; but when at last they agreed, as inevitably they did in the end, he marked the occasion by inviting Godfrey and Baldwin to attend the ceremony as his guests. The newcomers were boorish and ill-mannered, and when one of them presumed to seat himself upon the Emperor's throne, Baldwin sharply rebuked him. Abashed the man took refuge in aggression, loudly trying to justify himself by complaining that the Emperor should not be seated while so many brave men were left standing. Alexius, who had overheard the man's words, asked to be introduced to him, and when, blustering, he began to boast of his successes in single combat, the Emperor mildly advised him to be careful when he met the Turks, who were unlikely to obey the chivalrous rules which governed single combat between Christian knights. When the party was over and all those present had taken the oath of allegiance, they were ferried across the Bosphorus to join Godfrey's army of Crusaders.

Once again, Alexius was only just in time. A few days later, the Norman prince, Bohemund of Taranto, arrived in Constantinople after a comparatively peaceful and uneventful journey at the head of a smaller army than Godfrey's but one that was well armed and well trained and made up of Normans who were born soldiers. Of all the Crusaders, the Emperor feared Bohemund the most. He was the son of a notorious Norman adventurer, Robert Guiscard ('Robert the Crafty' or 'Robert the Weasel'), who had carved out a dukedom for himself in the southern Italian province of Apulia by force of arms, and not so long before had invaded the Byzantine Empire and, ably assisted by Bohemund, spread terror wherever he went. As for Bohemund, physically he was a magnificent creature; Anna Comnena was bowled over by him. 'Such a man had never been seen before in the lands of the Romans,' she wrote, 'for he was marvellous to look at. He was taller than anyone else by a foot or more, slender waisted and narrow hipped, with wide shoulders, a deep chest, and great powerful arms...He had strong hands, a full, muscular throat, and he stood firmly poised on his feet, stooping a little. His hair was red-gold and did not hang down to his shoulders like that of the other barbarians, for he was not too vain about it to cut it short above his ears, and his face likewise was clean-shaven. His clear blue eyes betrayed spirit and dignity, as did his nostrils. A peculiar charm hung about this man, and yet there was something horrible about him, for the size of his body and the glint in his eye revealed both power and savagery; even his laughter sounded like snorting... For this man was cunning and swift to suspect others. Moody and sad in mind, he had left his country, where he possessed no lands, to worship, or so he said, at the Holy Sepulchre; yet he was in need of everything. He meant, really, to follow in his father's footsteps and to conquer, if he could, an empire in the East.' She was right. However, Bohemund had no intention of revealing his hand before he must, and on arrival in Constantinople he made no difficulty about taking an oath of allegiance to Anna's father; kneeling before Alexius he solemnly swore fealty to him regardless of any plans he might secretly be entertaining for his own future.

The next private army to travel eastwards was the largest of them all. It was led by Raymond IV of Saint-Gilles, Count of Toulouse and Marquis of Provence, and Adhemar of Monteil, the Bishop of Le Puy, who was regarded by everyone as the spiritual leader of the whole Crusade, responsible only to the Pope himself. Raymond of Toulouse was a man of about sixty with enormous estates in Languedoc and Provence, whom the Byzantines came to regard as both more civilised and more reliable than the other western leaders. They were accompanied by many nobles from the south of France, and they had a rough journey. Unlike those who had gone before him, Raymond led his men through northern Italy and down through the mountains of Dalmatia. It was not a wise choice of routes; the roads were bad, the country difficult, and the local people, most of whom were half-civilised Slavs, were hostile. The barbarity of the times is well shown by an incident during their journey; it was described by a priest, Raymond of Aguilers, who was chaplain to Raymond of Toulouse. The Count was with the men of the rearguard, when 'he was cut off for some time with several of his men by the Slavs,' wrote his chaplain. 'He made a charge, and took six of them prisoner. When on this account the other Slavs thronged in on him savagely, forcing him to ride back to the army, he commanded that the eyes of some of the captives be torn out, and the feet of others cut off, and the noses and hands of the rest mutilated. So the pursuers were delayed by the sight of the captives and by grieving at their suffering, while the Count was able to escape unharmed with his companions. And in this way, by God's mercy, he was delivered from the agony of death and the hazards of that place.' It is difficult for people of a later and a different age to understand what God's mercy had to do with this bloody little incident, but we shall never understand either the middle ages or the Crusaders if we fail to grasp how completely sincere they were in seeing God's mercy at work in such events.

Even after Raymond's Crusaders had passed through the country of the Slavs and had entered the Byzantine Empire near Dyrrhachium, their troubles were not over. They were hopelessly undisciplined, and their repeated attempts to pillage the country through which they passed eventually brought them into conflict with the Pecheneg police, who as usual had been ordered to watch over their progress. People were killed on both sides; the Bishop of Le Puy was wounded and captured for a time, although he was returned as soon as the Pechenegs discovered who he was; and passions began to run higher and higher as tempers became more and more frayed. In the end there was a pitched battle between the Crusaders and some Byzantine troops who had been sent to reinforce the Pechenegs, and the Franks were routed. The survivors were so chastened that they caused no more trouble during what remained of the journey to Constantinople, where they arrived towards the end of April shortly after Bohemund's men had crossed the Bosphorus.

There were three more private armies, each of which may have been about ten thousand strong, although once again it must be said that numbers are notoriously difficult to determine, for the contemporary records are always exaggerated. They were led by Robert, Duke of Normandy, his brother-in-law Stephen, Count of Blois, and his cousin Robert of Flanders, and they travelled most of the way together. They were men of very different temperaments and abilities. Robert of Normandy, William the Conqueror's eldest son, rather surprisingly was a gentle, unimpressive man in early middle age, who had been at war with his brother William Rufus off and on ever since their father's death: a state of affairs for which Robert could not be blamed, for the younger man made a habit of invading his brother's duchy, and this Robert resented. He had responded to Urban's call for a Crusade with genuine and pious enthusiasm, and he took Odo, the Bishop of Bayeux, with him as well as a large number of nobles from Normandy and a few from

The Balkans and Asia Minor at the time of the First Crusade

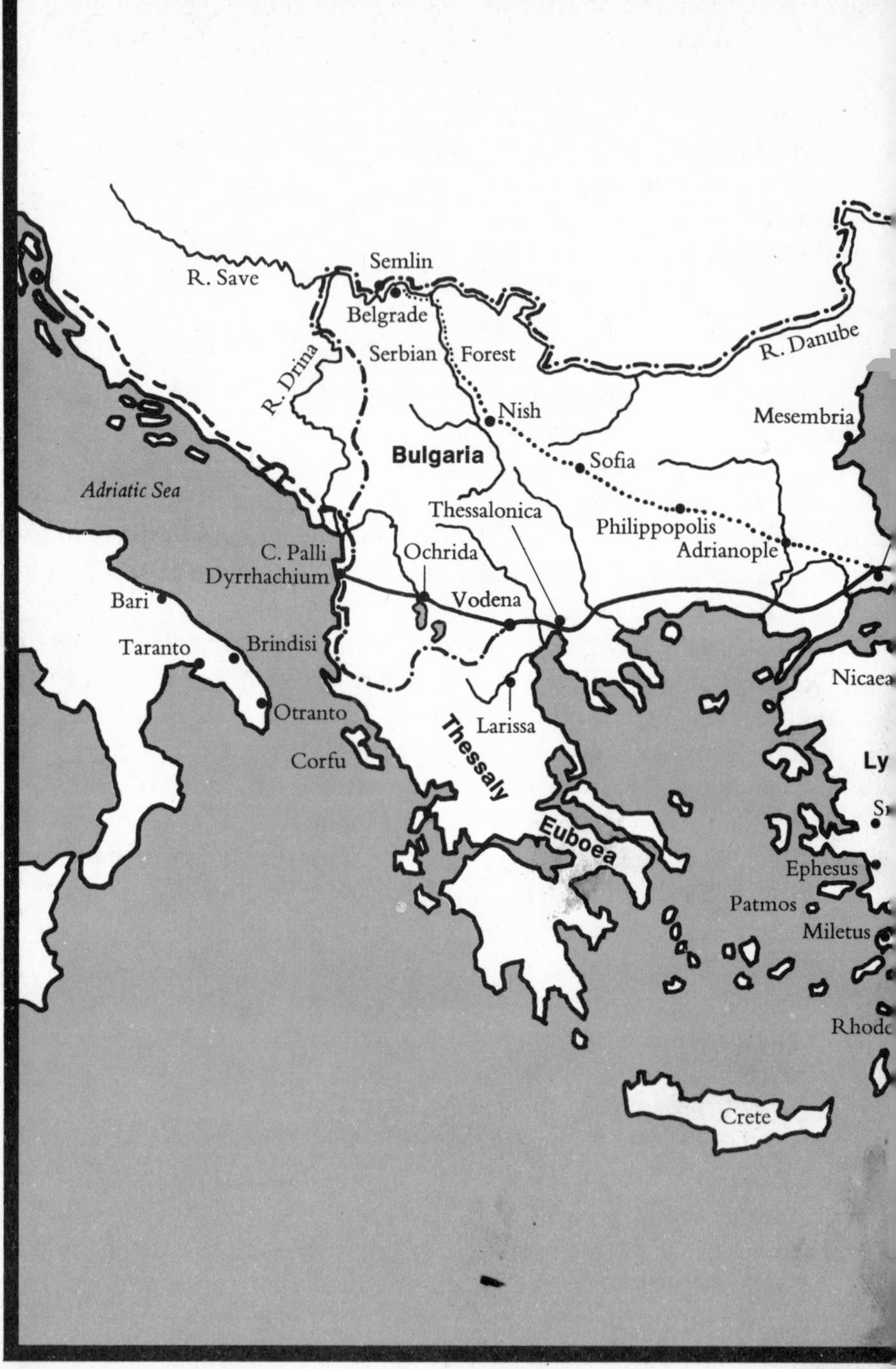

Black Sea

Sinope

Trebizond

Castra Comnenon
(Kastamuni)

Erzerum

nbria

tantinople

Sebastea
(Sivas)

Manzikert

Nicomedia

Ancyra

Cappadocia

aeum

Caesarea Mazacha

Edessa

hrygia

iladelphia

Laodicea

Marash

Jezireh

Mamistra

icea

Antioch
in Pisidia

Iconium
(Konya)

Heraclea
Tarsus

Adana

Mamistra

Turbessel

Alexandretta

Attalia

Seleucia

St. Symeon

Aleppo
Antioch

R. Euphrates

Cyprus

Lattakieh

Tortosa

Shaizar (Caesarea)

Homs

diterranean

Route followed by Raymond,
Robert of Flanders, Robert of
Normandy and Stephen of Blois
from Dyrrhachium to
Constantinople, by Bohemond
from Vodena and by First
Crusaders onward from
Constantinople.

Route followed by Peter the
Hermit and by Godfrey ••••••

Route followed by Raymond to
Dyrrhachium ▬ ▬ ▬

Route followed by Bohemond
to Vodena ▬•▬•▬•

Route of Baldwin of Boulogne
in 1097-8 ▬••▬••▬••

Miles
0   100   200

0   80   160 240 320
Kilometres

England, including the Earl of Norfolk, who was living in exile in Brittany at the time.

Stephen of Blois was a very different character. He had no enthusiasm for the Crusade, but he had married William the Conqueror's daughter, Adela, who considered that he ought to go, so he went. There was never any nonsense in their household about who made the decisions: she did. With him went a priest named Fulcher of Chartres, who became the principal historian of the events which were to follow. Count Robert of Flanders, who was younger than the other two, had a more formidable personality than either of them. In joining the Crusade, there was a sense in which he was following in his father's footsteps, for the older man had made a pilgrimage to Jerusalem some ten years previously, and on his way back he had stayed for a time in Constantinople.

Having marched south through Italy together, the army split into two groups. Robert of Flanders embarked at once with his own followers at Bari, and led them safely and without incident to Constantinople, which he reached shortly after Bohemund's arrival. But Robert of Normandy and his brother-in-law decided to spend the winter comfortably in southern Italy before continuing on their way, and as the months passed their army began slowly to melt away, as the men's enthusiasm waned and little groups decided to make their way home again. When at last the two leaders decided to embark their men at Brindisi, disaster struck them; it was a very medieval kind of disaster. The first ship to leave port capsized and sank with the loss of all hands, together with many pack animals, stores and chests of money, and understandably those who were waiting to embark on the other vessels were appalled; but it was not long before the news spread that the corpses of the men who had been drowned were being washed ashore marked with the sign of the Cross 'in the flesh of their shoulders', in the words of Fulcher of Chartres. Nor did this miracle much surprise anyone, for, to quote Fulcher once again, 'reason made it plain to those reflecting on it, that it was appropriate that by such a miracle those dead had already by God's mercy obtained the peace of everlasting life in the clearly evident fulfilment of the prophecy which had been written: "The just, though taken prematurely by death, shall find peace".' But although the other Crusaders were not surprised by this manifestation of the power of God, it did not entirely succeed in restoring the courage of all those who were waiting to board the remaining ships, and some deserted. Most, however, remained faithful to their vows as Crusaders, allowing themselves to be shipped to Dyrrhachium without further loss of life after a rough and unpleasant crossing, and thence to Constantinople, which they reached in May. The city enchanted them.

Fulcher of Chartres was enraptured by it. 'O, what a noble and beautiful city!' he wrote. 'How many monasteries, how many palaces in it, all marvellously well built! How many extraordinary things to see, even in the streets and squares! It would be tiresome to relate what quantities of gold, silver, varied vestments and sacred relics are to be seen there. All things needed by men are brought here incessantly by boats.' Stephen of Blois was no less impressed by the city, but he reserved his greatest admiration for the Emperor Alexius, who was as generous and kind to him as he had been to the other western lords once they had sworn allegiance, overwhelming him with gifts. 'Your father, my beloved,' he wrote to Adela his wife, 'made many gifts, but he was almost nothing compared to this man.' One cannot help wondering how the formidable Adela reacted to this remark about her father, William the Conqueror, but since her husband was the better part of two thousand miles away, perhaps for once he himself did not much mind how she reacted.

Meanwhile, the subject of his admiration, Alexius, was doubtless heaving an enormous sigh of relief as the last of the great crusading armies was ferried safely across the Bosphorus into Asia. By exercising a remarkable combination of patience, firmness, forbearance, diplomacy and generosity, he had somehow succeeded in assimilating a series of formidable foreign armies into his Empire without disaster, while sending them on their way to fight his enemies; moreover, he had done everything humanly possible to ensure that, when they did so, they would act as his vassals. That most of them would eventually break their vows of allegiance to him was not his fault, and it could be argued that it was not entirely the fault of the perjurors either; for oaths are fragile things at the best of times, and when those who make them are caught up in one of the great movements of history, they are seldom strong enough to prevent men from straying from the hard road of fidelity and honour. As the restless, half-organised, savage, and yet visionary chivalry of western Christendom crossed the Bosphorus under the watchful eyes of Alexius and his fellow Byzantines, two cultures were beginning to come into collision; one was very old, immensely civilised and past the peak of its physical strength, while the other, which was just emerging from total barbarism, was filled with the callous and boundless energy and creativity of youth. The younger was destined to play a large part in the destruction of the older, but no one knew that yet. They still believed themselves to be allies.

Captions for following pages

These two pictures were originally illustrations to an early nineteenth-century travel book. Although they are in the romantic pictorial style of the day, they probably give a correct representation of the ancient buildings which remained at the time. The first is of the walls of Antioch as they were in 1840, and the second is of the market place as it appeared at that time under Turkish rule. The figures wearing turbans and the man in the foreground in the tall hat are Turks.

Sonia Halliday

View of Jerusalem from the east showing the walls of the old city, the Temple area with the Dome of the Rock and the Mosque of al-Aqsa to the left, and a Jewish cemetery in the foreground. The Mount of Olives is just outside the picture to the right.

Ronald Sheridan

The Dome of the Rock in the Temple area of Jerusalem. One of the great buildings of the world, it was built by Byzantine craftsmen commissioned by the Moslem Caliph Abd el-Malik in 691; the Crusaders mistakenly believed it to be the Temple of Solomon.

Ronald Sheridan

VI

♣♣♣

Onward Christian Soldiers

Onward Christian soldiers, marching as to war,
With the Cross of Jesus going on before.
Christ the royal Master leads against the foe;
Forward into battle see his banners go!
                                    S. Baring-Gould

Once the Crusaders had all gathered together in a great military camp on
the Asiatic side of the Bosphorus, they were eager to begin the long
march east to the holy land. The Emperor Alexius was equally eager to
see them go, and he promised to supply them with guides who knew the
way across the great Anatolian plateau. But there was one thing which
had to be done before they could safely set out on their march to
Jerusalem a thousand miles away; they had to capture the fortified city of
Nicaea barely fifty miles from Constantinople as the crow flies, for it lay
across the road which would be their main supply route, and it was held
by the Seljuk Turks. It was built on the shores of a lake named Lake
Ascania; it was surrounded by formidable defensive walls and, since the
Turks regarded it as their capital city, it was bound to be strongly
garrisoned. The Crusaders could not simply by-pass it; it would be too
dangerous a stronghold to leave in their rear.

The Crusaders' army was the greatest military force to be assembled by
the people of western Europe since the end of the western Roman
Empire. Probably it numbered a hundred thousand men, women and
camp followers, and even though it lacked an overall commander, it was a

very formidable force indeed. For their first venture against the Turks, luck was on the side of the Crusaders; for the Seljuk Sultan, Kilij Arslan (Arslan means 'Lion'), was away on his eastern frontier fighting some Danishmend Turks, rivals of the Seljuks, for the overlordship of a petty Armenian state in that part of the world. The division of the Turks into clans is extremely confusing; there were Seljuks, Danishmends, Khwariz-mians, Ghaznevids, Kipchaks, Pechenegs, Karakhanids and, later, Otto-mans, and all were originally nomadic shepherds from central Asia who had become Moslem and had founded an Empire, over which they some-times bickered and which they sometimes defended together as allies. At the time of the First Crusade, the Seljuks were dominant, and their Sultan, Kilij Arslan, had heard of the coming of this new host of western Christians; but Peter the Hermit and his rabble had convinced him that he had nothing to fear from such undisciplined riff-raff, and he had not bothered to hurry back to meet them; Nicaea was well garrisoned and could look after itself.

Godfrey of Bouillon was the first to leave the base camp on the Bosphorus and lead his men against the city. He was soon joined by Bohemund's army under the temporary command of his nephew, Tancred, deputising for his uncle, who was in Constantinople as the Emperor's guest. Peter the Hermit also joined them with a few survivors from the disaster into which he had led them a few months previously. Finally, some Byzantine engineers joined them to give advice and help if it became necessary to lay siege to the city. They all arrived below the walls on 6 May They were tower-studded, extremely strong, and four miles long; and it was not until Raymond of Toulouse joined them ten days later with his great host of Crusaders from Languedoc, followed by Robert of Normandy and Stephen of Blois in early June, that the place could be fully invested. Meanwhile, the Turks sent messengers, one of whom was captured, to tell Kilij Arslan of their arrival and to urge him to hurry to their assistance.

As it happened, he was already on his way, and as soon as he arrived he launched an attack on Raymond's army, which was guarding the southern wall of the city. The brunt of the Turkish assault fell on the Christian right flank, which was commanded, despite his holy orders, by the Bishop of Le Puy, whose men were hard pressed to hold their own until Robert of Flanders came to their assistance. The battle lasted all day, and there were losses on both sides, but in the end it was the Sultan who was forced to order his men to retire; to his astonishment, these newcomers had proved very different from Peter the Hermit's men and more than a match man for man with his Turks. Needless to say, the Crusaders were hugely elated by their success, even though many of them had been wounded and all of them were exhausted. They celebrated their victory by cutting off the heads of as many dead Turks as they could find and catapulting them over the city walls into the streets; others were set up on pikes in front of the city gates in full view of the depressed defenders.

It was a significant victory, but the city had not fallen, and it did not look like doing so; supplies were still reaching it by boat across Lake Ascania, and when the Byzantine engineers tried to undermine the walls, they failed. Eventually, the Emperor's help was asked, and he ordered a small squadron of the Byzantine navy to prevent supplies reaching the place by way of the lake; the ships were commanded by an Admiral named Butumites, who also had instructions to open negotiations with the commander of the Turkish garrison for the surrender of the city. The Turk realised that he could not hope for relief from Kilij Arslan after his defeat and, seeing no point in prolonged resistance, he informed Butumites that he was prepared to hand over the city to him in return for the lives of his men. This was strictly an agreement between the Turkish commander and the Byzantine admiral; the leaders of the Crusade may have been kept informed of the progress of the negotiations, but their men knew nothing of what was going on. On the contrary, they were looking forward to making a general assault on the city, which was planned for 19 June, and as the day approached their excitement mounted. During the night of 18 June, however, the Turks opened one of the gates to Butumites' men, so that, when the Crusaders woke on the morrow, it was to discover that they had been cheated of their prey. They had been looking forward to sacking the place, and they were furious. They became even angrier when they saw how the Turkish prisoners were treated by the Byzantines; some were allowed to buy their freedom, while others were allowed to return to their families without even having to pay for the privilege of doing so. To the Crusaders, who would have slaughtered them all out of hand as the enemies of Christ, this ill-judged and inexplicable generosity seemed akin to treachery and even to blasphemy. They could not understand, as the Byzantines did, the diplomatic value of such gentleness.

Angry as they were, however, none of the Crusaders doubted that the capture of Nicaea was a major victory, and everyone was heartened and encouraged by it. Stephen of Blois wrote to his wife Adela in high spirits. 'In five weeks' time we shall be in Jerusalem,' he said, adding with what proved to be unpleasantly perceptive foresight, 'unless we are held up at Antioch.' But the shadow of Antioch did not yet darken the optimism of the Crusaders as they set out from Nicaea a week after it had been captured, although the problem of how to keep such a vast host of people and animals alive on so formidable a journey was well known to their Byzantine guides, who knew what an inhospitable place Anatolia was. In winter, its seemingly endless steppe, rolling away into Asia as treeless as the Gobi desert or the steppes of southern Russia, was swept by icy winds from Siberia and buried in snowdrifts which could be fifty feet deep in places; in summer its sparse grass lands, its stony volcanic plains, and its dry and lifeless salt flats were baked by the sun, their horizons either lost in a shimmer of heat or smothered in dust storms. Nomadic shepherds were at home in such country; they lived off their flocks, and they knew where water could be found; but feeding an entire army with all its hangers-on and its pack animals was a very different task, and so was watering it. The women were as tough as the men, and most of them were prepared to march on foot like everyone else, although a few rode donkeys; the knights were mounted, although many of them walked most of the way too to spare their horses, which were led by grooms; and everyone's belongings, together with the expedition's military stores, were carried on great lumbering ox carts or on the backs of mules. Meanwhile, somehow or other, soldiers, women, knights, priests, camp followers and animals all had to be given food and water, and since there was no commissariat, they had to live off the country through which they passed. The problem was so acute that before they had travelled very far they decided to split into two groups; the Normans and the northern French with a Byzantine contingent marched ahead under the command of Bohemund, and they were followed a day later by the rest under Raymond of Toulouse.

When Bohemund and his Normans had travelled about fifty miles, they reached a city named Dorylaeum, and made camp beside some springs of water; there they spent the night of 29 June 1097. At dawn the next day, they were attacked by the army of Kilij Arslan, who had been waiting for them, the lightly armed Turkish cavalry sweeping in from all sides and showering the Crusaders with arrows. Bohemund immediately despatched a rider to tell Raymond that he was under attack and to urge him to hurry to his assistance, and having done so, he turned to the task of organising the defence. He gathered the women and non-combatants in the centre of the camp by the springs with orders to keep the fighting men supplied with water during the battle, and he ordered the knights to dismount and remain on the defensive until help could arrive. The only man to disobey him was the knight who had been rebuked by Baldwin for sitting on Alexius' throne; with forty of his personal followers he charged the Turks in a fine fury of martial belligerence, only to fall almost at once with a multitude of wounds from which he later died. Fortunately both for themselves and the Christian cause, everyone else obeyed Bohemund, and the first wave of Turks was thrown back.

As the hours passed, and the Anatolian sun rose higher and higher into a blue and cloudless sky, the heat became almost unbearable to the men in armour, and the Christians began to wonder whether any of them would survive under the incessant showers of Turkish arrows; but since retreat was impossible and surrender unthinkable, with the courage which was perhaps their greatest virtue, they resolved to die fighting. Some did so, but shortly after mid-day some horsemen appeared in a cloud of dust to the north, barely visible and strangely distorted by the moving heat haze, and the Turkish attack faltered. The Sultan knew that the newcomers could not be Turks; he had no reserves in the area; yet until this moment he had imagined that he was fighting the whole Crusader army, and that they, too, could not expect reinforcements. But as the shimmering cloud of golden dust drew nearer, and the low thundering noise of horses' hoofs began to be discernible over the sounds of the battle – the whirring of arrows, the neighing and terrified whinnying of horses, the clash of steel on steel, and the cries of men in anger or in agony – the battle standards of Toulouse, of the Rhineland and of Vermandois could be seen fluttering over the dense, steel-clad ranks of armoured knights who were approaching. In a slow gallop the chivalry of Provence and Lorraine bore down on the Turks and, tired as they were, the Normans, who had been in battle all day, went over to the offensive in a magnificent display of indomitable pugnacity. With Bohemund, Robert of Normandy and Stephen of Blois on the left flank, Raymond of Toulouse and Robert of Flanders in the centre, and Godfrey, Baldwin and Hugh on the right, the massed nobility of western Christendom rode into the attack. The Turks, who were now in their turn greatly outnumbered, were wholly unprepared for the weight of such an onslaught, and they reeled under its impact. When they suddenly saw what appeared to be yet another army of Crusaders under the redoubtable Bishop of Le Puy appearing across their line of retreat on the hills behind them, they fell into a panic and fled. The Crusaders' victory was complete.

Anatolia now lay open to them. They had captured a vast booty from the Sultan's camp, which they had overrun after the battle, and their morale was even higher than it had been after the fall of Nicaea; nothing, it seemed, could stand in their triumphant, God-assisted way. But that way was still a long and hard one, and the retreating Turks made it harder by laying waste the country, burning the crops and destroying or befouling the wells. The weather was still painfully hot, and it was not long before hunger and thirst began to take their toll. The horses were the first to die; knights were reduced to walking on foot, and sheep, goats and even dogs were pressed into service to carry their personal luggage. People rubbed the coarse grass, which grew at the wayside, through their hands, and ate the seeds, but even so their hunger was unsatisfied. After passing through Pisidian Antioch the road became even worse; with the Taurus mountains on one side and a salt desert on the other, the only vegetation to be seen was thorn bushes, whose branches the exhausted Crusaders chewed in the hope of finding a little moisture. Raymond of Toulouse fell ill, and had to be carried in a litter; as the days passed, he got worse, and it looked as though he was going to die. Godfrey of Bouillon was wounded by a bear, which he had been hunting, and the men of the rank and file began to die of privation, although as yet only in small numbers. Their bodies were loaded onto wagons to be buried each evening in common graves, while their comrades stood around as the Bishop of Le Puy and the other priests who had taken the Cross sang the office of the dead over them in the failing light. It was a mournful performance, but it did not depress the Crusaders too deeply; they had no doubt that the souls of the dead travelled straight to God, for Pope Urban had promised all who died on the way to Jerusalem absolution and remission of their sins; and no one could want anything more from life than such a death. Seen in such a light, the dead were lucky.

So morale remained high, and when the army reached Iconium (the modern Konya), everyone went wild with delight; the Turkish inhabitants had taken to the hills in their terror of the Frankish invaders, deserting the city; but since they hoped to return one day, they had left it undamaged. The sight of its gardens, streams and orchards was like a glimpse of paradise to the weary and thirsty Crusaders, who marched into the place like the children of Israel entering the promised land; if the city was not flowing with milk and honey, it was well supplied with food and fruit of all kinds, and everyone settled down to enjoy a few days' rest. Even Raymond of Toulouse, who had become so ill that he was given the last rites of the Church as he lay at death's door, rallied and began to recover, and to everyone's astonishment proved well enough to continue the journey when the others eventually departed.

At Heraclea, eighty miles east of Iconium, they again met the Turks, who seem to have hoped to frighten them into crossing the Taurus mountains towards the coast, thus leaving much Turkish territory un-invaded on the rest of their way to the Holy Land; but Bohemund had no intention of being diverted from his chosen path by men whom he and his fellow Christians had twice defeated in recent days, and he immediately led the entire army into the attack. The Turks, who did not want to risk another encounter with the heavy Christian cavalry, hastily retired, abandoning southern Cappadocia to the Crusaders. Their victory was marked that night by a comet which blazed its splendid and portentous way across the eastern sky in token of God's approval of the day's events.

So far the Crusaders had been completely united, but the battle of Heraclea was followed by an argument about the road forward. The shortest way into Syria lay across the Taurus mountains by way of a pass known as the Cilician Gate; but it was rugged and extremely steep, and the majority of the princes were against attempting to follow it. Now that the Turks had once again been defeated, the way through Caesarea Mazacha (the modern Kayseri), the capital city of Cappadocia, lay open; and from there a good road ran across the Anti-Taurus down onto the Syrian plain and thence to Antioch. The majority were in favour of travelling that way, but a small number could not be persuaded to agree, and they decided to go their own way without the others. Bohemund's nephew, Tancred, with some of the Normans from southern Italy, and Godfrey's brother, Baldwin, with some Lorrainers and some men from Brabant, announced their intention of moving south into Cilicia inde-pendently of the main army; and since their decision proved to be a turning point in the affairs of the Christians in the Middle East, the course of events which followed their departure must be described before the story of the main body of Crusaders is told.

VII
♣♣♣
Fortune in the Making

Every man is the maker of his own fortune.
Sir Richard Steele, *The Tatler*

Tancred set out on 15 September with about three hundred men, of whom a third were knights. He was followed by Baldwin, who was accompanied by his namesake and cousin Baldwin of Le Bourg, with five hundred knights and two thousand infantrymen; they moved more slowly than Tancred's smaller force, and they took a slightly different road over the mountains down onto the coastal plain. The aim was to capture the city of Tarsus, the principal city of Cilicia, where St Paul had been born. Tancred arrived first to find it occupied by Turkish troops, who came out in strength to meet him only to be savagely driven back into the city by the Crusaders. The inhabitants, who were mostly Christians, were delighted at the prospect of being liberated from the Turks, and sent messengers to Tancred begging him to take the city as soon as possible; but his small force was not strong enough to storm its fortifications, and he sat down to await the arrival of Baldwin.

He did not have to wait very long. Three days after his own arrival, Baldwin and his army came into sight in the distance, moving slowly across the plain in a great cloud of dust, and the sight of them terrified the Turks. Very sensibly, they decided to get out of the city while there was still time to do so, and as soon as darkness fell they fled. The people of Tarsus immediately opened the gates, and rushed out to tell Tancred that the garrison had gone and to invite him to enter the place in triumph, which he did, not waiting for Baldwin. The result was that, when the sun came up the next morning, Baldwin and his men were greeted by the sight of Tancred's banner flying over the city in proud and defiant possession. It did not improve their tempers.

Baldwin had no intention of allowing Tancred to keep Tarsus for himself. Icily, he demanded that the city should be handed over to him at once, and since he had a force many times larger than Tancred's behind him, the younger man had no alternative but to do as he was told. He was furious, but he handed the city over to Baldwin, and then rode out of the place in a rage with his men following him. There were other cities waiting to be liberated from the Turks, and in future he would do without Baldwin's assistance in taking them.

Baldwin had as little intention of handing Tarsus over to the Emperor Alexius as he had had of allowing Tancred to keep it; despite his oath of allegiance and his promise to return all Byzantine territory to its former owners, he meant to keep the city as the nucleus of the kingdom which he intended to build for himself. So, when three hundred Normans arrived before the city gates, saying that they had come to reinforce Tancred, Baldwin refused to allow them entry; Tancred had gone, he told them, and they had better follow him. It was getting dark, and the Normans decided to camp outside the city walls for the night. Neither they nor Baldwin knew that the Turkish garrison was still in the neighbourhood, but the unfortunate Normans were destined very soon to discover that the Turks had not gone far, for under cover of darkness they crept quietly back and massacred every single one of them.

Their deaths shocked the Crusaders, and Baldwin came in for a good deal of criticism, even from his own men, for not allowing them to enter the city. Their reproaches became even more bitter when, after a time, Baldwin decided to abandon the city to some Christian pirates who happened to be in the vicinity. Why had the Normans had to die, people asked themselves, if Baldwin had had no intention of holding Tarsus for longer than a day or two, but meant to hand it over to this riff-raff from the sea? But abandon it he did, perhaps because it lay amidst malarial swamps and its climate was oppressively hot; or perhaps because he came to the conclusion that there were better cities waiting to be conquered farther east, as Tancred had already discovered. Whatever his reasons, he followed Tancred's example, rode out of Tarsus, and marched after him.

They met at a place named Mamistra, the ancient Mopsuestia, a few miles east of Tarsus. When he heard of Baldwin's arrival, Tancred and his men immediately attacked him; but Baldwin was much the stronger, and Tancred was decisively repulsed. It was a foolish thing to do, and when the main body of the Crusaders and their leaders heard of this unseemly strife between fellow Christians they were furious; such squabbling could not be tolerated, and Baldwin and Tancred were forced by public opinion into a reluctant reconciliation. Everyone then hoped that the whole unedifying episode would be forgotten; but the Byzantines did not forget it, for it had demonstrated quite clearly that at least two of the leading Crusaders, who had sworn allegiance to the Emperor, were interested only in founding independent kingdoms for themselves in lands which had been Byzantine for centuries before the advent of the Turks, whatever promises they might have made to return them to their rightful masters.

Having patched up his quarrel with Tancred, Baldwin hurried back to rejoin the main army, which by this time had crossed the Anti-Taurus mountains and was approaching the Syrian frontier; for he had heard that his wife and children were seriously ill. His wife died before he could reach her, and his children died soon afterwards. However, he did not allow this disaster to affect his determination to do what he had come so far to do, and once again he left the main army with a force of his own, although this time it was a smaller one than that which he had taken with him to Tarsus. He marched east towards the river Euphrates through country inhabited by Armenians. All of them were Christians, and as Baldwin approached they rose up against the Turks, whom they loathed, massacring them with the greatest enjoyment and greeting the Crusaders rapturously as God-sent deliverers from their evil dominion. Reinforced by small contingents of pugnacious Armenians under their local leaders, Baldwin's little army grew in strength as he went along, and it was not long before he had conquered all the country up to the river itself, placing garrisons of Armenians in two strategic castles, one of which commanded the road to Antioch and the other the crossing of the Euphrates at Carchemish. Shortly afterwards, at the invitation of the independent Armenian Prince of Edessa, who was terrified of what the Turks might do by way of reprisals if he did not make war on Baldwin, and even more terrified of what Baldwin would do to him if he did, he crossed the river and agreed to become the man's adopted son and co-ruler of Edessa with him. The ceremony of adoption was a peculiar one; the Armenian Prince, whose name was Thoros, and Baldwin both stripped to the waist, whereupon together they donned a gargantuan shirt, and within its privacy they rubbed their bare breasts together. This, however, was not the end of the matter, for having performed the ritual with Thoros, Baldwin was expected to repeat the ceremony with his wife: a procedure which, one would have thought, must have had some embarrassing aspects.

As co-ruler of Edessa with Thoros, Baldwin had now won half a kingdom for himself, and shortly he was to have all of it. Thoros was unpopular with the people of Edessa, and they had longed to get rid of him for years, but they had had to put up with him for want of anyone to take his place. The arrival of Baldwin entirely changed the situation, and he had not been there for long when they rose up against Thoros and laid siege to the citadel in which he lived. Whether Baldwin was privy to this revolt against his adopted father is not known, but he did not lift a finger to protect him; on the contrary, he advised him to surrender to the rebels, while promising to see that his life was spared. Thoros duly surrendered, and was imprisoned in his own palace, from which after a while he decided to try to escape; but his attempt to save himself was discovered by the people of the city, who caught the wretched man and tore him to pieces. On the morrow, they invited Baldwin to become their sole ruler with the title of Count of Edessa.

His reign began most auspiciously. By a combination of diplomacy, military force and economic inducement he managed to enlarge his country by winning, conquering or buying the neighbouring petty states, and in the process he greatly strengthened his own position. As a result, when a major counter-attack was launched against him by a ferocious and much-feared Turk named Kerbogha, the Atabeg of Mosul, it failed. (In origin, the office of *atabeg* was that of tutor to the Sultan's son, held by senior military officers.) The failure of Kerbogha's attack proved to be of great value to the main army of Crusaders who by this time had reached Antioch. These successes greatly increased Baldwin's authority, and he further reinforced it by marrying a local Armenian princess, the daughter of a man named Thatoul, who brought a huge dowry with her. Meanwhile, he acted with statesmanship in his treatment of his subjects, doing everything he could to weld the very mixed people of his new realm into one harmonious whole, and even treating the local Moslems with respect and fairness: a policy which shocked some of his own followers.

However, some people grew to dislike him, and foremost amongst his critics were the Armenians, who became progressively disillusioned with their so-called liberator. They resented the arrogance of Baldwin's knights, who tended to treat them as racially inferior and socially unacceptable, and they disliked his policy of employing those Moslems who were prepared to take service under him. As a result, after a time some of them began secretly to plot his downfall. Their plan was to depose him and to put his new Armenian father-in-law Thatoul into power in his place; if this failed, they hoped at the very least to force him to accept Thatoul as co-ruler. But they were betrayed to Baldwin, who struck back at them with speed and ruthless efficiency; the two leading conspirators were arrested and blinded, while their fellow conspirators had either their noses or their feet cut off. All others upon whom suspicion fell were thrown into prison, and their fortunes were confiscated: all, that is to say, except Thatoul, who hastily retired to the mountains, where he was surrounded by his own retainers and so felt safe from the vengeance of his savage son-in-law.

When the story of the crushing of the conspiracy in Edessa spread throughout the region, Baldwin's fame spread with it, and since ruthlessness was a quality greatly admired in a ruler, his prestige rose to new and dizzy heights far beyond the frontiers of his new realm. He had joined the Crusade as a junior prince and a younger son with no prospects. Now, alone amongst those who had taken the Cross in response to Urban's call, he had founded the first Crusader kingdom. It was a remarkable achievement.

VIII

♣♣♣

Behold, a People from the North

Thus saith the Lord, Behold, a people cometh from the north country; and a great nation shall be raised from the sides of the earth.
They shall lay hold on bow and spear; they are cruel, and have no mercy; their voice roareth like the sea; and they ride upon horses, set in array as men for war.

Jeremiah, 6, 22–3

While Baldwin had been busy on the Euphrates' plain, the main army had made the slow and difficult journey south across the Amanus mountains of northern Syria to arrive before the walls of Antioch on 21 October 1097. It had taken them four months to march and fight their way across Anatolia from Nicaea, and they had lost some of their number *en route* both from disease and in battle, but they arrived in high spirits full of hope and confidence in themselves. The sight of the city, however, daunted them; apart from their brief glimpse of Constantinople, none of them had ever seen a city like Antioch. It had been founded in 300 B.C. by one of Alexander's generals, Seleucus, and named after his father Antiochus. For centuries it had rivalled Alexandria, both cities claiming to be the second city of the Roman world, and in one respect at least it had literally outshone its rival; for Antioch had been the first city in the world to be lit by street lamps at night. To Christians it was remarkable as the place where they had first received the name of Christian, and although earthquakes and wars had somewhat diminished its former glory, it was still one of the great cities of the world and immensely strong.

Captions for following pages

The Mosque of al-Aqsa in Jerusalem. Here, when the Crusaders captured Jerusalem, a host of Moslems took refuge and were promised safety by Tancred; but they were massacred, and the next morning the building was knee-deep in blood and corpses. The Knights Templar used it as a palace in which to dwell, and stabled their horses in the vaults nearby.

Sonia Halliday

View of the dome of the Mosque of al-Aqsa in Jerusalem, taken from below the old Temple area upon which it is built.

MEPhA

The keep of Shaizar Castle. An Arab castle, Shaizar was the home of the Munqidh family, of whom Usamah ibn-Munqidh was a member. His *Memoirs* are an invaluable source of information about the Crusaders and their kingdoms.

A. F. Kersting

A painting of knights fighting from a *History of the World* produced in Acre in the late thirteenth century. Although the artist's subject was the battle between Alexander the Great and the Indian King Porus, he portrayed them in the armour and accoutrements of knights of Outremer in his own day.

British Museum

Knights in single combat from the same *History of the World*.

British Museum

It lay twelve miles from the sea on the banks of the river Orontes, covering an area three miles long and a mile wide between the river and the rugged mountainous country of Syria to the south, and with its southern quarter built on the shoulder of a hill named Mount Silpius. Justinian had surrounded it with formidable walls in the sixth century, and the Byzantines had modernised and repaired them in recent years. With the river to one side and on the other the tower-studded walls climbing superbly up Mount Silpius to a magnificently placed citadel a thousand feet above the plain, the place was virtually impregnable. It was equally well placed to resist a siege, for it was almost too big to invest, and it never ran out of water; streams tumbled down the sides of Mount Silpius, and although they dried up in summer, thunder in the hills always resulted in sudden floods which replenished the city's reservoirs and endangered the lives of any animals which happened to be caught unawares in the stream beds. One such stream was called Onopnicles or Donkey-killer because of the number of beasts which had died at one time or another in its flash-floods. Food seldom ran short during a siege either, for great quantities could be stored in the city; and anyway there were market gardens, orchards and even a few fields within the city walls.

With the exception of Raymond of Toulouse, who wanted to attack the place at once, the leaders of the Crusade were in favour of waiting for reinforcements; Tancred had not yet joined them, the Emperor Alexius might send some of his engineers with siege weapons if asked to do so, and there were rumours that a Genoese fleet was on its way. The fortifications were so formidably strong that it seemed madness to gamble the lives of the Crusaders in a desperate bid to take the place by assault until every other possibility had been explored. This was a conclusion with which the rank and file heartily agreed, and which they greeted with relief. Instead of hurling themselves at the walls, they settled down to the enjoyable task of looting the suburbs and robbing the many luxurious country houses and villas which lay outside the city. Food was abundant; poultry, pigs, sheep and cattle were there for the taking; wine was to be found in every cellar; and gardens, orchards and vineyards were still laden with the fruit of late summer and autumn. After the previous four months of hunger and austerity, when everyone had come close to starvation, an orgy of over-eating and drinking was very welcome.

But the army with its hangers-on was still nearly a hundred thousand strong, and it was not long before the immediate countryside had been stripped bare. As supplies began to run out, the Crusaders were forced to

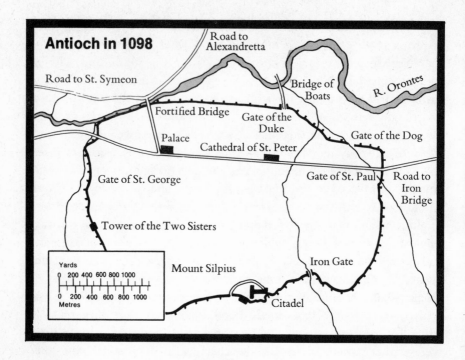

forage ever farther and farther afield for food, and this gave the Turks more and more opportunities to steal out of the city at night and then lie in wait for small parties of Christians and for stragglers, whom they slaughtered. The arrival of the Genoese and their capture of the small port of St Symeon on the coast was very welcome, both because it brought new strength to the army, and because the port could now be used by ships bringing supplies; but until such ships began to arrive, the only result of the coming of the Italians was to make the problem of feeding the army even more acute. So, at Christmas time, it was decided to send Bohemund and Robert of Flanders with about twenty thousand men on a grand foraging expedition, while the rest of the army under the command of Raymond and the Bishop of Le Puy stayed behind to invest the city. The news soon reached the Turkish commander in Antioch, a man named Yaghi-Siyan, who launched a night attack on some of Raymond's men as they were camped north of the river Orontes. They were taken by surprise, but as soon as Raymond was told of the Turkish attack, he reacted with exemplary speed; gathering a group of knights around him and not waiting to raise a larger force, he charged out of the darkness, taking the Turks by surprise in their turn, and routing them. Indeed, as he chased them back across the river into the city, he nearly succeeded in storming into the gate after them, but a bolting horse threw his small party of mounted knights into confusion and the chance was lost. It was a sharp and bloody little encounter while it lasted, and people were killed on both sides, including some of Raymond's knights, whom the Crusade could ill afford to lose.

While this battle was being fought under the walls of Antioch, Bohemund and Robert and their foraging party were unwittingly riding into the arms of a large Moslem army, which had been gathered for the relief of Antioch and was marching north from Damascus up the Orontes valley. They met on the last day of the year 1097. Robert's men, who were ahead of Bohemund, were taken completely by surprise and virtually surrounded before they realised that the enemy was anywhere near them; they fought with their usual courage and ferocity, but they would have been annihilated if Bohemund had not come on the scene and charged the Moslems just when they thought that they had won the battle. His sudden onslaught took such a devastating toll of the men from Damascus that they were forced to turn tail and run for their lives. So, once again, the victory was the Crusaders'; but they, too, had suffered heavy losses, and were forced to abandon their expedition. They returned to Antioch with none of the food the army so desperately needed.

At about this time, there was an earthquake, followed the same evening by a spectacular display of the *aurora borealis*, and the Crusaders were terrified. Since the stability of the earth and the darkness of night were part of the God-given order of things, they concluded reasonably enough that any interruption in their even tenor must be due to some extreme agitation on God's part; plainly, he was angry with his people, and had sent these signs of his wrath to warn them of the danger in which they stood. This was a conclusion which was reinforced when it began to rain, for no one but an angry God could have sent them such weather. Yet after the earthquake and the terrible night when the fiery glow of divine displeasure had banished the natural darkness, the heavens were opened, and it rained as it had not rained since the days of Noah, when all flesh had been destroyed because the earth had been full of violence. The Bishop of Le Puy declared a fast in the hope of turning away the wrath of God, but since there was no food to be found in the camp or in the surrounding countryside, it made little difference to the hungry Crusaders as they huddled together for warmth in whatever shelter they could find. Everyone and everything became sodden and wet; the camp itself turned into a quagmire in which people could hardly keep to their feet as they slithered and slid about in the mud; water and mud oozed up through the blankets on which men tried to sleep, and their tents no longer kept out the water; armour rusted, bow-strings softened and became flaccid, leather harness became mildewy, and Stephen of Blois wrote to Adela his wife to say that it was a great mistake to imagine that the sun always shone in Syria, for 'throughout this winter we have endured intense cold and incessant rain'.

With the failure of the foraging party led by Bohemund and Robert, famine was soon added to the Crusaders' other miseries. Christian villagers brought in what food they could spare, and so did some of the monks in the Syrian hills; but only the wealthiest of the Crusaders could afford to buy their goods, for neither monks nor villagers were philanthropists; on the contrary, they knew a sellers' market when they saw one. Small foraging parties were sent ever farther and farther afield in a quest for food, but although they had some success, they could not collect enough to prevent horses and men from dying. As time passed, food began to arrive from Cyprus, but it was not enough to satisfy the hunger of so large an army, and people still died. A surer way of ensuring their own survival was adopted by some half-civilised Flemings known as Tafurs, who had originally travelled east with Peter the Hermit; they collected the carcasses of dead Turks and ate them. When the supply of Turkish corpses was exhausted, they hunted live Turks, and killed them for the pot.

By the end of January 1098, things had become so bad that men began to desert, and one of the first to do so was Peter the Hermit. He was not allowed to get far, however; he was brought back a virtual prisoner, and his prestige, which had already sunk very low indeed, never recovered. A little later a Byzantine general, who had been the Emperor's representative on the Crusade, announced that he was leaving; his motives were probably entirely honourable, but nevertheless his departure was regarded as desertion, and the Crusaders' suspicion of the Greeks deepened. But worse was to come, for the next to begin talking about going home was Bohemund. That he had not the smallest intention of doing so is as sure as anything can be, but his announcement caused something like panic in the army, as no doubt he intended that it should; everyone immediately begged him to change his mind, and this he graciously consented to do on the strict understanding that, when Antioch was captured, the lordship of the city should be his. Some of the other leading Crusaders were not deceived by this charade, but there was little they could do to call Bohemund's bluff, for at about this time news reached the camp that a large Turkish army was marching to the relief of Antioch.

The Turks were coming from Aleppo, and the news put the Crusaders in a quandary; for if they marched out to meet them in force, leaving Antioch unguarded, Yaghi-Siyan's beleaguered garrison would be free to make a sortie and destroy their camp; while if they left a sufficient number of men to contain the Turks in the city, they would hardly be strong enough to defeat the men from Aleppo. A conference was held, and at Bohemund's suggestion it was decided to leave the infantry to contain the city while the knights alone would march out to meet the advancing enemy, even though by this time there were only seven hundred of them fit for service. If they could surprise their opponents, they stood a chance of success. It was an astonishingly bold plan, and it nearly failed. The knights rode out of the camp under cover of darkness, and met the advancing Turks at dawn, charging them before their archers had time to move into battle positions; but the enemy was so numerous that the charge by the Crusaders did not break them, and Bohemund was forced to retreat. This could have been disastrous, but he had chosen his ground carefully with just such a possible reverse in mind, and he lured the triumphant and excited Turks after him as he withdrew, until he had led them onto a narrow neck of land between the Orontes and a lake; his right and left wings were now protected, and the Turks could not outflank him. Bohemund then turned on his pursuers, and once again the knights charged them. Their impact was enormous, for although they were hugely outnumbered, on a narrow front their weight and resolution were irresistible, and the Turks were thrown into complete confusion. Within minutes they were in flight with the knights pursuing them and killing them as they ran. But Bohemund did not allow his companions to chase them far, for he was worried about the army below the walls of Antioch. It was just as well, for when they rode into camp, elated by their spectacular victory, they arrived just in time to come to the aid of the infantry, which was under heavy attack by Yaghi-Siyan's men, who had made a sortie from the city in strength. The Turks were pressing hard, but at the sight of the approaching knights they withdrew again into the city as quickly as they could.

The defeat of the army from Aleppo was yet another proof that the Crusaders were formidable fighting men, whose reserves of sheer courage were both impressive and apparently unfathomable; indeed, even the

Turks were unable to withhold their admiration from men so prodigiously brave. But their victory did little to alleviate the difficulty of their position, and famine still stalked their camp. At last, however, at the beginning of March, the tide of their ill fortune turned; food began to arrive from Cyprus in sufficient quantities to feed them all, and a large English fleet put into the port of St Symeon with a cargo of siege materials and Byzantine engineers, sent by Alexius to their aid. The Turks did their best to prevent these supplies from reaching the famished men below the walls of Antioch, and there was a critical battle on the road from the coast; but after an initial reverse the Crusaders once again totally defeated their opponents. It was said at the time that they killed over fifteen hundred Turks, including nine Emirs, but this may have been an exaggeration. On the evening of the battle they allowed the Turks to creep out of the city to bury their dead, but this sudden access of compassion was short lived; the next morning they dug them all up again, and robbed the bodies of everything of value found on them.

Antioch was now totally cut off from the outside world, and for the first time its inhabitants began to suffer from hunger, while with the coming of spring weather and more supplies from Cyprus the Crusaders were at last better off than the Antiochenes; but even with the siege weapons brought by the Byzantines the prospect of taking the city by assault seemed as remote as ever. Bohemund was clear minded enough to have realised for some time that, if the city was to be captured, other measures would have to be taken to reduce it. He had already made contact with a leading member of Yaghi-Siyan's staff, an Armenian convert to Islam named Firouz who had a grudge against his Turkish master, and now in the greatest secrecy he began to try to persuade the Armenian to betray the city, promising him a large sum of money if he would do so. It was none too soon, for news began to arrive at this time of the coming of the ferocious Kerbogha with yet another large Turkish army, which was reported to be so strong that something like panic began to spread through the ranks of the Crusaders; all through the month of May deserters drifted away in parties of ten to a hundred men trying to reach the safety of the coast, and in early June Stephen of Blois and his northern Frenchmen marched off to Alexandretta, which was firmly in Crusader hands. He saw no point in waiting to be massacred by the Atabeg of Mosul; it was better to save lives than to throw them away to no purpose.

On the very day of Stephen's departure, for which later he was to be bitterly rebuked by the formidable Adela, Bohemund received a secret message from Firouz agreeing to hand the city over to him that night. The Armenian had just discovered that his wife had been seduced by a senior Turk, and the discovery had thrown him into a rage; furious and embittered, he decided to hesitate no longer, and he sent a messenger to Bohemund to say that if his men scaled the city wall at a place known as the Tower of the Two Sisters, he would let them in. Bohemund immediately called a conference of the leading Crusaders and described his plan: that evening, under the eyes of the Turks, he would lead the army ostentatiously out of camp eastwards, as if marching to meet Kerbogha; but as soon as darkness fell, he would double back on his tracks and gather the men as silently as possible under the walls of Antioch at the spot chosen by the traitor Firouz. The others listened in silence, and when he had finished speaking, they all agreed to support him. Even Raymond of Toulouse raised no objections, although he hated Bohemund and was desperately jealous of him.

The plan worked well. It was nearly daybreak when the army arrived below the Tower of the Two Sisters, the men moving as stealthily as the rocky ground and their armour would allow. A ladder was set up against the wall of the Tower by an open window, and sixty knights scaled it one after another, led by a man named Fulk of Chartres (not to be confused with the historian, Fulcher of the same city). Firouz, who was in a state of extreme agitation, met them, but they took little notice of him; instead, they ran along the top of the wall and captured two more towers before the alarm could be raised. Ladders were then placed against all three towers and against those parts of the wall captured by the knights, and as more and more Crusaders swarmed up them some knights descended into the city and threw open one of the gates to the waiting army. Nothing could now stop the Crusaders, and they poured into the place to be greeted rapturously by the Greek and Armenian citizens, who, as Christians, loathed their Moslem overlords and were only too happy to join in the massacre which followed. It was a barbarous affair, in which no one was spared; Turkish women and children were butchered along with their men, and a good many Greek and Armenian Christians were killed by mistake. Yaghi-Siyan tried to escape with a bodyguard of horsemen, but he did not get far; thrown from his horse and half stunned on a mountain track outside the city, he was found by an Armenian, who killed him at once, cut off his head, and carried it to Bohemund, who paid him handsomely for his gruesome trophy. By mid-day there was not a Turk left alive in the city except for some who had taken refuge in the citadel and held out against all attempts to storm its formidable defences; the streets were so littered with corpses that in places it was difficult not to stumble over them, and as the sun grew hotter the air began to reek of blood and rotting flesh; but Antioch had been won for Christ again by the Franks.

Their position, however, was precarious in the extreme, for they had hardly occupied the city before Kerbogha and his army arrived and laid siege to it. With the citadel still in the hands of the Turks who had taken refuge there, the danger that the city might fall to the newcomers was greatly increased; but although they launched a violent attack on the city's defences, very nearly breaching them, eventually they were thrown back with heavy losses by Hugh of Vermandois' Flemings and Robert's Normans. A few days later the Crusaders mounted an equally violent attack on the Turks, but they were driven back into the city having achieved nothing. Their failure deeply depressed them, and their despondency was amply justified; for if they had often been hungry in the past, now they were famished. A small loaf, when it could be found, cost so much that few could afford it, and the poorer Crusaders were reduced to munching grass and the leaves of trees. They faced starvation and surrender, their only ground for hope the possibility that the Byzantine Emperor might come to their aid. It was known that a large Byzantine army had reoccupied much of Anatolia in the wake of the Crusaders' advance, and messengers were despatched begging him to help; but Alexius, who had heard tales of mass desertions, the flight of Stephen of Blois and the desperate straits to which the rest had been reduced before the fall of Antioch, was not prepared to risk his own army on a hazardous bid to rescue them. Even though Hugh of Vermandois, at great risk to himself, went to Constantinople to beg him to intervene, he refused. He knew that the fate of his entire Empire depended upon the preservation of his armed forces, and if his army was to go to the aid of the Crusaders only to find that they had been defeated before it could arrive, it would be in real danger of annihilation by the Turks. It was a sensible decision, but when the men besieged in Antioch heard of it, their bitterness was extreme, and they vowed never to trust the Byzantines again. Meanwhile, Hugh of Vermandois followed Stephen's prudent example and went home.

Half-starved, angry, and afraid for the first time that God had deserted them, the spirits of the men in Antioch were suddenly raised by the eruption of the supernatural into the darkness of their daily lives. Exactly a week after they had captured the city, a ragged young peasant named Peter Bartholomew sought an interview with Raymond of Toulouse and the Bishop of Le Puy to announce that he had had a miraculous vision. On the night of the earthquake he had been terrified, and had taken refuge in a hut, whereupon two men in shining garments had suddenly appeared to him, frightening him even more. The older of the two had then declared that he was the apostle St Andrew, and that he had come to show Peter where the lance which had pierced Christ's side during the Crucifixion was to be found; almost at once he had been miraculously transported, clad only in a shirt, to the Cathedral Church of St Peter in Antioch, which the Moslems had converted into a mosque, where St Andrew had shown the trembling peasant the place where the holy lance was buried under the floor of a chapel. Peter had wanted to take possession of it at once, but he had been told to wait until the city had been captured by the Crusaders, and then to come back in search of it. St Andrew and his angelic companion had then led Peter back to the camp and disappeared. But Peter had been too afraid to obey the divine commands of the saint; he was a poor man and feared ridicule. So he had gone about his daily business, only to be visited by St Andrew on no fewer than three more occasions to be roundly rebuked for his disobedience and to be ordered to do as he was told.

Adhemar of Le Puy was suspicious; the story was rambling and improbable, and the story-teller illiterate, shifty and unimpressive. As a churchman the Bishop had been trained to distrust private visions, and he was in favour of rejecting this one as the product of an imagination made over active by fear and hunger. But Raymond of Toulouse was less sceptical, and his namesake and chaplain, Raymond of Aguilers, devoutly believed every word of Peter's story. The tale soon got about, and soon someone else also had a vision: Christ, accompanied by Mary his mother and St Peter, appeared to a French priest named Stephen while he was praying one night in the Church of Our Lady. If the Crusaders would give up their drunken and adulterous ways, Stephen was told, they would soon receive divine protection again, and all their troubles would be over. Stephen was a respectable cleric, and even Adhemar was impressed. When, a few nights later, in the words of the chaplain Raymond of Aguilers, 'a great star flamed over the whole city, and then divided into three, and fell down on the Turks', all scepticism vanished; plainly God was at work. He had acted first through Peter Bartholomew, then through

7

the priest Stephen, and lastly through this great and wonderful meteor. It was time to obey his divine commands.

The next day Peter Bartholomew and a small number of specially picked men, including Count Raymond and Raymond his chaplain, went to St Peter's Cathedral and began to dig up the floor of the chapel where St Andrew had allegedly shown Peter the lance. They dug for hours and found nothing; Raymond of Toulouse went home bitterly disappointed, and everyone began to wonder whether they had been duped. Then, quite suddenly, Peter himself, clad only in a shirt as he had been on the night of his miraculous vision, leapt into the trench; calling on everyone to pray as they had never prayed before, he bent down and triumphantly produced a pointed metal object and held it aloft. The chaplain Raymond later swore that he had kissed its tip while the rest had still been embedded in the earth, but predictably others, including the Moslem chronicler Ibn al-Athir, roundly accused Peter Bartholomew of faking the whole thing or at the very least of burying the lance himself. Whether he did so or not, we shall never know; certainly, at the time the vast majority of the Crusaders were convinced that the holy lance which had pierced the Lord's side on Calvary had been miraculously revealed to them as a sign of God's favour.

As time went by, however, more and more people began to doubt Peter. If his original excursion into the realm of supernatural experience had not been repeated, they might never have questioned his credibility, but it was matched by a number of subsequent miraculous visions of ever more doubtful authenticity, and many people grew sceptical. One of them, however, was of considerable practical value; it was a vision in which St Andrew appeared once again to Peter and predicted that, if the Crusaders attacked the Turks in five days' time, they would be victorious. In fact, this was not as improbable a prospect as might have been imagined, for the Turks had troubles of their own; their leaders were deeply divided, they too were short of food, and more and more of Kerbogha's men were growing tired of the siege and its discomforts and were deserting. On the off chance, an embassy under Peter the Hermit was sent to persuade Kerbogha to abandon the siege, but it failed; despite his own problems Kerbogha would settle for nothing less than the unconditional surrender of the Christians. Since this was wholly unacceptable, the Christians, headed by Bohemund, who was in sole command during the sickness of Raymond of Toulouse, decided that they had no alternative but to stake everything upon a battle.

Early on the morning of 28 June, while some priests said Mass on the walls of the city, the Crusaders marched out of Antioch by way of a gate which led directly onto a fortified bridge over the Orontes. Most of them were half-starved, thin and in rags, but their morale was high, for they knew that the holy lance was being carried into battle tied securely to a banner, and with such a relic at their head the idea of defeat was both blasphemous and absurd. Their women marched with them carrying water in leather bottles and bladders, and even a few children stumbled along with the host. The knights were shabbier than they had been when they set out from Europe; some were reduced to going into battle on foot, having lost their horses, while others rode mules or even donkeys; their armour was red with rust in places, and their banners were faded and very much the worse for wear, but if they looked less formidable than they had in the past, their appearance belied them; they were as unafraid and dangerous as they had ever been. They were organised in six army groups, each under the command of its own lord, and as they crossed the bridge in a seemingly endless river of humanity, they spread slowly and deliberately out across the plain to form a line of attack.

Kerbogha's army was also very numerous, and he had some of the finest cavalry in Asia under his command; they were Seljuk Turks, and they wore Persian chain mail and high damascened steel helmets. Although there was no love lost between Turks and Arabs, a large number of Arab princes had brought their desert warriors to Kerbogha's aid against the common enemy of Islam; and of course the Turkish rulers of Aleppo, Damascus and Homs were there with their private armies, men in heavy turbans armed with curved scimitars and short bows, even though they disliked Kerbogha and were deeply suspicious of one another. Kerbogha resisted the temptation to attack the Crusaders as they crossed the bridge, lest he should simply destroy a few of them while allowing the remainder to retreat into the safety of the city; but it was a mistake, and when he saw the host of Christians forming up to attack him he sent a belated messenger to offer them a truce if they still wanted it. It was too late. The Crusaders ignored the man and his message, and fighting began on the right flank near the river, the sound of men roaring at each other and the clash of steel being heard over the whole battlefield.

In a matter of minutes the two armies were engaged along the entire front, the Turkish cavalry pouring in arrows and trying to outflank their enemies on the Crusaders' left wing, where they were unprotected by the Orontes; but the Christian advance was heavy and inexorable, and the

Turkish line began to waver. At the height of the battle, with casualties mounting on both sides, a rumour spread through the ranks of the Crusaders that a company of knights on white horses with white banners fluttering over them had been seen fighting furiously on the left flank, and that their leaders had been identified as the three great warrior saints of Christendom, St George, St Demetrius, and St Mercury. Elated by this renewed proof of divine favour, the men of Normandy, Provence and Flanders pressed on with dogged ferocity and murderous courage. The Arabs were the first to begin to melt away, unwilling to die for the sake of their Turkish overlords, and it was not long before the Emirs of Damascus, Homs and Aleppo decided to save themselves and what was left of their armies and leave the Atabeg of Mosul to his fate; they had been wildly jealous of him for years, and they had had enough. As the Moslem line began to crumble, and the Christian rank and file saw the crimson standard of the Normans suddenly surge forward, marking the charge of Bohemund and his knights, they began to run after them, stumbling over the wounded and the bodies of the dead, weeping for joy and screaming with excitement. Tancred and his knights followed Bohemund in a thunderous cloud of dust, and as the Crusaders' last reserves were thrown into the fray the Turks broke and ran. The battle was won.

IX

♣♣♣

The Gates of Jerusalem

I was glad when they said unto me: We will go into the house
of the Lord. Our feet shall stand in thy gates: O Jerusalem.

Psalm 122

The victory over the combined forces of Islam below the walls of Antioch
was decisive, but the subsequent celebrations were marred by two events:
the death of the Bishop of Le Puy, and a bitter quarrel between Bohemund
and Raymond of Toulouse over the lordship of the conquered city. These
two things were not unrelated, for Adhemar of Le Puy had been the one
man in the Christian camp who had been admired and loved by everyone,
and he had always managed to stand above the factional quarrels and
disputes which had recurrently threatened to disrupt the fragile unity of
the Crusaders. As the nearest thing to an official representative of the Pope,
his authority had been immense, and when he died there was no one to
take his place: no one to mediate between the power-hungry lords or to
control their violent animosities. If he had lived, things would probably
have been very different; the proper claims of the Byzantine Emperor to
the lordship of Antioch, which all the leading Crusaders had sworn to
respect, might even have been remembered, and some sort of harmony
between them might have been maintained. In his absence, none of them
cared a fig for Alexius or for their vows of loyalty to him, with the exception of Raymond of Toulouse, who became more and more angry as

Bohemund set about establishing what he considered to be his right to the city. Nearly all the other great lords took sides, thus exacerbating the hatred and the squabbling. It was a depressing spectacle, and one which was to be seen only too often during the long history of the Crusader kingdoms of Outremer, as the lands conquered by the Christians came to be called. That history was just beginning.

The rivalry between Bohemund and Raymond was reflected in the mutual dislike of the Normans and the southern French; this grew as the months passed, and no attempt was made to press on towards the original goal of the Crusade, namely Jerusalem, because the leaders were too busy bickering over the fate of Antioch. During this time, in one typical incident, Raymond's men captured the key city of Maarat an-Numan in northern Syria after a short but costly siege, whereupon by a combination of trickery and speed Bohemund's men, who had had little to do with the capture of the place, looted it before Raymond's Provençals realised what was happening. As a result, the hatred between the two leaders and their men became even more bitter, until a point was reached when they would hardly speak to each other. Eventually, some of the lords who had managed to stand aside from the battle between the two factions wrote to Pope Urban begging him to come and take over the leadership of the Crusade himself, but he was not prepared to leave Rome. Instead, after some delay, he sent the Archbishop of Pisa, a man named Daimbert, to act on his behalf. It was a bad choice, and when eventually Daimbert arrived, he turned out to be an almost unmitigated disaster. But events did not wait upon his arrival: the ordinary rank and file of the army became so disgusted by the perpetual bickering of their leaders that they decided to intervene. At about Christmas time in 1098 they demanded to see Raymond, and offered to recognise him as their supreme commander if he would lead them to Jerusalem. Raymond knew that to agree would mean abandoning Antioch to Bohemund, but to his eternal credit he did agree, and on 13 January 1099 he led an emaciated and greatly reduced army southwards on the road to the Holy City; it may have numbered no more than about thirty thousand people, of whom only about half were fighting men. As if to remind his fellow princes, many of whom refused to accompany him, of their original Christian vows, he walked barefoot at the head of his men in the garb of a pilgrim.

At first all went well; the local people, who hated the Turks, greeted Raymond and his men as liberators, and did all they could to help them on the way. This benevolence may have been also due, at least partly, to the fact that they had heard terrible tales of the Crusaders, and were desperately eager not to offend them. But some of the coastal cities were still ruled by Turkish garrisons, and Raymond was forced to lay siege to them. He captured the ports of Marqiye and Tortosa without much difficulty, and these early successes persuaded Godfrey of Bouillon and Robert of Flanders to follow the examples set by Robert of Normandy and Tancred, who had already joined him, and the strength of his army was nearly doubled by these new recruits. But even with these reinforcements he failed to take the city of Arqa near Tripoli; and as the Crusaders became bored and frustrated below the city walls, quarrels broke out again between the Provençals and the Normans, while the Norman lords disagreed with Raymond's conduct of the siege and wished to abandon it. It was at this point that Peter Bartholomew took a hand once again. Ever since the fall of Antioch he had been reporting encounters with St Andrew and other saints, who had invariably and conveniently ordered him to pass on messages favourable either to himself or to his patron, Raymond, and many people had grown sceptical of his claims to supernatural experiences and had come to regard him as merely one of Raymond's political allies in his struggle with the Normans. Some were even beginning to doubt the authenticity of the holy lance, and when Peter claimed to have received yet another revelation from St Andrew, backed this time by St Peter and by Christ himself, that urged the Crusaders to obey Raymond's orders and follow his advice over the siege of Arqa, scepticism reached new heights, and Peter was openly accused of fraud.

Furiously angry, he demanded the right to defend himself against his accusers in a trial by fire, and this was granted. On Good Friday the ceremony took place. Two great piles of firewood were arranged like the walls of a passage with a narrow path between them, and after prayers had been said by a bishop, the wood was set alight. News of the coming ordeal had spread throughout the Christian camp, and the army had assembled *en masse* to witness the outcome. Peter, clad only in a linen tunic and clutching the holy lance in his hand, plainly believed in his own coming vindication, for after kneeling for a moment and crossing himself, he approached the blaze with no sign of fear. By this time the heat was so intense that a bird flying over the fire fluttered down into it and perished. Peter, however, did not hesitate for an instant; rising from his knees, he ran through the flames, stopping for a brief moment at the half-way point, and emerged the other end, where he fell to the ground desperately

The Church of the Holy Sepulchre in Jerusalem. The first church on this site was built by the Emperor Constantine's mother, Helena, in the fourth century; the present building was built by the Crusaders and consecrated in 1149. Fire, earthquake and restoration have not succeeded in destroying its austere splendour.

Sonia Halliday

Crusader graffiti on the walls of the Church of the Holy Sepulchre in Jerusalem.

Top: Ronald Sheridan   Bottom: Sonia Halliday

The Coronation of Baldwin I. Below: the story of his kindness to a woman he had captured is illustrated. She was the wife of a sheikh, and he treated her with great courtesy. The picture comes from an early fourteenth-century French MS of William of Tyre's *History of Outremer*.

Giraudon

Sunrise over the Sea of Galilee.

Sonia Halliday

sour le leu demonte caluaire ou
nře sires fu mis en croiz. al leu lē
gardez toz popres por enterrer les
rois de ierlm. iusqau ior dui
ois fu
lidus
Godef.
de ierla.
li pm-
ers des
latins.
mesnē
uolt pf
auoir
le non. Lors fu li reaumes sanz roi
apres lui. iij. mois. Au derrenier
fu enuoiez querre baudoins ses
freres li cuens de roes. por uenir

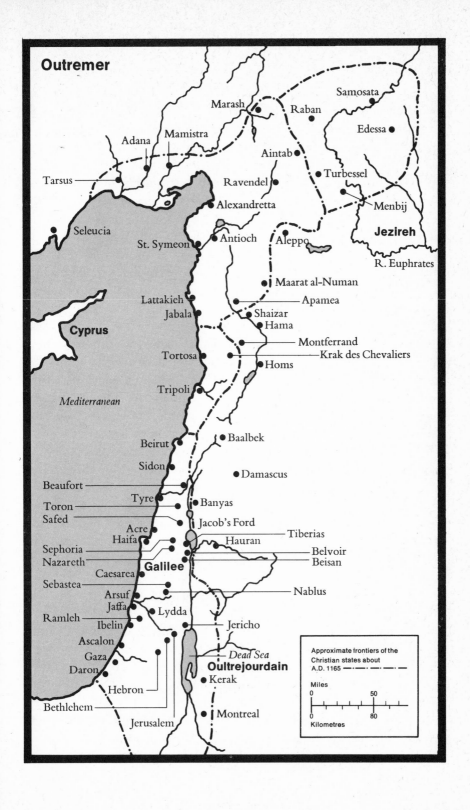

burnt. He died a few days later, and except among the Provençals, who swore that he had been pushed back into the flames by people eager to touch the hem of his miraculous garment, both he and the lance he had discovered were wholly discredited.

After Peter's death, Raymond reluctantly abandoned the siege of Arqa, and led the army south by way of the coastal road. The governor of Tripoli hastened to assure the Christians of his friendship, providing them with money, horses, supplies and guides, and the citizens of Beirut proved equally keen to please. One after another the great cities along the Mediterranean coast – Sidon, Tyre, Acre, Haifa and Jaffa – made friends with the Crusaders, or fell to them, or were left behind in embattled isolation. The Fatimids of Egypt, who were the nominal masters of this part of the country, were as unpopular with the local people as were the Turks farther north, and few of them made much trouble for Raymond. The inhabitants of Ramleh fled, and a Latin bishop was installed there and made secular lord of the place as well; in early June Tancred rode into Bethlehem and ran up his standard over the Church of the Nativity; and the next day the army climbed a hill, which they later named Montjoie, from which they could see Jerusalem. It had been three years since Godfrey of Bouillon had left Lorraine, but at last he and the Crusaders who had survived the hazards of the journey had arrived. They were hungry, tired and ragged, and shortly they were once again to prove themselves to be both murderous and barbarous; but as they gazed across the valley which separated them from the holiest city in the world with its honey-coloured stone walls, its clustered roofs and the great Dome of the Rock looking as resplendent as the Temple of Solomon, which many of them took it to be, there was not a man among them who was not genuinely moved to the bottom of his soul, and many had tears in their eyes. God had not deserted his people.

But if God had led them to the gates of Jerusalem, those gates remained obstinately shut against them, and they had no divine key with which to open them. Jerusalem had always been a formidably fortified city, and the walls which confronted the Crusaders were daunting; built originally by Hadrian, they had been strengthened and brought up to date with every new device of military engineering by Byzantines, Ommayads and Fatimids. The walls of the old city as we know it today were built at a later date by the Ottoman Turk, Suleiman the Magnificent; but they probably follow the same line as those of the Crusaders' time, and the city they besieged must have looked remarkably like the old city of

Jerusalem today. The Fatimid governor of the place had had ample warning of their coming, and had taken every possible precaution to make the city as impregnable as possible; he had expelled the local Christians, lest they should prove to be unreliable; he had laid in a vast store of food and water; he had poisoned the wells outside the city, thus destroying his enemy's water supply; and he had driven the flocks of sheep and goats and the herds of cattle from the surrounding countryside into the city, where they would feed his garrison of Egyptian and Sudanese soldiers while the Crusaders starved. Lastly, he had sent messengers to Egypt calling for help and impressing on the Caliph the need for haste in sending an army to the relief of the city. (A map of Jerusalem is on p. 131.)

Despite their very understandable fear of attacking so formidable a place without the aid of proper siege weapons, the leading Crusaders were encouraged to do so by an ancient Christian hermit who lived somewhere near the Mount of Olives. This old man advised them to attack the place at once, armed with absolute faith in God, and assured them that they would be victorious. They believed him. On the next day they stormed the walls on the north side of the city, and so impetuous was their attack that it proved irresistible. They overran the outer defences in an astonishingly short time, but there they were stopped; under a hail of arrows and stones from the defenders on the inner wall of the city, their faith, unsupported by enough scaling ladders, proved inadequate to take the Crusaders any farther. They fought for three hours, but then they bowed to the inevitable and retreated, carrying the dead and wounded with them.

It was a bitter disappointment, and the army succumbed to depression. Having failed to storm the city, they had no alternative but to besiege it until they could somehow find the materials to build proper weapons with which to renew their assault, and they had no idea where such materials could be found. They were cheered a little by the arrival of a mixed English and Genoese fleet in the port of Jaffa, bringing both food and war materials, but there was only enough of each to tide them over for a short time. What they needed was enough heavy timber to build movable assault towers which could be rolled up to the walls, and expeditions were despatched all over the country in search of it. But trees were exceedingly scarce, and it was not until some Crusaders reached the well-wooded hills round Nablus fifty miles north of Jerusalem that they found what they wanted. Even then the problem of how to carry a lot of heavy timber over the rough roads of Samaria and Judea remained, but in the end it was solved by using both Moslem prisoners and pack animals to drag the wood laboriously through the dust.

As work began on two great assault towers and a large number of scaling ladders, the weather became extremely hot. May and June are notorious in the eastern Mediterranean for a burning wind which blows from the deserts of north Africa for days on end, bringing unbearable temperatures and making life intolerable to both man and beast; known by the Arabs as the *khamsin*, its breath is like a blast of hot air from an electric hair-drier. The Crusaders, who had never experienced anything like it, were stifled, roasted and maddened by it. Whipped up into little tornados, it covered them in choking dust, filling their nostrils and their ears, getting into their eyes and their hair, and covering them when they were asleep; their food was coated with fine grit which grated between their teeth, and what water could be found was yellow and tasted of mud. But water was in such short supply that the men were perpetually thirsty and the animals soon began to die; parties of men were sent as far as the Jordan to fetch water, but they seldom came back with enough to quench the men's thirst, and after a time a few people began to desert.

Under such conditions, tempers became frayed, and arguments broke out as to why God should once again be chastening his people. Some thought that it was because Tancred had flown his own personal standard from the roof of the Church of the Nativity in Bethlehem in a moment of almost blasphemous arrogance; others believed that it was because so many of the lords of the Crusade had put their own personal ambition above their Christian duty; indeed, they were still behaving in the same self-seeking way, arguing about who should become King of Jerusalem when the city eventually fell. The clergy were adamant that no man ought to take such a title; there could be only one King of Jerusalem, and he had died on a Cross, upon which his title to such kingship had been pinned by order of Pontius Pilate over a thousand years previously. Most people agreed with the clergy, and the great lords bowed to public opinion; but the arguments did not make anyone better tempered. It was a bad summer.

In early July news arrived that a large Egyptian army was marching north to the relief of Jerusalem, and everyone began to wonder how the Crusaders, reduced now to about fifteen thousand men and weakened by privation and disease, could survive an encounter with them. It seemed that after they had come literally within a stone's throw of their goal, God was about to deny them the victory, and their spirits sank lower than ever. But they lived in a world in which the membrane which separated time from eternity, nature from God, was infinitely thin and liable to rupture at any moment, especially in hours of crisis, when consciousness was heightened by anxiety, and on the night of 5 July a priest named Peter Desiderius had a miraculous encounter with Adhemar of Le Puy, who had been dead for some months. The late bishop told Desiderius that if the Crusaders would give up their selfish ways, observe a day of fasting and walk around the city in procession barefoot, they would capture it in nine days. Without hesitation the entire army accepted this vision as genuine, and a fast was ordered at once; then, on 8 July, everyone joined in a solemn procession round the walls of Jerusalem. Led by the bishops and the priests, who were closely followed by the knights, the Crusaders and their women stumbled painfully on bare feet over the rocky hills round Jerusalem, while the Moslem defenders of the city crowded onto its walls to watch them. They were hugely amused by the antics of their Christian enemies, and mockingly carried crosses on their own backs in derision, while their women threw dung at them and screamed unintelligible abuse; but the Crusaders ignored them. When they reached the Mount of Olives, Peter the Hermit, Raymond the chaplain and a celebrated preacher named Arnulf of Rohes preached to the assembled multitude one after the other, and did so so well that everyone went home confident that soon the city would be theirs.

During the next two days everyone lent a hand in finishing the great wooden siege towers. There were three of them, one smaller than the others, and they were armoured with oxhide against the Greek fire used by the defenders: a chemical compound of highly inflammable materials which was ignited and directed at attackers by machines like modern flame-throwers. The towers had been built out of sight of the Moslems, who were appalled when they suddenly saw these enormous and menacing mobile castles being trundled slowly but inexorably towards the walls of the city. The military governor ordered his men to strengthen the defences at the points which seemed to be menaced, and as his men worked frantically to raise and reinforce the wall, others kept up a steady bombardment with stones and Greek fire against the siege towers as they drew nearer; but for the time being most of their ammunition was wasted, for the Crusaders and their towers were out of range. Before they could push the towers into place and launch their attack, the outer wall had to be destroyed, and the ditch at the foot of the main wall had to be filled in; then and only then could the mobile towers be pushed right up to their allotted battle stations. This was dangerous work, but most of it was done on the night of 13 July and during the following day; both sides maintained a heavy bombardment, and the men working at the foot of the wall inevitably suffered casualties, but by the night of 14 July one of the towers had been wheeled into position, and Raymond of Toulouse tried to launch an attack from its summit. But the defenders fought with courage and ferocity, and Raymond's men could make no headway. It seemed that stalemate had been reached.

No one slept much that night. 'It was a night of fear for both sides,' wrote Raymond of Aguilers later. 'The Saracens dreaded that we might storm the city during the darkness, since their outer wall had been broken down and the ditch filled up; and we on our part feared that they would set fire to the towers which were now close to the inner wall. So it was a night of watching and work and unsleeping care.' As dawn broke the next morning, 15 July, the task of pushing the second of the great towers towards the foot of the north wall was begun. Godfrey of Bouillon and his brother Eustace of Boulogne were in command of the upper storey, but the resistance of the defenders was as fierce as ever, and as the morning wore on it looked as though they might prove too strong for the attackers. Some of Godfrey's knights urged him to abandon the tower and withdraw, but he would have none of it, and although the men who were painfully inching the huge construction nearer to its objective were suffering heavier and heavier casualties, he would not give the order to retreat. Stones and fire rained down on them, and the heat of the sun was becoming so intolerable that some men stripped off their armour in sheer desperation, preferring to be killed by an arrow than to be roasted to death; but like Godfrey they had no intention of giving up, and at noon they brought the tower to within three feet of the inner wall. As the watching army cheered wildly and the Moslems roared their defiance, a wooden platform at the top of the wall, from which the defenders had been hurling stones at the Crusaders, was set alight by arrows wrapped in flaming cotton; as the flames and the smoke spread, the defenders were thrown into momentary confusion, and Godfrey seized his opportunity. He ordered someone to cut the ropes which held up the drawbridge, and it crashed down onto the flaming rampart. Immediately, two Flemish knights from the city of Tournai ran across it onto the top of the wall, and Godfrey followed with a handful of picked men who had been waiting for this moment. As they spread out and captured a small sector of the wall, the men below raised scaling ladders against it, and swarmed up to join them, while others clambered up the tower and streamed across the drawbridge to reinforce Godfrey's advance party. The defences had been breached, and nothing could now save Jerusalem.

While Godfrey and his Lorrainers consolidated their position on the wall, Tancred led a party of Normans down into the city and threw open one of the city gates to the waiting army. As the Crusaders poured into the streets the Moslem defenders retreated to the old Temple area, where the Dome of the Rock and the sacred Mosque of al-Aqsa stood and where they intended to make a last stand against the invading Christians, but Tancred and his men caught many of them before they could resist, and they surrendered to him. He promised them their lives in return for a huge ransom, and when they agreed, he gave them his banner to fly over the mosque in token that they were under his protection; but in the event it did them little good, for once the Crusaders were let loose inside the city, they succumbed to an immense and terrible blood lust. For months they had suffered great privations; they had watched their comrades die of disease, of hunger and of thirst, and they had seen them killed in battle; they had just won a great victory, and after the heat, fear and blood of the last two or three days they were in a state of almost hysterical exaltation; moreover, they did not doubt for a moment that the Moslem defenders of Jerusalem were hateful to God, profaners of the holy places, servants of anti-Christ and worshippers of the abomination of desolation mentioned in the Bible; so they killed every man, woman and child whom they could find in the city with enjoyment and a complete assurance that they were doing the will of God. The massacre went on and on throughout the day and far into the following night. When the chaplain Raymond of Aguilers went to visit the Temple area the next morning he found it a wilderness of corpses; the Mosque of al-Aqsa with Tancred's banner still fluttering from its roof and the Dome of the Rock were both so full of the bodies of the slain that blood came up to his knees. The only people who escaped from the city with their lives were the governor and his bodyguard, whom Raymond allowed to leave after paying him a huge bribe and handing over an enormous treasure. Everyone else was slaughtered, including the Jews, who were first herded into their chief synagogue and then burnt alive as the building was set on fire. When there was no one else to kill, the victors went in procession through the streets of the city, still littered with corpses and stinking of death, to the Church of the Holy Sepulchre to give thanks to God for His manifold and great mercies and for the triumph of the Cross which they had just won in His name.

X

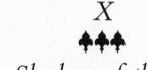

The Shadow of the Crown

Titles are shadows, crowns are empty things.
Daniel Defoe, *The True-Born Englishman*

The capture of Jerusalem was the supreme achievement of the Crusade; it was for that it had set out, fought and striven, and it was the answer to the prayers of every Christian in western Europe. But Pope Urban, who had called upon the Crusaders to march east under the banner of the Cross to free the holy places from the dominion of the Turks, was not destined to lead the victory celebrations or the prayers of thanksgiving for this triumph of Christian arms, for he died a fortnight after the fall of the city and before the news reached Europe. Despite his death, however, when the news did eventually arrive everyone went wild with delight. God had forgiven the mistakes and sins of the past and had led his people to a great victory.

This was a conclusion with which the Crusaders in Jerusalem entirely agreed; but curiously enough, now that they had reached their goal, they were at a loss as to what to do next. No one had ever questioned the supreme importance of capturing Jerusalem; it was the holy city of Christian faith, and therefore self-evidently it should be in Christian hands, but what those hands should do with it, now that they held it, no one knew. Meanwhile, however, there were two urgent tasks to be

8

done: the city had to be cleared of thousands of rotting corpses, and some sort of defence against a Moslem counter-attack must be prepared. The first was unpleasant but comparatively easily done, but the second was more difficult, for the rivalry between the princes was as bad as ever, and until the leadership of the army had been decided, no proper plans could be made. If Adhemar of Le Puy had been alive, almost certainly he would have been made Archbishop and Patriarch of Jerusalem, and under his guidance the problem of the secular leadership would have been solved amicably and quickly; probably Raymond of Toulouse would have been chosen, and with Adhemar's authority behind him the other leaders would have accepted him without too much animosity. But Adhemar was dead, and there was no one with his authority to take his place.

When the leaders met, they succeeded in agreeing about only one thing: a Patriarch should be elected at once, for the spiritual leadership of the city and the army was paramount. Symeon, the Greek Patriarch of Jerusalem, had just died in Cyprus; but even if he had been alive, he would have been too far away to be of any use to them, and they set about trying to choose one of their own number to fill the archiepiscopal throne. But this was too much for their fragile unity, and the Provençals, led by Raymond, were soon squabbling with the Normans over the appointment. Arnulf of Rohes, one of the men who had preached to the assembled Crusaders on the eve of the assault upon Jerusalem, was favoured for the post by the Normans; he was chaplain to Robert of Normandy and had been tutor to some of William the Conqueror's children, but there were serious objections to his candidacy, and Raymond allowed no one to forget them. Admittedly he was a well educated man, but he was illegitimate, his morals were notoriously lax, and he was not even a sub-deacon. Tempers became so frayed that the selection of an archbishop was abandoned for the time being, and the even more divisive issue of who should become secular leader was tackled instead. Only two of the many men who had set out from Constantinople were serious contenders; Baldwin was not in the running, for he was in Edessa; Bohemund was in Antioch; both Stephen of Blois and Hugh of Vermandois had gone home, and neither Eustace of Boulogne nor Tancred had a large enough following to be a serious candidate. The field was further reduced by the fact that both Robert of Normandy and Robert of Flanders had announced that they wanted to return home as soon as possible, now that the main objective of the Crusade had been achieved, and this left only Raymond of Toulouse and Godfrey of Bouillon.

Even if all the original leaders had been starters in the race for power, Raymond of Toulouse would probably have been the favourite, for in many ways he was the obvious candidate; he was immensely rich, senior to the others in both age and experience, and he had been Adhemar's friend. But the Normans disliked him, and he had proved unsuccessful as a general; moreover, he had backed Peter Bartholomew and consistently argued in favour of the authenticity of the holy lance, and when both were rejected as spurious by most people, his reputation and standing had suffered. Lastly, it was said that many of his own followers did not want him to be chosen, for they wanted to go home. Nevertheless, the Council of bishops and lords, which was charged with the election, eventually decided to offer the throne to Raymond. To everyone's surprise he refused it on the ground that he did not want to be King of Jerusalem; there could be only one King of Jerusalem, he said, and that was Christ. He may have suspected that the offer was half-hearted, and he may have hoped by his reply to make it impossible for Godfrey to be made king in his place. The electors, however, turned at once to his rival, who agreed to assume the leadership, but refused to be called 'King'; instead, he let it be known that he would like to be called *Advocatus Sancti Sepulchri*, the Defender of the Holy Sepulchre, and thus the affair was settled.

Raymond was furious, and behaved like a spoilt child, refusing to accept Godfrey of Bouillon's authority or to hand over the citadel of Jerusalem, a building known as the Tower of David, of which he had taken charge. This exhibition of pettiness shocked even his supporters, and it was not long before he was tricked into leaving the Tower, whereupon he flew into a rage and marched out of Jerusalem with all his men, whom he led down to the Jordan and thence to Jericho, where he stayed sulking.

Relieved of his somewhat awkward presence, the lords in Jerusalem returned to the task of appointing an archbishop of the city, and despite his obvious faults Arnulf of Rohes was eventually chosen and consecrated. Not surprisingly, in view of his secular background, he proved to be acceptable to Godfrey and the other secular authorities but hopelessly insensitive and tactless with the Greek clergy and the native Christians, who had been delighted to be liberated from the Turks but soon began to regret their change of masters. Arnulf's one aim seemed to be to put western clergy, who practised the Latin rite, into every vacant post in place of the Greek clergy of the Orthodox Church, who had always been there; he even forbade the priests of the Greek rite entry into the Church of the Holy Sepulchre, and he bitterly antagonised members of the smaller churches such as the Armenians, the Copts and the Jacobites by treating them as heretics. They had been better treated by the Moslems.

Godfrey had not taken the reins of government into his hands for long before news began to arrive of an enormous Egyptian army which had crossed the Sinai desert into Palestine; it was commanded by the Vizier of Egypt himself, an Armenian by the name of Al-Afdal, and it was advancing on the coastal town of Ascalon. Tancred and Eustace of Boulogne were away from Jerusalem, having gone to Nablus to accept the submission of its inhabitants, but when a messenger from Godfrey brought them the news, they moved down onto the coastal plain near Caesarea and thence marched south towards the advancing Egyptians, capturing some of their scouts on the way. From these unfortunates they extracted the information that the Vizier was not expecting the Christians to attack him; taking his time, he was waiting for his fleet to catch up with him with supplies, while his men recovered from their long march across the Sinai. Realising the crucial importance of this information, Tancred and Eustace sent a message to Godfrey advising him to join them with every man he could muster as quickly as he possibly could; the situation was potentially extremely dangerous, and by far the best hope of success lay in taking al-Afdal and his greatly superior force by surprise.

It is a measure of how widely divided by jealousy the lords of the Crusade had become that Raymond, who was still sulking in Jericho, and Robert of Normandy, who had also fallen out with Godfrey for some reason, refused to march with him until the news from Tancred and Eustace had been independently confirmed. Robert of Flanders alone responded at once, and on 9 August 1099 he and Godfrey marched out of Jerusalem with all their men. Archbishop Arnulf and most of the clergy went with them, for prayer was as much a weapon of war as a suit of armour or a sword, and it would have been unthinkable to every Crusader to neglect the spiritual side of the coming battle. When they reached Ramleh, where Tancred and Eustace were waiting for them, there was no doubt left in anyone's mind that the fate of the Crusade would be decided within the next few days, and one of the bishops accompanying Arnulf was sent back to Jerusalem to urge the others to join them as soon as they could. Convinced at last, Raymond and Robert of Normandy set out on 10 August with almost every man who could bear arms, although a tiny garrison was left behind, and Peter the Hermit was ordered to mobilise every Christian in the city, both Greeks and Latins, to pray without ceasing for victory. By the next morning Raymond and his Provençals and Robert with his Normans made contact with Godfrey, Robert of Flanders, Tancred and Eustace of Boulogne, and the entire Christian army set out together to march south. It was much smaller than it had once been; now it numbered no more than twelve thousand knights and about nine thousand infantrymen.

They marched steadily through the dust and heat of a typical Palestinian summer day, and as the afternoon wore on and the sun sank lower in a cloudless sky their scouts suddenly raised an alarm; ahead of them through the heat haze, shimmering in the glare of a hot and breathless early evening, they seemed to discern an army of men and horses; but the light was so dazzling and disruptive that it was like seeing an army in a mirage. Two hundred knights rode out to investigate, and as they drew nearer they found themselves surrounded by great herds of camels, cattle, sheep and goats, tended by a few terrified Arabs who fled at their approach; they were the herds brought by the Vizier to feed his army, and they fell into the Crusaders' hands. The result was that everyone fed well that night. 'We passed the night uncomfortably, for we had no tents and no wine. Some of us had bread, and a few had grain and salt; but meat was as plentiful as the sand itself. We ate beef, and eked it out with fat mutton for bread,' wrote Raymond the chaplain.

In the first light of dawn the next day they formed up on the plain north of Ascalon, where the Egyptian army was still asleep in camp. The Vizier's men were taken entirely by surprise, and although they were twice as numerous as the Christians, they put up no resistance worthy of the name; some were killed where they lay sleeping, while others fled for their lives in wild panic. Few escaped; a large number hid in a copse of sycamore trees, but the Crusaders set fire to it and they were burnt to death; others were driven into the sea, either to be killed in the shallows or drowned; Robert of Normandy and Tancred smashed their way into the centre of the enemy camp with a handful of mounted knights, killing al-Afdal's standard bearer and capturing his tent and all his personal belongings, while the rest of the knights chased the scattered remnants of the terrified Egyptian army down the road to Ascalon, killing them as they fled. The Vizier with one or two of his personal attendants was one of the few people to reach the safety of the city, where he hastily took a ship for Egypt. Everyone else was either killed or captured, and the victory of the Crusaders was complete.

Once again it was spoiled by an outbreak of violent quarrelling between the triumphant leaders, who seemed quite incapable of working together except in moments of crisis. Jerusalem had been saved, and Ascalon, the most important port within easy distance of Jerusalem, should now have fallen into their hands like a ripe plum; indeed, the Moslem governor offered to surrender the city, but he made his offer to Raymond of Toulouse, not to Godfrey. He probably chose the Provençal because he had a higher reputation than the others, whose names had been stained by the barbarity of their actions during the massacre after the fall of Jerusalem. Godfrey was both furious and deeply suspicious of Raymond's intentions if the city were to surrender to him, and he refused to have anything to do with such an arrangement This was too much for Raymond, who decided to wash his hands of the whole matter, marching his men away northwards in a mood of angry resentment and hurt pride; and both Robert of Normandy and Robert of Flanders were so appalled by Godfrey's small-mindedness that they too left him. Without them Godfrey was far too weak to attack Ascalon, and the chance of capturing it was lost; it did not recur for over fifty years.

As Godfrey returned to Jerusalem the two Roberts announced that they were going home, and marched their men north on the first stage of their long journey; they had performed their vows, and they had no wish to serve under Godfrey. Raymond of Toulouse marched north with them, hoping to carve out a lordship for himself as Baldwin, Bohemund and Godfrey had all succeeded in doing, although unlike them he would probably have been content to hold it as the vassal of the Byzantine Emperor. He was horrified, therefore, as were the two Normans, when all three reached the city of Lattakieh on the Syrian coast to find Bohemund besieging it and its Byzantine garrison, while a fleet from Pisa with the new papal legate, Archbishop Daimbert, on board blockaded the place from the sea. The Pisans, who were a wild and savage lot, had agreed to carry the Archbishop to Outremer in the hope of gaining valuable trading concessions, yet on the way they had not hesitated to behave like pirates. They had raided a number of Byzantine ports and islands, to the fury of Alexius, who had ordered his own fleet to punish them; but they had been lucky, eluding the Greek ships. On arrival at Lattakieh, they found Bohemund already besieging it, and at his invitation they joined him. Raymond loathed Bohemund, and was furious, while the two Roberts, who realised that without the goodwill of the Byzantines they would never reach home, were equally appalled; all three were aghast too at the stupidity of Daimbert in allowing himself to become involved in a minor war with the Byzantines, who were, after all, his fellow Christians. Summoning Daimbert to their camp at Jabala, they managed to persuade him to call off his Pisan fleet, and since Bohemund could not possibly reduce Lattakieh without its aid, he retired with great ill will to Antioch. For the moment the crisis was over, but relations with the Byzantines had not been improved, and the new papal legate could scarcely have begun his career in Outremer in a more inauspicious manner.

As the two Roberts made their way home, Raymond settled down in Lattakieh as the honoured guest of the Byzantine governor. Meanwhile, Godfrey had time to assess his position in Jerusalem. It was not impressive. He was desperately short of men, and although his little kingdom was safe from a Moslem counter-attack for the time being, the coastal cities were still held by men who were his enemies, even if they had been behaving in a disarmingly friendly manner ever since the Egyptian army had been annihilated. So, when Daimbert, Bohemund and Baldwin of Edessa severally announced their intention of coming to Jerusalem to discharge their vows as pilgrims, Godfrey was pleased, hoping to persuade a few of their followers to stay and swell his pitifully small garrison. In the event, he succeeded in doing so, but the other results of their visit were not so happy. Daimbert deposed Arnulf as Archbishop of Jerusalem on the grounds that his election had been uncanonical, and arranged things in such a way that he himself was promptly elected Patriarch in his place. He then insisted that Godfrey should kneel before him to be invested as the legitimate ruler of Jerusalem; the fact that Bohemund agreed to submit to the same ceremony, to be invested by Daimbert as the legitimate ruler of Antioch, was little consolation to Godfrey, who knew that he would have to live with the new Patriarch and his overbearing ways when Bohemund had gone home. Moreover, by his action Godfrey tacitly acknowledged Daimbert as his feudal superior, even if the acknowledgement was no more than tacit. Baldwin of Edessa, however, was a man of a different stamp, and he was conspicuous by his absence during the investiture; he had no intention of kneeling before any man.

Encouraged by his success in persuading some of the visiting knights to stay in Jerusalem, Godfrey felt strong enough after the departure of Bohemund and his brother Baldwin to take the offensive against some of the coastal cities still held by the Moslems, and one by one they came to terms with him. At one point the Egyptians tried to intervene by

A secret underground passage below the Crusader castle in Acre.

Ronald Sheridan

Modern stained glass in the ancient Church of St Denis near Paris showing Peter the Hermit preaching and Louis VII trouncing the Moslems in battle. While it is highly misleading historically, it is a good example of the romantic version of events which gained both credence and popularity in Christian countries, where latterly it was widely propagated both by the Church and by historians.

Bulloz

The sea walls at Acre. After the loss of Jerusalem to Saladin, Acre became the principal Crusader city in Outremer and the seat of the Kings of Jerusalem. When it fell to the Mameluks in May 1291, it was from the harbour here that those who could do so escaped to the waiting ships.

Ronald Sheridan

The refectory of the Knights of St John in Acre. Until recently these buildings were entirely filled with dust and rubble, and it was only after they were excavated that anyone discovered how extensive and splendid they were.

Ronald Sheridan

PIERRE·L'ERMITE·PRECHE·LA·
PREMIERE·CROISADE·

LES·CROISES·METTENT·EN·
FVITE·LES·MVSVLMANS·

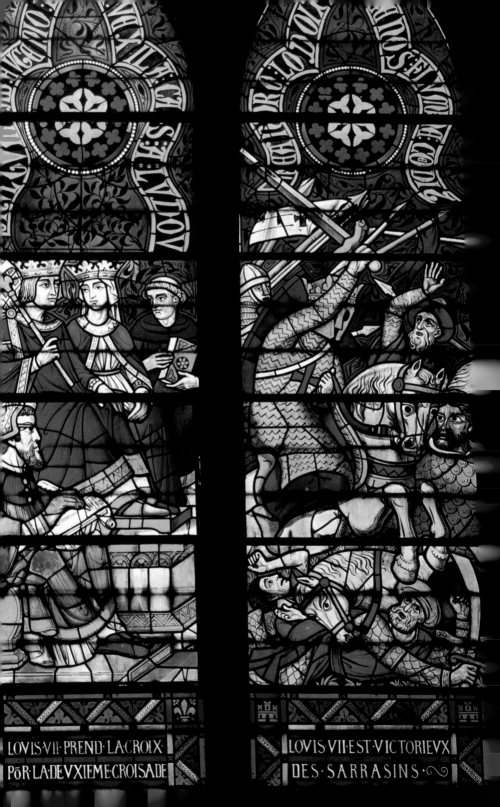

LOVIS · VII · PREND · LA · CROIX
PÓR · LA · DEVXIEME · CROISADE

LOVIS · VII · EST · VICTORIEVX
DES · SARRASINS ·

sending some troops to reinforce one of the places which Godfrey was besieging, but their arrival merely encouraged the hungry garrison to sally forth and try conclusions with Godfrey's men, who ambushed and destroyed them. In despair the citizens begged for terms, and Godfrey accepted their submission without making impossible demands upon them. Encouraged by this example, it was not long before the Emirs of Ascalon, Caesarea and Acre also decided to submit to him and to pay him tribute, and a little later the Arabs of Transjordan approached him too in the hope of establishing some sort of friendly relations; their livelihood depended on their trade with the Moslems of the coastal plain, and since Godfrey's new state lay across their trade routes, it was important for them to make friends with their new Christian neighbours. Godfrey had the good sense to realise that, if a Christian presence was to be firmly established in the Holy Land, perpetual war with Islam would be politically impossible, and he welcomed the Arab overtures, allowing their caravans to cross his domain, and encouraging their merchants to trade with his people. As a result, not only did the citizens of the new Crusader state become increasingly prosperous, but their relations with their Moslem neighbours improved almost daily as the facts of geography and economics forced both sides to discover the advantages of co-operation.

Godfrey's biggest trouble was caused by the papal legate, Daimbert, who as time passed showed clearly enough that he had no intention of restricting himself to the role of Patriarch and Archbishop of Jerusalem, or of allowing Godfrey to treat him as merely his nominal suzerain; on the contrary, he took every opportunity to grasp the reality of secular power. Godfrey did not dare to stand up to him, partly because he was in awe of the Church, and partly because he was afraid of offending the Pisans, upon whose continued naval support he depended for the security of his realm; so, when he heard that a large Venetian squadron had put in at Jaffa, he hurried down to the coast to meet them, for if he could secure their support he could free himself of his dependence on the Pisans. He took the road through Tiberias and Caesarea, where the Emir proved eager to honour him as his guest and invited him to a banquet. He was treated with the greatest respect, and the fare was sumptuous, but by the time he bade farewell to his host Godfrey was feeling unwell, and when he arrived at Jaffa he collapsed. He felt a little better the next day, and at his own request he was carried back to Jerusalem in a litter, but on arrival he was extremely weak, and everyone feared the worst.

But he did not die at once. While Daimbert waited impatiently for his death in order to seize supreme power for himself, Godfrey, although still very weak, continued to conduct the day-to-day business of government; he gave the Venetians far-reaching concessions in return for their support, and despite his friendly relations with the Emirs on the coast, he ordered an attack on Acre. He gave command of the army to one of his knights, a certain Warner of Gray, and when Tancred arrived from Galilee to join the expedition they rode out of Jerusalem together. Daimbert went with them, almost certainly hoping and intending to take command of the army as soon as the long delayed event for which he was waiting should take place in Jerusalem. He did not have to wait much longer. On 18 July 1100, Godfrey of Bouillon, Duke of Lower Lorraine and *Advocatus Sancti Sepulchri*, quietly died.

If Daimbert had been in the city, he would have seized his opportunity, and it is doubtful if anyone could have stopped him. As things were, however, a group of Godfrey's own Lorrainers, who hated the papal legate, took control of the city, and sent a messenger to Baldwin of Edessa, Godfrey's brother, inviting him to come at once and take over his rightful inheritance as next of kin. Distances were huge and communications slow, but although it took him a long time to do so and Daimbert tried to stop him on the way, Baldwin eventually reached Jerusalem to claim the inheritance from his brother. He, however, had no religious scruples about claiming the kingship, and on Christmas Day 1100, although he swore to defend the Holy Sepulchre, he was crowned King of Jerusalem.

XI

♣♣♣

Times and Seasons

To everything there is a season, and a time...a time to be born
and a time to die; a time to plant, and a time to pluck up that
which is planted; a time to kill, and a time to heal...a time of
war, and a time of peace.

Ecclesiastes, 3, 1-8

Baldwin I of Jerusalem reigned for eighteen years. He did more than any
man to consolidate the victories of the First Crusade and to establish the
Crusader kingdoms of Outremer as lasting political realities. When he
succeeded his brother Godfrey, the little kingdom which he inherited
was totally unorganised, virtually bankrupt, served by a handful of lawless
knights from Lorraine and a few unreliable local mercenaries, and beset
by enemies within and without. He knew that the Moslems would
inevitably mount a counter-attack one day and that the other Christian
princes were both jealous of him and determined to carve out their own
petty kingdoms, even if they had to do so at his expense; and the one
organised power in the land, the Church, was headed by Archbishop
Daimbert, who loathed him. Almost his only assets were his own
very considerable talents and the reputation which he had gained for
both invincibility and utter ruthlessness, and these he exploited to the
utmost.

He cowed the Arabs to the south and east of Jerusalem in a number of
ferocious raids; he captured some coastal cities, and butchered their
inhabitants to increase the fear of his name; and he defeated an Egyptian

army of over thirty thousand men with the aid of only two hundred and sixty knights and less than a thousand infantry, although he nearly lost both his life and his kingdom in a subsequent encounter with another Egyptian army. Five years after his coronation he captured Acre, and thus secured what he needed most: a port which was safe in all weathers; and he went on to capture Sidon, providing both his Genoese and Venetian allies with safe anchorages for their fleets, on which he depended for naval power and for communications with Europe by sea. He was so successful in consolidating his kingdom that towards the end of his life he even decided to invade Egypt in an effort to destroy his most powerful enemy; but although his campaign began well he was struck down by a mortal disease before he could finish it. His men tried to carry him home to die, but he died at the little frontier town of el-Arish. His body was brought back to Jerusalem and, on Palm Sunday 1118, he was buried in the Church of the Holy Sepulchre next to his brother Godfrey. At his death his kingdom stretched from Beirut in the north to Beersheba in the south, and from the river Jordan in the east to the Mediterranean coast, where only Ascalon and Tyre remained in the hands of his enemies. His was a truly remarkable achievement.

During Baldwin's reign, many of the original Crusaders went home, but others settled down to spend the rest of their lives in Outremer. Many of the minor knights and most of the rank and file had little or no incentive to make the return journey. But perhaps the words 'settled down' are misleading, for life in the Crusader kingdoms throughout their history was turbulent and unsettled. Internally it was beset by dynastic quarrels between the great ruling families, who were violently jealous of one another and chronically incapable of living in peace together, while externally it was lived against a background of almost perpetual war with the Moslems. Most histories of the Crusades have concentrated on the tortuous and bewildering course of these internal and external wars, and unavoidably so; for, as Runciman, the greatest recent English historian of the period, remarked in his *History of the Crusades*, 'war was the background to life in Outremer, and the hazards of the battlefield often decided its history'. But the repetitively homicidal events of the time were, after all, no more than a background to that life, which evolved a style of its own as the years went by. On the whole, the chroniclers do not describe it; how their contemporaries lived when they were not fighting battles was unimportant to them. But scattered throughout the records and the literature of the times there are scraps of information from which a picture of daily life in the Crusader kingdoms can be built up, especially that of the noble families and the wealthier classes.

The first Crusaders were nearly all either Norman or French, and the states they founded were unmistakably created by Frenchmen; everyone spoke French, and the feudal structure of contemporary French society was faithfully reproduced in Outremer, while the Orthodox Church and its Greek liturgy was ousted by the Catholic Church and its Latin rite. During the two centuries of their existence, the Crusader kingdoms did not change in these respects. In all sorts of other ways, however, the way of life there was profoundly changed by the climate, the physical conditions and the natural resources of the land, and as the years went by the Franks of Outremer succumbed to a slow process of orientalisation, the results of which regularly shocked newcomers from the West. Perhaps if they had been more numerous, more of their western ways and customs might have remained unchanged over the years, but during the whole course of their history they were a tiny minority both racially and socially in the lands which they ruled. It has been estimated that there were never as many as a thousand knights resident in the Kingdom of Jerusalem, although their numbers were swollen by visitors from time to time; and much the same was true of the entire knightly population of the Principality of Antioch and the Counties of Edessa and Tripoli taken together. The rank and file were more numerous, but even they were vastly outnumbered by the local people. These consisted of Greek-speaking Christians alongside Armenians, Jews, Egyptians and Arabs, some of whom were Christians and some Moslem, but there was not much social contact between the Franks and those whom they ruled. Inter-marriage was exceedingly rare; in aristocratic circles members of the ruling families tended to marry only members of similar families, although a few of them married well-bred Armenians or Byzantines, all of them Christian. Any kind of sexual intercourse with a Moslem, in marriage or in concubinage, was strictly outlawed; indeed, the Council of Nablus in 1120 decreed that a man found guilty of going to bed with a Moslem woman should both be castrated and have his nose cut off. But members of less exalted Frankish families felt free to marry the daughters of local Christians, whatever their ethnic origins might have been; and the result was that, as time went by, their descendants, who were known as *poulains*, were often difficult to distinguish from other members of the native population. In contrast, the Venetians, the Pisans and the Genoese, who as time went by were to be found acting as merchants and *entrepreneurs* in almost every city, kept their identity better than most of the Franks, partly because they lived together in streets allocated to them by the various princes with whom they had made treaties, and partly because they travelled to and from Italy on their mercantile occasions, and so never lost touch with their native cities.

Life in the villages was much the same as it had been in Old Testament times, so little had it changed, but very few Franks settled in them. Wherever it was possible, they were built on the tops of hills, both because such sites were more easily defended than more accessible settings, and also because they were windier and thus both cooler in summer and better suited for winnowing at harvest time. Those Franks who did live in the villages had to endure the primitive conditions endured by the native villagers, and this was one reason why they were unpopular. Those who lived in the towns enjoyed much better amenities. Some lived in simple, single-storeyed houses, but most had homes with two floors, and the rich lived in much grander abodes, which they called 'palaces'; these were built in a style inherited from Graeco-Roman days, as much else had been by Arab civilisation in that part of the world. Usually they consisted of a square of rooms on two floors surrounding a central *patio*; apart from the main entrance, all the doors and windows opened onto the central court, as did a row of verandas in the more luxurious houses, and their roofs were flat. People slept upstairs, while the living-rooms, dining-rooms and kitchens were on the ground floor. Unlike their oriental subjects, who reclined to eat their meals as the Romans had before them, the Franks sat around a table when they ate together; the table was covered with a cloth, lit by candles or oil lamps at night and, as the years went by and old prejudices slowly died, it was furnished with just such luxuries as knives, spoons and forks, glass decanters and goblets, elegant dishes and plates, as had aroused the angry derision of the first Crusaders to pass through Constantinople and observe the 'effeminate' table manners of Alexius' court.

The Franks personal habits changed in many ways too, although not in all. The men continued to wear their hair long to their shoulders and to shave their chins, although a few grew beards like those of the Greeks and Syrians. In Jerusalem there was a barbers' quarter near the Church of the Holy Sepulchre, to which many people went to be shaved once or twice a week, while others were shaved by attendants at the public baths; and presumably other cities had similar amenities. The women wore their hair in two long plaits, painted their faces and dressed superbly. A Spanish traveller who was in the Kingdom of Jerusalem in 1181, a man named Ibn Jubayr, was dazzled by a Frankish bride whom he saw on her wedding day in Tyre. 'She was most elegantly arrayed in a beautiful dress,' he wrote, 'from which there floated, according to their traditional style, a long train of silk. On her head she wore a golden diadem covered by a net of woven gold, and on her breast there was a similar ornament.' The men were scarcely less splendid; for some time they continued to wear European clothes, which consisted of long stockings, a shirt with long tight sleeves, and over it a short jacket with short sleeves, but whether these garments were made of fine wool, cotton, linen or silk, invariably they were brilliantly coloured and embroidered with gold or silver thread. But as the years passed most of the knights abandoned Western fashions altogether and, returning from whatever battlefield happened to have been claiming their professional attention at the time, removed their armour and put on a silk burnous in summer and furs in winter.

But perhaps the single biggest change in their habits took place in their attitude to personal hygiene. In Europe, washing had been despised, but in the climate of Outremer they began to patronise the public baths, to be found in every city. They were similar to the Turkish baths of today or the Roman baths of antiquity; the bather first undressed, and then donned a towel and sandals, although apparently some of the Franks sometimes dispensed with the towel; the Prince Usamah, a member of an independent dynasty of Munqidhite Arabs with a castle at Shaizar near Hama, who travelled widely through Outremer, made many Frankish friends, and wrote his *Memoirs*, complained that some people did not bother with a towel but bathed naked. But whether clothed or not, the bather entered a heated room, where he began to sweat; then, when he had sweated enough, he called an attendant, who soaped him all over, rubbed him down, and dried him with another towel. Before leaving he rested in an ante-room where couches were provided on which he could lie in comfort. Bathing became so much a part of everyone's way of life that it was even required on certain occasions; for instance, young men seeking admission as novices to one or other of the Military Orders were obliged to bathe in a communal bath-house before they were formally admitted. Women bathed as frequently as men, going to the baths two or three times a week, although needless to say they bathed separately from the men.

If the Franks were cleaner in Outremer than they had been at home in Europe, they were much better fed too; for not only was their food rich and varied, but it was cooked by local people who were artists in the kitchen. Chicken, crane, quail, pigeon and partridge were plentiful; mutton, beef, wild boar, ibex, roebuck and hare were cooked with garlic and herbs and seasoned with mustard and pepper, or served with delicious sauces; there was an abundance of freshwater fish, and eels were much prized as delicacies; cooked vegetables included such things as beans, peas, artichokes, asparagus and rice, while lettuces and cucumbers were eaten raw. When they first arrived, the Franks were astonished by the novelty and variety of the various kinds of fruit which they found growing everywhere, many of which they had never even heard of let alone seen or eaten; there were bananas, oranges, lemons, dates, carobs, the fruit of the sycamore tree which they named 'Pharaoh's figs', grapes, peaches, plums, quinces and ordinary figs, and with them various nuts including almonds. Since wine was forbidden to Moslems, there were no vineyards, but that was a deficiency soon remedied, and after the first few years wine was plentiful and much of it was good. In the heat of summer it was chilled with snow from the mountains of Lebanon, which was brought south protected from the heat of the sun by straw, and it was drunk both in private houses and in taverns. Beer brewed from barley was also popular, and fruit juices were cheap and easily available.

In the intervals between wars, some of the Franks practised trades of various kinds. They were great builders, as both their churches and their castles still testify, and although much of the work of building them must have been done by local Arabs and other native people, the masons' marks to be found on some of their stones proves that Frankish craftsmen were also active. The area around Tyre was famous for its pottery and glass, and a Frankish glass-smelting furnace has been found at Samariya near Acre, so some of the Crusaders must have learned how to blow glass from their Arab neighbours, who had been manufacturing it since Roman days and before; the Venetians, who held large parts of Tyre and the country round it, seem to have learned to be glass-makers there. There was a thriving textile industry in Outremer too, and probably some Franks were employed in the manufacture of silk and cotton fabrics. But then as now the most thriving industry was the manufacture of religious souvenirs for the pilgrims who came in large numbers to visit the holy places of the Christian faith, and the resident Franks must have been involved in this highly lucrative trade.

But if involvement in trade was not beneath the dignity of some of the less aristocratic Frankish citizens of Outremer, the knights scorned it as unworthy of their nobility; war was their profession, and when they were not fighting one another or their Moslem neighbours, they spent most of their time hunting. Mounted and armed with spears, they pursued such beasts of prey as lions, leopards, bears and wolves for the sheer enjoyment of the chase, while they also hunted wild boar, deer, ibex and hares for the pot. Needless to say, there were accidents from time to time and men were hurt or even killed; but this deterred no one. Foxes were also hunted with packs of hounds, and some parts of the country became famous for the excellence of the sport to be had there; Mount Tabor, the forests of Banyas on the foot hills of Mount Hermon, and the plain of Acre were all celebrated for their fox hunting. But the favourite sport of the nobility was falconry, and high prices were paid for good falcons. Usamah described a hunt near Acre at which a Genoese noble flew his falcon at cranes. 'Whenever the falcon was flown at the cranes,' he wrote, 'a bitch would run right below the falcon, so that the moment the falcon clutched a crane and brought it down, the hound would grab the crane in its teeth, and the bird could not escape.'

After the pleasures of the chase, race meetings and tourneys held pride of place. Tourneys were particularly popular. Generally they were held on race courses just outside one of the large towns or cities, and people would come from miles away to take part in them, while the local people flocked to watch them, so that a tourney was always a colourful affair. Essentially it consisted of war games; single combat between matched knights was popular, and so too were mock fights between groups of knights. The rival sides formed up on the open field, and each knight chose his opponent; when the sign to charge was given, both sides went into combat with their lances levelled, and as the ranks were thinned the few who still remained in the saddle charged each other again and again, until at last the knight who had unseated the largest number of 'enemies' was declared the champion. Such events were useful as training for the more serious business of war, but there was a lighter side to the tourneys too, and some of the games were nearer to buffoonery than to military training. Usamah described how, on one occasion when he was present as a spectator, 'the cavaliers went out to exercise with lances, but with them went two decrepit old women, whom they stationed at one end of the race course. At the other end of the field they left a pig which had been scalded and laid on a rock. Then they made the two old women run a race while each one was accompanied by a detachment of horsemen urging her on. At each step they took, the old women would fall down

9

and get up again, while the spectators roared with laughter. Finally, one of them got ahead of the other and won the pig'.

When they were not enjoying themselves out of doors, the Franks spent their time at home or visiting their friends, and as the years passed some of their houses became astonishingly luxurious: so luxurious indeed that they shocked newcomers from the West. Like the houses of wealthy Byzantines, the palaces of some of the richer Franks were adorned with Persian carpets, damask hangings, mosaic floors, inlaid marble walls, carved furniture of ivory or rare wood and dinner services of silver or Chinese porcelain brought by caravan from the East. Their owners slept in comfortable beds between fine linen sheets, and in some of the northern cities, where water was abundant the biggest houses had their own private bathrooms with running water. People played dice a great deal, and such games as chess were also played; they drank a lot, both at home and in taverns, and drunkenness was common. Musicians, strolling players and mimes performed in the squares of the cities and in other open spaces; their performances were popular and well attended, but the performers themselves were regarded as the lowest of the low, little better than prostitutes. These, too, were to be found on the streets of every city.

Most of these pursuits were, however, masculine preserves; it is difficult to discover what the Frankish women did in their spare time. No doubt the greater part of their lives was spent either preparing to be married or, after their marriages, bearing children, even if desperately few of their babies survived to the age of five. But everyone was used to the fact that in the midst of life they were in death, and they took the deaths of many of their children as much for granted as they took the way in which their marriages were arranged for them. It was not at all unusual for the children of the upper classes to be married when they were five or six years old in the hope that one day they might grow up to consummate their union and produce some dynastically desirable children, while on other occasions a child might be married to a much older adult in order to join two dynasties in a desirable political union; for instance, Baldwin III of Jerusalem married a little Byzantine princess named Theodora when she was thirteen years old and he was twenty-seven; he did this for entirely political reasons, although, as it happened, he fell deeply in love with her after the event and the marriage was an extremely happy one while it lasted. In fact, it did not last very long, for Baldwin died four years later. His still youthful widow then went on to show that marriage and childbirth were not the only pastimes open to women in

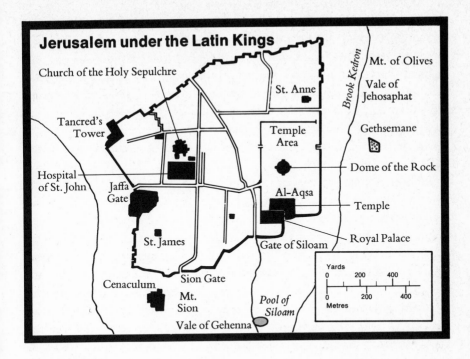

Jerusalem under the Latin Kings

Outremer, for she had a scandalous affair with a handsome but middle-aged Byzantine nobleman named Andronicus Comnenus. Andronicus seems to have been addicted to such illicit affairs; before meeting Theodora, he had already seduced the Byzantine Emperor's niece, a girl named Eudocia, as well as Bohemund's sister, the Princess Philippa, to the fury of their respective kinsmen.

Just as the standard of living of the Franks in Outremer was much higher than anything they had ever known at home in Europe, so they enjoyed a much higher standard of medical care too. The skill of their physicians was borrowed over the years from the Arabs, who were far in advance of doctors in the West. Indeed during the early years of the Crusader kingdoms everyone consulted local physicians in preference to men of their own race; the chronicler, William of Tyre, noticed how his contemporaries 'scorned the medicines and practice of our Latin physicians and believed only in the Jews, Samaritans, Syrians, and Saracens'. At the height of their prosperity and power, the Crusader kingdoms probably had more hospitals than any other countries of comparable size; in Jerusalem alone there were four, and Acre, Nablus, Ascalon, Jaffa and Tyre each had its own. The most famous medical institutions were run by the knights of the Order of the Hospital of St John the Baptist in Jerusalem, whose lives were devoted to the care and cure of the sick and whose military duties were always supposed to take second place to their medical tasks. Pilgrims were their special charge, and their first hospitals were built to accommodate sick visitors to the holy places. Each had four physicians and four surgeons, and the rules of the Order laid down in great detail how their patients should be fed, how their beds should be made, when they should be treated and what sort of medicines and drugs should be given to them.

The Hospitallers, as they came to be known, were founded by a monk named Gerard, who was in Jerusalem when the Crusaders besieged it; he was in charge of a small Christian hospital, and it was said of him afterwards that he had helped his fellow Christians outside the city by throwing loaves of bread to them from the walls when they were at their hungriest, while telling the Moslem defenders that he was bombarding them with stones. His trick was discovered, however, and he was dragged before the Moslem governor of the city and accused of treachery; but when the incriminating loaves were produced in evidence, they had been miraculously turned into stone, and Gerard was acquitted. The story won him immense popularity after the capture of the city, and he took the opportunity to enlarge and reconstitute his hospital and to recruit more monks to serve in it. Godfrey of Bouillon granted him and his new order of Hospitallers a castle and two bakehouses in Jerusalem itself, and it was not long before kings, grandees and princes of the Church throughout western Christendom were showering Gerard with properties in Provence, Spain, England, Italy and Portugal, where an entire province was made over to him, to endow his Order. Recruits also flowed in, for the new Order, being semi-monastic and semi-military, fulfilled a need for many men who longed to dedicate themselves to the religious life but whose only skills were military, and who were better adapted to an active rather than a passive or a contemplative life.

The Knights Templar, or the Poor Knights of Christ and the Temple of Solomon to give them their full title, were founded at about the same time as the Hospitallers by a Burgundian knight, Hugh of Payens, with the object of protecting pilgrims from attack by Moslems or robbers on their way to Jerusalem and the other holy places. At first there were only eight knights, but from this tiny beginning the Order soon grew to be immensely powerful and extremely wealthy, despite its official dedication to poverty. Both these Orders, the Templars and the Hospitallers, had the same structure, being divided into three classes: the knights, from whose number was chosen a Grand Master who ruled with autocratic powers and who had to be of noble birth; the Sergeants, who sprang from less aristocratic families; and, finally, the clergy, who acted as chaplains and performed other non-military duties. Vowed to poverty, chastity and obedience, as time went by the members of each Order became a corps of utterly dedicated professional soldiers who had no rivals in the world of the day; they were an *élite* body, and they knew it. Their courage became a by-word amongst friends and enemies alike; they were willing to go anywhere at any time and at a moment's notice, and they were invariably found fighting in the most dangerous places. At their best, some of the Hospitallers and Templars probably came as close to being like Chaucer's 'verray parfit gentil knight' – that is to say, the ideal knight of popular romantic imagination – as any of the Crusaders. Needless to say, they were extremely valuable to the rulers of Outremer, who used them rather as Commando units are used today. Unfortunately, as the years passed they developed glaring faults which tarnished their record: the natural rivalry between the two Orders gradually grew into a bitter mutual hatred, so that each loathed the other; and as their power grew each tended to consider itself a law unto itself. The welfare of the Order came to be regarded as much more important than the common good, and if the members of the Order did not like any particular command issued by the King, they simply disregarded it.

The Templars and Hospitallers, later supplemented by the Order of Teutonic Knights, were the only Military Orders, but they were by no means the only religious Orders in Outremer, for nearly all the great monastic Orders of the Catholic Church had houses there. Jerusalem was full of monasteries, amongst which the Augustinian abbeys on Mount Sion and the Mount of Olives and the Benedictine abbey of St Mary Latina were perhaps the most important. The Benedictines also had an abbey at Bethany, the Cluniacs one on Mount Tabor, the Premonstratensians on Montjoie, the Carmelities on Mount Carmel, the Cistercians in Tripoli and in Antioch, and there were other smaller monastic houses scattered all over the country. These were in addition to the many Greek Orthodox monasteries, which had existed long before the Crusaders had arrived, and the houses of such heretical Churches as the Jacobite Church, the Maronite Church and the Coptic Church, which had been tolerated by the Moslems. Church buildings were even more numerous than religious houses; there were about twenty-seven in Jerusalem alone, forty in Acre and twelve in Tyre, and these cities were not exceptional in this respect. Religion was at the centre of everyone's life, and so, in the words of James of Vitry, who was Bishop of Acre in the thirteenth century, 'the Holy Land flourished like a garden with many regular clergy, religious persons, hermits, monks, canons, nuns, cloistered virgins, and chaste and holy widows.' The focal point for all this religious devotion and activity was Jerusalem, but Christmas was celebrated at Bethlehem, and the other great festivals of the Church were observed in places traditionally associated with them: Ascension on the Mount of Olives, Whitsun on Mount Sion, Good Friday on Calvary and Easter Day in the Church of the Holy Sepulchre, where great crowds gathered annually to witness 'the miracle of the Sacred Fire', when flames kindled by God were used to light the lamps of the church.

In their daily lives, the Franks were capable of both appalling cruelty and great generosity and chivalry, as indeed were their Moslem enemies and neighbours, and on neither side were these extremes of behaviour confined to times of war. To give one example only of the kind of cruelty the Franks were capable of, in 1332 a Breton knight was arrested for attempted murder; since his victim was known to be an enemy of the incumbent King of Jerusalem, some suspicion fell on the monarch, who was understandably eager to clear his own name. The Breton was arrested and confessed his guilt, swearing that the King had had nothing to do with the crime; but this was not enough to satisfy the King. The man was condemned to death by having his limbs cut off one by one. The sentence was duly carried out in public and, when his arms and legs had been hacked off one after the other but his head remained, he was asked once again whether the King had been accessory to the crime; once again he denied it, and this at last satisfied his tormentors, who beheaded him.

Ghastly as such cruelty may have been, it was tempered from time to time by deeds of splendid magnanimity and compassion, of which once again only one example can be given here, although it is typical of many more. Just after his coronation as King of Jerusalem in 1100, Baldwin I was told that a rich tribe of Arabs was travelling through Transjordan, and he decided to attack it. He led a small force of knights across the Jordan and fell on the Arabs at night while they were asleep in their tents. Few of them escaped; most of them were killed, while the women and children were taken prisoner together with a huge booty of money and precious stuffs. Amongst the captive women there was the wife of one of the sheiks of the tribe. She was pregnant, and about to give birth to her child. When Baldwin heard of her condition, he gave orders that she should be set free at once together with her personal maid, two camels, and an ample supply of food and drink. She gave birth by the side of the road soon after her release, and there her husband found her; he was so moved by Baldwin's gallantry that he hurried after him to thank him.

Throughout their whole history the Franks in Outremer remained a conquering race. Rather like the British in India, especially the first nabobs, they found themselves far better off in their new home than they had ever been in Europe, and so there was a fairly constant stream of new arrivals from the West. Fulcher of Chartres described the situation. 'Every day our dependents and our relatives follow us, leaving behind, unwillingly perhaps, all their belongings. For he who was poor there now finds that God has made him rich here. He who had little money now possesses countless gold coins. He who did not hold even a village over there now enjoys a town which God has given him. Why should anyone return to the West, who has found an Orient like this?' Why indeed! Moreover, as time went by, in many little ways the Franks learned to live on friendly terms with their Moslem neighbours, and as the process of orientalisation continued to change their habits, the superficial differences between them diminished, and an ever firmer *modus vivendi* was established by the two sides. 'We who had been occidentals have become orientals,' wrote Fulcher of Chartres; 'the man who had been a Roman or a Frank has here become a Galilean or a Palestinian; and the man who used to live in Rheims or Chartres now finds himself a citizen of Tyre or Acre. We have already forgotten the places where we were born; already many of us know them not, or at any rate no longer hear them spoken of. Some among us already possess in this country houses and servants which belong to them as of hereditary right. Another has married a wife who is not his compatriot: a Syrian or an Armenian woman perhaps, or even a Saracen, who has received the grace of baptism. He who was once a stranger here is now a native.'

But two things prevented this process of slow assimilation from resulting in a full acceptance of the Franks by their non-Christian neighbours: the Moslems never forgot the massacres of their compatriots by the Christians in Antioch and Jerusalem; and during the whole history of the Crusader kingdoms there was a steady influx of newcomers from the West, whose first question on arrival was, 'Where are some Moslems that I may kill them?' Again and again, enthusiastic knights would arrive

This is thought to be a portrait of Saladin by an Egyptian artist of the Fatimid school, perhaps because the man portrayed appears to be blind in one eye, as was Saladin.

Fotomas Index

Masyaf Castle, the stronghold of the Assassins. They were members of a strict Moslem religious order, who brought political murder to a fine art under the leadership of Sheikh Rashid ed-Din Sinan, who was known to the Crusaders as the Old Man of the Mountains.

A. F. Kersting

The Castle of Kerak in the stony desert east of the Dead Sea. It commanded the pilgrim route from Damascus to the Red Sea and on to Mecca, by which route caravans also passed between Egypt and Syria. They were frequently raided by Reynald of Châtillon. It was besieged by Saladin at the time of the marriage of Humphrey of Toron to the Princess Isabella of Jerusalem, who did not allow the hostilities to interrupt their wedding celebrations.

A. F. Kersting

bursting with determination to do God service by slaughtering some of the enemies of Christ, with whom the citizens of Outremer might just have made a treaty or concluded a truce, which was not only necessary to their own welfare but sometimes essential to their survival. But such political arrangements seemed almost blasphemous to the less sophisticated Christians from the West, and usually nothing deterred them from charging out of Christian held territory in a fine flurry and fury of faith, hell-bent on a little godly bloodshed. The fact that they often got themselves killed in the process was little consolation to the long-suffering Franks, who had to live with the consequences of their aggression, which often included renewed warfare with their neighbours when they least wished it. Yet they could not afford to discourage immigrants from the West, for they were perennially short of manpower, and only reinforcements from overseas made up for the twin evils of a chronically low birth rate and a chronically high rate of infant mortality, which between them crippled Outremer. It was a dilemma which was destined never to be solved except by the eventual extinction of the kingdoms founded by the first Crusaders; for while recruits from the West could still be found who were willing to fight for the triumph of the Cross, as they understood it, Moslem hostility was inevitably replenished; and when their enthusiasm eventually faded, and no more recruits were forthcoming, the fate of the Crusader kingdoms was sealed.

XII

A Full Sea

There is a tide in the affairs of men,
Which, taken at the flood, leads on to fortune;
Omitted, all the voyage of their life
Is bound in shallows and in miseries.
On such a full sea are we now afloat,
And we must take the current when it serves,
Or lose our ventures.

Shakespeare, *Julius Caesar*

After a certain amount of bickering, Baldwin I was succeeded, in 1118, by his cousin Baldwin of Le Bourg, who took the title of Baldwin II. He was one of the original Crusaders, who had come from Europe with Godfrey of Bouillon, and when Baldwin I had been made King of Jerusalem he had taken his place as Count of Edessa. His courage and his practical ability were not in doubt, but it was not for these qualities that he was chosen; his principal virtue was that he was on the spot, while Eustace of Boulogne, the late King's brother and next of kin, had returned to France. Baldwin of Le Bourg was a large, fair-haired man with a blond beard, and his tastes were simple. He was religious to the point of being pious; his private life was entirely virtuous, unlike that of his predecessor, and he was married to an Armenian lady who was blessed with the name of Morphia, to whom he was genuinely and deeply devoted.

By the time of his coronation, most of the original great lords who had not already gone home to their estates in Europe, had died. Raymond of Toulouse, who had eventually founded a small dominion for himself in the Lebanon with Tortosa as its capital, had died in 1105 from wounds received a few months previously while trying to capture Tripoli.

Bohemund, who had spent two years as a prisoner of the Turks, had returned to Europe on his release, where he had tried to persuade the Pope to preach a Crusade against the Byzantines, and had had some success in doing so; but when he had led an attack against the great Byzantine fortress of Dyrrhachium, the modern Durazzo in Albania, he had been soundly beaten. Discredited by his defeat and not daring to return to the East for fear of the Byzantine Emperor, he had retired to his estates in southern Italy, where he had died in obscurity in 1111. Tancred, who had proved to be both the most belligerent and one of the most able of the first Crusaders, and who like Baldwin I had set out as a penniless adventurer, had died a year later just before Christmas at the age of thirty-six, but not before he had achieved real power for himself as Prince of Galilee and Regent of Antioch in Bohemund's absence. Stephen of Blois, who had been forced by the inexorable Adela to return to the East and there to redeem his tarnished reputation, had done so by dying in battle at Ramleh. A similar fate had overtaken Hugh of Vermandois, who had also decided to return to the Holy Land and discharge his vow to go to Jerusalem; he had died of wounds received in battle with the Turks on the journey there, before he could keep his vow.

Despite the deaths of the old guard and the appearance of a new cast on the stage of events in Outremer, the Franks there felt themselves to be highly successful. When Baldwin II came to the throne Frankish rule stretched from the plain of the Euphrates around Edessa in the north through Antioch and most of the coastal cities of Syria and Palestine down to Hebron and the deserts of the Dead Sea in the south, even if every little Moslem enclave in this huge area had not yet been subjugated. Moreover, news of the success of the First Crusade had been greeted with such wild enthusiasm in Europe that there had been a small flood of new recruits for the East; many of these had been killed by the Turks during their passage through Anatolia, but some had arrived to strengthen the resident Franks, and even the death of the others did not destroy the general atmosphere of confidence and success which prevailed. But there were forces at work, both in Frankish society itself and in the various Moslem countries and principalities by which the Franks were surrounded, which were soon radically to change the balance of power between them and their enemies.

Up to this time, although the leaders of the Crusade had constantly squabbled and bickered among themselves, when a crisis had arisen, they had always come together again and fought shoulder to shoulder literally for dear life; unity had been forced upon them by necessity. At the same time, their Moslem adversaries had never been so disunited in their entire history as they were when the first Crusaders erupted into their world. Some of their disunity was due to racial antagonism, some to political rivalry, and some to religious sectarianism; the Arabs, who had conquered the Byzantine provinces of Syria, Palestine and Egypt, hated the Turks by whom they themselves had been conquered in their turn, and regarded them as barbarians; farther north the Persians disliked them even more, and had even greater reason to despise them as uncivilised savages. The Turks themselves were split into rival clans, between whom little love was lost, and the Seljuk Turks were at daggers drawn with their compatriots, the Danishmends. Needless to say, the local people of Syria and Palestine, who had been conquered by both the Arabs and the Turks, loathed them both; the vast majority of them were Christians, but even those who were Moslems welcomed the Crusaders, so delighted were they by the discomfiture of their erstwhile conquerors.

These racial hatreds were made worse by the acute political rivalry of the various Turkish provincial governors, who were bitterly jealous of one another's power. They were headed by a Turkish aristocracy, whose members ruled from such important cities as Aleppo and Damascus, and watched each other like lynxes in their determination not to allow one of their number to become stronger than the others; below them a large number of minor potentates and power-hungry officials followed the example of their superiors, and were at perpetual odds with one another. Although as Moslems they all looked upon themselves as enemies of the Crusaders, at a pinch individual rulers were prepared to make arrangements with the invaders, if by doing so they could save their own skins or score a point or two over their Moslem rivals.

But perhaps the worst cause of disunity in the Moslem camp was the religious dissension between the Sunni Moslems and the Shi'ites. There is no need to describe their doctrinal differences, but they tore the Moslem world apart in much the same way as doctrinal differences between Catholics and Protestants were later to ravage western Christendom; and as in the West, so in Islam, the religious disagreement between the two embattled sects was used by those who played at power politics to further their own ends. The Seljuk Turks had taken the Abbassid Caliphs of Baghdad under their wing in the course of their conquest of Persia, and the Abbassids were Sunni Moslems; their great rivals were the Fatimids of Egypt, who were Shi'ites, and this had proved to be a convenient excuse for the Seljuks to invade Syria and drive the Fatimids out, even though it was a part of the world which had been theirs for many years; the resulting bitterness between the two Moslem factions had become sour in the extreme. These religious hatreds were compounded by the existence of the Druzes, an odd sect of people who believed in the divinity of a mad Arab named Hakim, who had been Caliph of Jerusalem at the turn of the tenth and eleventh centuries, and by the rise of the sect known as the Assassins, who specialised in murder as a political and religious weapon. Their real name was the Hashishiyun, and they were Shi'ites.

If it had not been for this disunity of the Moslem world, it is doubtful whether the Crusaders would have succeeded in conquering so much of their territory; but once they had done so, the tables began to turn. With the spur of necessity removed, the Christian princes could indulge in the luxury of unfettered bickering without having to unite against the common foe in order to survive, while the Moslems began to realise that, if they were to regain the lands they had lost, they would have to patch up their own quarrels and unite to do so. They did not succeed overnight, but the first signs that there was a new spirit abroad in the Moslem camp were seen in 1119, the year after Baldwin of Le Bourg was crowned Baldwin II of Jerusalem. In the north, the Franks under Tancred's nephew Roger, who had inherited the principality of Antioch, were pressing the Moslems of Aleppo so hard that the defenders of the city were forced to make an alliance with a Turk named Ilghazi, with whom hitherto they had not been on very good terms. Ilghazi came to Aleppo at once, and on arrival he made a further alliance with the Turkish ruler of Damascus. News of this closing of the Moslem ranks so alarmed Roger that he sent messengers to Baldwin urging him to come to his assistance in defeating this formidable new coalition while there was still time. Baldwin, who was in Tiberias at the time, replied that he would come as quickly as he could.

But Roger was impatient and decided not to wait for him. Despite a warning from the Patriarch of Antioch not to take unnecessary risks, he led the army of Antioch out to meet Ilghazi, although it numbered no more than four thousand infantrymen and less than a thousand knights. Meanwhile Ilghazi commanded a force of forty thousand Moslems. Roger made camp in broken country, hoping that Baldwin would join him there before the arrival of his enemies, but Ilghazi was told by spies disguised as merchants exactly where he was and how many men he had with him, and he had no intention of waiting until Baldwin arrived.

Instead, on 27 June, he led his whole force towards the Christian position, which he reached just after dusk, and during the night he surrounded it.

At daybreak the next morning, some scouts brought the news to Roger that the enemy were all round him. There was little food and less water in the camp, and Roger realised that he had no alternative but to try to break out of the trap in which he found himself. It was a stifling day, dusty and heavy, with a *khamsin* blowing from the south and getting on everyone's nerves. The Archbishop of Apamea, who was with the army, preached to the assembled troops; after hearing a general confession, he gave them absolution, and blessed them as they formed up in readiness to attack. Then in perfect order they charged the massed ranks of Moslems; but for once their enemies were united and ready for them, and the Franks did not stand a chance. About a hundred knights managed to break their way out through the Moslem ranks and reach Antioch with news of the disaster, and later in the battle another handful of knights escaped for a time, although they were captured later; the rest were either killed or made prisoner. Roger died surrounded by his knights, who died with him, fighting below the standard of a large jewelled Cross. By mid-day the battle was over, and the victorious Moslem troops began to torture and kill the prisoners; those who were not slaughtered immediately after the battle were dragged back to Aleppo, where the people went mad with delight as they watched them being tortured to death in the streets of the city. Only one man was spared: a knight named Reynald Mazoir, whose courage in the battle had taken Ilghazi's fancy, and he was forced to listen to the cries of his fellow Christians as they were butchered publicly to provide a spectacle for the people of Aleppo.

The consequences of this battle, which the Franks called the *Ager Sanguinis* or the Field of Blood, were considerable, and they would have been greater if Ilghazi had followed up his victory by an immediate attack on Antioch, which was left virtually defenceless; but he missed his opportunity, and Baldwin arrived in time to save the city. Even so, the myth of Frankish invincibility had been shattered, and the Moslems had learned that they could defeat their enemies if they united against them. The balance was partly redressed five years later, in 1124, when the Franks captured Tyre with the help of a large Venetian fleet which had joined them since the battle of the Field of Blood; it was the last great coastal city to remain in Moslem hands, and its loss was a bitter blow to them. Meanwhile, however, in one of those ups and downs of fortune which were the background to life in Outremer, both Baldwin II and the new

Count of Edessa, his cousin Joscelin of Courtenay who had succeeded him there, had had the bad luck to be captured by their enemies and held prisoner for a time. However, Joscelin managed to escape, and shortly afterwards Baldwin was ransomed by his wife Morphia and returned to his kingdom in Jerusalem.

He had not been back for long before two more events took place which had far-reaching consequences for the Franks of Outremer. Baldwin was prevented from capturing Damascus, when it might well have fallen to him, by an accident of the weather; it was in November 1129, during an attack launched by Baldwin at a moment of Moslem weakness. Just when it looked as though nothing could stand between the large Frankish army and the fall of the city, the heavens opened, and the ground was turned into a morass by torrential rain; the attackers slid and slithered about in the mud, while the horses sank hock-deep into the mire, and there was nothing Baldwin could do but admit defeat.

The other event took place further north, and was even more unfortunate. Joscelin of Edessa and the new Prince of Antioch, Bohemund's son, who had recently arrived from Europe to take up his inheritance, did not get on well together. Each was bitterly jealous of the other, and they took every opportunity which presented itself to quarrel. The result was that, when Aleppo was thrown into chaos by the assassination of its ruler, a golden opportunity to capture the city was thrown away by the refusal of the two Frankish leaders to co-operate. When Baldwin heard the news, he was furious, but the damage had been done. It was a calamity, and it could not have happened at a worse moment, for a new star was beginning to rise over the Moslem horizon. A man named Imad ad-Din Zengi was made deputy governor of Mosul by the Seljuk Sultan, and he had not been there long before he marched on Aleppo and claimed it for the Sultan. The citizens of the place welcomed him, and he followed up his success by dealing so skilfully and ruthlessly with his potential Moslem rivals in the area that he was soon the acknowledged master of northern Syria.

It was doubly unfortunate for the Franks of Outremer that the beginning of Zengi's career happened to coincide with a series of personal disaster for the Christian princes. Bohemund II, the new Prince of Antioch, was the first to suffer. In February 1130, he was engaged in a minor campaign against one of his Armenian neighbours when he was surprised by some Danishmend Turks and killed with all his men; the Turks cut off his head, and the Danishmend Emir had it embalmed and sent as a present to the Caliph of Baghdad, who was delighted with it. In August the next year, 1131, Baldwin died after a short period of failing health, and a few weeks later his cousin and old friend Joscelin of Edessa died of wounds he had received while besieging a small castle near Aleppo. Baldwin was one of the first Crusaders; he had taken the Cross nearly forty years previously in response to Pope Urban's call, and he had travelled from Europe with his cousins Godfrey of Bouillon and Baldwin I. Joscelin was not quite so experienced as Baldwin, but he had been in Outremer for nearly thirty years and knew its ways and those of the Moslems well. The two men could ill be spared, particularly at this juncture, just as the Moslems were beginning to unite under their new leader, Zengi; and as fate would have it, they were destined to be succeeded by newcomers from the West who were both stupidly aggressive and aggressively stupid from time to time. Fulk, the Count of Anjou and the head of the powerful Angevin clan, had been brought out to Outremer especially to marry Baldwin's daughter, Melisende, on the understanding that, when she succeeded her father and became Queen of Jerusalem, he would become not just her consort, but King of Jerusalem with her; and in September 1131 they were duly crowned in the Church of the Holy Sepulchre. Fulk was the least disastrous of the new generation of rulers, but that is not saying much, for some of the others were ghastly.

The early part of his reign was beset by troubles. Joscelin of Edessa's son, also called Joscelin and now become Joscelin II, gave every sign of wanting to throw off his feudal allegiance to King Fulk, even though he was plainly inadequate to rule the most important Christian outpost in the north in isolation from his fellow Christians further south. He was an unattractive little man, short, dark and thick-set with a pock-marked face, a huge nose, and protruberant eyes like those of a fish. Nearer home, scandal linked the name of Fulk's wife with that of the lord of Jaffa, a certain Hugh of Le Puiset, with whom it was widely believed she was having an affair; the country was divided into two factions, and so high did partisan feeling run that there was a risk of civil war between those who backed the Count of Jaffa and those who took the King's side. Fulk had trouble in Antioch too. Since the death of Bohemund II the city had been without a prince, but unfortunately not without a princess, for he had left a young widow named Alice and a small daughter, Constance, who was his heir. Ever since her young husband's head had been sent to the Caliph of Baghdad, Alice had been engaged in an attempt to secure the regency of the city for herself during her daughter's childhood, an

10

arrangement which would have excluded Fulk from the affairs of Antioch altogether, and this he was determined to prevent since by law he was the rightful regent.

Meanwhile, Zengi took every opportunity presented to him by the disarray of the Franks to make things worse for them, attacking and capturing a number of strategic castles while Fulk was too busy with his internal troubles to rush to their defence. The height of Zengi's success at this time was reached when he defeated a Frankish army near the castle of Montferrand, capturing the Count of Tripoli in the process, and driving Fulk and a few survivors into the fortress, which he then besieged. Eventually, to Fulk's immense relief and equal astonishment, Zengi let him go in return for possession of the castle; but although Fulk considered that he had much the best of the bargain, the Moslem leader knew what he was doing, for Montferrand was of great strategic importance.

There is no telling where Zengi's formidable talents and even more formidable ambitions might have led him, if the affairs of Outremer and its neighbours had not been rudely interrupted by the eruption of a new and unexpected factor in the political situation. For years both the Franks and the Moslems had ignored the Byzantine Emperor and his claims, and Alexius had been too busy on his western frontiers to do more than follow in the wake of the Crusaders, regaining much of Anatolia as he did so. But Alexius had died in 1118, and had been succeeded by his son, John Comnenus, who was thirty years old when he became Emperor. He was an austere little man, very dark-haired and dark-skinned; but although he was self-disciplined and frugal in his personal habits to the point of asceticism, he was generous and kind to others and an able and just ruler. He was remarkable, too, for being one of the very few great public figures of the day of whom no one had anything unpleasant to say; he was nicknamed *Kaloioannes* or John the Good by his subjects, and only his sister Anna Comnena disliked him, through jealousy.

The Emperor John inherited from his father Alexius a powerful navy, a large and well organised if somewhat polyglot army, and a full treasury. By temperament he was a soldier rather than a courtier, and he spent the first years of his reign reducing the enemies of Byzantium in the West and dealing with the Danishmend Turks of Anatolia; but as soon as he had made the Empire secure from attack in these quarters, he turned his attention to Syria, where he intended to reassert his authority over Antioch and come to the aid of the Franks against Zengi. These were partly contradictory aims, but they were forced on John by the facts of the political situation; the Franks had to be forcibly reminded that Antioch and the other lands they had conquered had been parts of the Byzantine Empire for centuries, and that they themselves had sworn to win them back for Christendom as faithful vassals of the Byzantine Emperor; but although they had brazenly broken their vows, they were still Christians, and John as head of the oldest and greatest Christian state on earth was morally bound to come to their assistance against their Moslem enemies. So in 1137 he marched east at the head of a large Byzantine army, while his fleet guarded his right flank; he passed through Cilicia, where city after city submitted to him, and reduced the few Armenian castles which had the temerity to resist him without allowing them to hinder his triumphal progress. The news of his coming terrified Zengi, and deeply alarmed the Franks, who were only too conscious of how many vows of allegiance to John's father had been blithely broken over the years.

The prince of Antioch at the time was Raymond of Poitiers, the younger son of the Duke of Aquitaine, who had been smuggled into the country at the age of thirty-seven especially to marry the little Princess Constance, outwitting her mother Alice, who had had other plans for her daughter. It worried no one that Constance was only nine years old. Raymond was handsome, vigorous and endowed with all the qualities which make a man popular, but few which make one wise. He was away from Antioch when the Byzantine army arrived below its walls, and so the citizens, who were unsure of what to do in the absence of their prince, shut the gates against the Emperor John, who immediately laid siege to the city. Before it could be wholly invested, however, Raymond hurried back and managed to slip into the place and take charge of its defence. As the Byzantine siege engines began to pound the walls, he sent a letter to King Fulk asking his advice, and Fulk, who did not want to antagonise a potentially powerful ally against Zengi, replied advising him to recognise the Emperor's just claims. Rather reluctantly, Raymond sent messengers to the Emperor John to tell him that he was willing to submit to him, to swear allegiance to him and to pay him homage, and John pressed him no further; he did not even insist on entering the city, although he did give orders for the imperial standard to be raised over the citadel for all the world to see who its true master was.

Even at this late date, if the leaders of the Franks had decided to co-operate whole-heartedly with the Byzantines, Zengi's plans would have been frustrated, and the Crusader kingdoms might have endured much longer than they did; but personal jealousy and short-term advantage blinded them, and they returned to their old ways as soon as John returned to Constantinople. When he led his army into Syria again the next year, this time to fight the Moslems, Raymond of Antioch and Joscelin II of Edessa grudgingly agreed to help him in his campaign but, when it came to the actual fighting, they held back, leaving it to the Byzantines, who were cheated of the success they might have won if their allies had played their part honestly. But not only were Raymond and Joscelin sullenly resentful of the Emperor's greater power and standing, they were also violently jealous, each determined not to allow the other to gain an advantage by working with John. As a result, little of importance was achieved, and John eventually returned home.

In the years that followed, he met with nothing but dishonesty and hostility from both Raymond and Joscelin, and in 1142 he decided to return once again and punish them by force if necessary, but before he could do so he died as a result of an accident which befell him while he was hunting wild boar. His death came as a great relief to Raymond and Joscelin, and even King Fulk of Jerusalem was not sorry to hear the news; but their relief was nothing to that of the longer-sighted Zengi, who realised that nothing now stood between him and the Franks. The Emperor's death was followed a few months later by that of King Fulk; he was thrown from his horse while chasing a hare, and died soon after-wards. His widow, Queen Melisende, took the reins of government into her own hands, but not all the leading lords of the kingdom were happy at the idea of petticoat government and, partly at their insistence, Fulk's eldest son, even though he was only thirteen years of age, was crowned King Baldwin III.

Zengi was not the man to miss such a golden opportunity as that presented by the deaths of his two most powerful Christian opponents. Indeed, after the Emperor's death and before Fulk had been killed, he had already seized the military initiative by making an attempt to capture Damascus; but for once he had made a bad mistake, for he had so frightened the Damascenes that he had thrown them into the arms of his enemies, with whom they made a defensive treaty. But when Fulk died, Zengi made no mistake; he invaded the County of Edessa, and invested the city itself while Joscelin was elsewhere. As soon as Joscelin heard the news, he appealed urgently for help, both to Raymond of Antioch and to Queen Melisende of Jerusalem, and the latter sent an army to his aid. Raymond, who hated him, refused to do anything to help. Joscelin decided to do nothing until the army from Jerusalem arrived, trusting that Edessa with its massive walls would hold out until then. But it did not do so. After a siege lasting four weeks and before Melisende's troops could reach the city, it surrendered to Zengi, and the first of the Crusader kingdoms to be founded proved to be the first to be destroyed.

Zengi's troops were no more humane than the Christians had been after the capture of Antioch and the fall of Jerusalem. On Christmas Eve 1144, they poured into Edessa, massacring everyone who stood in their way. Thousands of Edessenes were trampled to death in the stampede to escape from the Moslem soldiers, and the city was filled with corpses. But Zengi was less bloodthirsty than his men, and when he had regained some measure of control over them, he gave orders that the native Christian inhabitants of the place were to be spared; only the Franks were to be killed. His orders were obeyed, and the Franks were wiped out to the last man, while their women and children were sold into slavery.

In the months which followed, Zengi mopped up most of the pockets of resistance in Frankish hands on the eastern side of the Euphrates, and he would certainly have gone on to attack the territory still held by the Franks west of the river and in northern Syria if he had not been murdered on the night of 14 September 1146, by a eunuch whom he had angrily reprimanded for drinking out of his own personal wine glass. Understandably, the news of his death was greeted with relief and delight by his enemies. They would have been less pleased, however, if they had known what they were destined to suffer at the hands of his son, Nur ed-Din, who succeeded his father after the usual period of dynastic plotting, counter-plotting and political murder. For if the words spoken by Solomon's son, Rehoboam, when he succeeded his father on the throne of Israel, had come from the mouth of Nur ed-Din, they could not have been more apposite from the point of view of the Franks: 'My father chastised you with whips,' he had said, 'but I shall chastise you with scorpions.'

XIII

♦♦♦

The Preachers and the Kings

The Lord gave the word: great was the company of the preachers. Kings with their armies did flee and were discomfited: and they of the household divided the spoil.

Psalm 68

The fall of Edessa deeply alarmed the Christian rulers of the Crusader kingdoms, who knew their own weakness. The Moslems were numerically vastly superior to them, and their apparent inability to reproduce themselves in sufficient numbers to make up for losses by death was a perpetually worrying problem and never more so than at this juncture in their affairs. Pilgrims were still coming to the holy places in good numbers, and some of them were persuaded to stay for a time, but they were not enough to make good the losses, and when they went home, usually a few of the resident Franks went with them in order to see their homelands once again before they died. Unless massive reinforcements were sent from the West to help them, the future looked bleak, and it was decided to send an ambassador to the Pope urging him to call a new Crusade.

The Bishop of Jabala, a man named Hugh of whom nothing much is known except that he disliked the Byzantines, was entrusted with the task; but despite the obvious urgency of obtaining help, he did not arrive in Italy until a year after the fall of Edessa. He found Pope Eugenius III, who had only just ascended the pontifical throne, at Viterbo, and his

Captions for following pages

Krak des Chevaliers from the east.

A. F. Kersting

Krak des Chevaliers, the greatest castle in Outremer and perhaps the greatest in the world, it was the headquarters of the Hospitallers – the Knights of St John. It stands 2,300 feet above sea level and commands the strategic valley between Homs and Tripoli. An Arab historian called it 'a bone in the throat of the Moslems'. An aqueduct (seen here just right of centre) brought water to the Krak des Chevaliers and filled its reservoirs in readiness for times of siege. The castle was never taken by storm; it surrendered to the Mameluk, Baibars, in 1271.

A. F. Kersting

Leander's Tower at the meeting of the waters where the Bosphorus, the Sea of Marmara, and the Golden Horn converge. It is misnamed, for Leander swam the Dardanelles, not the Bosphorus. The ships of the Fourth Crusade sailed past this little island on their way to attack Constantinople, some of the domes of which can be seen in the background against the sunset.

Sonia Halliday

Carved head of a Crusader from Montfort Castle near Acre. Montfort belonged to the Teutonic Knights.

Ronald Sheridan

Carving of an angel from Montfort Castle.

Ronald Sheridan

The tomb of Sir John Holcombe in Dorchester Abbey. He died of wounds received in the Holy Land during the Second Crusade. It used to be thought that the curious position of his legs, which is found on other Crusader tombs, was a sign that the dead man had visited Jerusalem, but doubt has been thrown on this idea.

Michael Holford

Made originally for Alexander the Great, these four bronze horses were brought from Alexandria to Rome by Augustus and then from Rome to Constantinople by Constantine, who set them up in the Hippodrome there. The Venetians of the Fourth Crusade took them back to Venice as loot after the capture of the city in 1204 and put them over the porch-entrance to St Mark's.

Sonia Halliday

news seriously disturbed him; the Pope agreed with Hugh of Jabala that nothing short of a new Crusade would suffice to restore the position of Christendom in the East. But to talk of a new Crusade was easier than to call one. Times had changed since Pope Urban's day, and although Eugenius duly issued a bull calling on the faithful to go to the rescue of their brothers in Outremer, no one took much notice of it. They were too busy with their own affairs, and the glamour which had surrounded the idea of taking the Cross in the old days had been somewhat tarnished by familiarity. Moreover, if anyone wanted to kill a few Moslems, they could do so by joining a Crusade in Spain; it was nearer and much easier to reach than the Kingdom of Jerusalem, and there were enough Moors there to satisfy any honest Christian longing for a little devout slaughter.

The failure of Eugenius' call for a new Crusade was unfortunate, for it emphasised his lack of authority. Rome itself was ruled by an anti-papal commune headed by a man named Arnold of Brescia, who would not even allow Eugenius to enter his own city, and he was at loggerheads with Roger II of Sicily, whose kingdom was so placed that he could either hinder or help the despatch of any expedition to the East by sea. Roger was an able, proud and passionate man but, like many other Normans, he was devoid of most of the graces of civilisation; the Pope was not the only person whom he had offended by the savagery of his manners. Fortunately however, Eugenius was on good terms with both Conrad III of Hohenstaufen, the King of Germany, and the pious King of France, Louis VII, and it had been to Louis that he had addressed his bull, *Quantum praedecessores*, calling for a new Crusade. Louis had been as disappointed as the Pope himself by the cool reception it had been given by the nobility of France, whom he had gathered at Bourges at Christmas time 1145 to hear it; but he had had the sense not to antagonise his subjects by pressing the matter. Instead, he had decided to wait until Easter, and then try again with the aid of the Abbot of Clairvaux.

Bernard of Clairvaux, who was fifty-six years old and at the height of his fame, had been born of a noble French family at Fontaines near Dijon in the last decade of the eleventh century; he had become a monk at the age of twenty-three and the founder of the Cistercian house of Clairvaux two years later. He was a child of his own world and time, a medieval man *par excellence*, with many of the greatest virtues of the middle ages and some of their limitations. Above all, he was a monk, genuinely and whole-heartedly dedicated to an austere life of self-mortification in order that he might devote himself to the pursuit of a sublime mysticism; his knowledge of the Bible was enormous, and as a theologian he was both clear-headed and penetrating. Moreover he was a spell-binding speaker and a preacher of great brilliance. His reputation for saintliness and the strength of his personality made him one of the most powerful and popular men in the Europe of his day; but there was a less attractive side to his character too, for there were times when he was so rigidly and severely orthodox that he seemed to be pitiless and utterly unloving. His judgement of Abelard was of this kind, and it has alienated many later historians, while his unbending hostility to Christians of the Greek Orthodox Church has done little to endear him to others. But these were the faults of his time and his society, and it would be obtuse not to acknowledge that by the standards of his own day he was a man of great sanctity, and by the standards of any day one of great distinction and stature.

Louis VII duly summoned another assembly bidding his vassals to come to Vézelay on 31 March 1146. The news that Bernard would be there spread rapidly, and this time people flocked from all over France in huge numbers to obey the King's summons. As when Urban had launched the First Crusade at Clermont, the Cathedral at Vézelay proved too small to accommodate the crowds of people who had come to hear Bernard preach, and he had to address them in the open air in a field outside the town. There is no record of what he said, but it is known that he read out the papal bull calling for a new Crusade and promising absolution to all who took the Cross before addressing the crowd in his own words and urging them to respond to the Pope's call. As an orator he was without peer, and it was not long before people were calling for crosses. 'Crosses, give us crosses!' they cried in a transport of enthusiasm as great as that aroused by Urban fifty-one years previously. The King was the first man to take the Cross, and many of the nobility, who had listened coldly to the Pope's appeal three months earlier, now stumbled over one another in their eagerness to follow his royal example. Soon there was no more stuff out of which to make crosses, as more and more people came forward to enlist in the army of Christ, and in a dramatic gesture Bernard took off his monk's habit and cut it up into crosses for the volunteers. Indeed, crosses were still being made out of whatever material could be found when darkness fell, so great was the excitement stirred up by Bernard, and by the end of the day the success of Pope Eugenius' call for a new Crusade was assured.

From Vézelay Bernard travelled north, where enthusiasm for the new

Crusade prompted another outburst of anti-Semitic hysteria. In Germany, a monk of Bernard's own Order named Rudolf was stirring up his countrymen against the Jews, who were being slaughtered in all the great cities of the Rhineland; Bernard ordered the murderous Cistercian back to his monastery, and the killing was soon stopped by the authorities, but not before a number of Jews were dead. Bernard then turned his attention to the south of Germany, moving from city to city and preaching where-ever he went, and although his sermons had to be translated into German, they were as successful as ever; men flocked to join the Crusade. But King Conrad was less enthusiastic, and without his active support no German army of Crusaders would have had much authority or military impor-tance; at worst, it might even have resembled Peter the Hermit's rabble. So Bernard approached the King, who agreed to meet him at Spier, where he was to hold a Diet at Christmas time. On Christmas Day, Bernard preached in front of Conrad with his usual verve, but for once he failed to influence his audience; the German King was unmoved. Defeat, however, was not a word understood by Bernard; two days later he preached again before the King, and this time he made sure of his man. He began gently enough, but as he developed his theme, he began to address himself more and more to Conrad personally, speaking to him as to one upon whom God had showered a multitude of favours. Then in a dramatic and tremendous climax, he turned to the King and spoke to him directly. 'Man,' he cried, 'what more could I have done unto thee that I have not done?' It was a quotation from the *Reproaches,* which were sung every Good Friday in cathedrals and churches throughout Christen-dom: the reproaches of Christ on the Cross for the ingratitude of his people, and Conrad was deeply moved. He promised to take the Cross and lead a German Crusade against the enemies of Christ, and as Bernard returned to France well pleased with the success which God had granted him, the nobility of Germany followed their King's example, competing with one another in their haste to pin crosses to their shoulders.

Pope Eugenius was less pleased with Bernard's success than Bernard himself; he had never intended to involve the Germans in the new Crusade, partly because he feared the consequences of an expedition under the dual command of the French and German monarchs, and partly because he needed Conrad's support against the republican aspirations of Arnold of Brescia and his anti-papal clique in Rome. Events were to prove his wisdom.

Conrad was the first to march to the help of his fellow Christians in

Outremer. He left in May, assembling his army at Regensburg and then setting out overland with about twenty thousand men by the route that had been taken by Godfrey of Bouillon and his brothers. The French King left Metz about a month later with a slightly smaller army. Roger II of Sicily, despite his feud with the Pope, offered to transport both armies by sea, but Louis did not trust him, and Conrad preferred to go by way of Constantinople, where the Emperor Manuel I Comnenus, who had succeeded his father John, was his ally.

Meanwhile, a small army of Englishmen, together with some men from the Low Countries, all of whom had taken the Cross, set sail from England for the Holy Land in a flotilla of English ships. As a military force it was not as important as either of the two great armies which were travelling overland, but it would have brought some very welcome naval support to them if only it had arrived. Unfortunately it did not do so. Bad weather forced it to take shelter in the estuary of the river Douro in Portugal, where the Count of Portugal had been at war with the Moslems of the Iberian peninsula for years, and here it was persuaded to join him in laying siege to Lisbon, which was held by the Moslems. With the help of the Flemings and the English the city was induced to surrender on condition that the defenders should be allowed to live; their lives were duly promised to them, but once the city gates were opened the Crusaders forgot their promise, and the enemies of Christ were zealously murdered.

The passage of the two great armies of Crusaders across Hungary was peaceful enough, but as soon as Conrad's Germans reached Byzantine territory, they began to make trouble. While Conrad himself was being persuaded by ambassadors from Constantinople to swear an oath of loyalty to the Emperor Manuel, his army of Germans began to pillage the countryside and to kill anyone who tried to stop them; at Philippopolis they made a riot and burnt the suburbs to the ground, and a few days later near Adrianople they burnt a monastery, killing all the monks in revenge for the death of one of their number, who had been killed by robbers. Manuel decided to prevent them from entering Constantinople by force; but he thought better of it at the last moment, and they arrived there at the beginning of September.

The French had less trouble with the local inhabitants, although they found it very hard to find enough food to eat; the Germans had consumed most of the available food, and had so frightened everyone by their brutalities that the peasants avoided this new army of Crusaders and hid what food they had left. The Byzantines were helpful, however, supplying what they could, and the journey of Louis' Frenchmen was uneventful until they drew near to Constantinople itself. Before reaching the city some of them hurried on ahead of the main body in the hope of buying some food from Conrad's Germans; but they were greeted with sullen and hostile looks, and no one would sell them any food at all. They were forced to wait, hungry and resentful, for the arrival of their compatriots. Some men from Lorraine had travelled with the Germans, and they made things worse by telling tales of the brutal way in which they had been treated on the journey, and it was not long before relations between the two western armies were strained almost to breaking point. The French and the Germans agreed about one thing and one thing only: they disliked their Byzantine hosts intensely and did not trust them an inch.

The Crusaders did not linger long in Constantinople. Conrad was the first to leave, marching at the head of his army to Nicaea. He was not an impressive man, and he had none of the qualities needed in a military commander; moreover, his health was not good, and he was well past his prime in years. The hostility between his men and the French was so great that he decided to make his way across Anatolia separately; it was an understandable decision, but splitting the Christian forces in this way was to court disaster, and the Emperor Manuel told him so. Conrad was adamant, however, and so Manuel supplied him with guides and gave him some good advice, all of which he later chose to ignore. But it was not until he set out from Nicaea that he made his greatest mistake; he split his army into two, ordering one party to march along the coast road with most of the non-combatants and some of the fighting troops under the command of the Bishop of Freisingen while he took command of the rest, much reduced in strength, meaning to take the road through central Anatolia. It was madness, but no one seems to have told him so, and in due course it had its predictable results.

For the first ten days, Conrad and his army marched through country held by the Byzantines, and all went well; but on 25 October they reached Dorylaeum, where the First Crusaders had won their first great victory over the Turks half a century previously, and once again the Turks were waiting for them. The Germans were tired by the day's journey and wholly unprepared for the sudden and violent onslaught of the Seljuk army, which was upon them before the weary infantry could form up for battle or the knights could mount their horses. The conclusion was foregone; there was almost no organised resistance, and many Crusaders were killed, while the few who had the presence of mind and courage to try to beat an orderly retreat were soon destroyed by the Turkish cavalry. Conrad and a pitifully small remnant of his army managed to reach Nicaea some days later, while the Turks were celebrating their triumph and counting the loot they had captured.

Meanwhile, unaware of the fate of their comrades, the Bishop of Freisingen's party marched along the Aegean coast, until the road turned inland to Philadelphia in a short cut to the Mediterranean across the south-west corner of Anatolia. All went well until they reached Laodicea, where they too were attacked by the Turks, and routed. Those who escaped managed to make their way south to the coast, although many died of hunger and privation on the way, and after yet another attack by the Turks in February 1148, in which more of them lost their lives, the Bishop and a few stragglers reached Attalia, whence they sailed to Syria.

While Conrad's Germans were being decimated by the Turks, Louis was preparing to leave Constantinople with his Frenchmen. He reached Nicaea at the beginning of November, and there he learned of the disaster which had overtaken Conrad. He was a pious young man as ill-fitted for military command as the German King and constitutionally unable, most of the time, to make up his mind about anything, but news of the destruction of the Germans shocked him into a resolve not to make the same mistakes. Accordingly he rode over to the remnant of the German camp as soon as Conrad had rested sufficiently to see him. The two Kings decided to join forces, and on about 8 November they set out along the coastal road, which ran south through Pergamum, Smyrna and Ephesus. It was a longer route to the Mediterranean than that followed by the Bishop of Freisingen, but for much of the way it passed through country controlled by the Byzantines, and so was safer than the shorter route through Phrygia.

All went tolerably well for the first few days, but by the time the army reached Ephesus relations between the French and the Germans had deteriorated. Not surprisingly, the Germans were tired after their recent experience, and they lagged nearly a day behind the Frenchmen, who taunted them with their slowness. '*Pousse Allemand! Pousse Allemand!*' they cried in derision; it was an insulting epithet normally reserved for broken-winded horses, and it did not increase the Germans' affection for their allies. At Ephesus Conrad fell ill. It was obvious that he could not continue the journey, and the army went on without him, leaving him to make his own way back to Constantinople, where eventually Manuel welcomed him with every sign of affection and regard; but without their

King the Germans felt at an even greater disadvantage than before. As the endless journey went on from week to week, their hatred of the French grew more and more bitter. By Christmas the Turks appeared and began to harry the long drawn-out column ,of weary Crusaders, picking off stragglers and galloping on their fast little horses near enough to shoot an arrow or two at their enemies, then retiring before they could retaliate.

On New Year's Day 1148, the Turks tried to prevent the Crusaders from crossing a river just outside the city of Antioch in Pisidia; they failed, but they inflicted some losses on the Frenchmen, and when three days later they attacked them again near Laodicea, the Crusaders' casualties were heavier. From then on, their journey was a nightmare; they were desperately short of food and water, the road was mountainous and hard, the weather was bitterly cold with icy winds sweeping down from Siberia out of heavy black skies, and the Turks hung onto their flanks like avenging furies, picking off the sick, the old, the tired and the careless with savage efficiency. A company of German pilgrims had tried to pass that way some months earlier, but the Turks had got them, and their rotting corpses did nothing to cheer King Louis' men as they struggled on towards the haven of Attalia on the Mediterranean coast. By the beginning of February, although they were much reduced in numbers, they reached it, and heaved a sigh of relief.

They sighed too soon. The citizens were short of food, and there was little to spare for the Frenchmen; there was no room to accommodate them in the city, and they were forced to camp outside the walls; no sooner had they done so than the Turks swooped down and attacked them. Angry, disappointed, and still very hungry, the Crusaders blamed the perfidious Byzantines, hurling accusations of treachery at them, while the Byzantines regarded the Crusaders contemptuously as barbarians; they had not invited them to invade their city in this way, bringing the Turks down on them, and the sooner they departed the better pleased the people of Attalia would be. Eventually they did leave. There were not enough ships to take the whole army, so Louis embarked with his household and the greater part of the cavalry, and sailed for Syria, where he arrived half-way through March. The rest of the cavalry and the knights followed by sea a few weeks later, telling the infantry to make their way east as best they could, and eventually that is what they did. Deserted by their leaders, many died on the way, and many more were killed by the Turks, while the lucky ones straggled into Antioch in the late spring, half-starved, demoralised, and looking like scarecrows. They had been incredibly badly treated, and they were angry and bitter; but they had arrived.

Louis and his household were welcomed by Raymond of Antioch, who escorted the royal party into the city, where he entertained them with a splendour befitting their station. The King and the Queen with the principal nobles and their ladies were housed in the lap of luxury, the weather was superb, and everyone soon forgot the terrors and the hardships of the journey. But when it came to discussing the immediate future and how best to attack the Moslems, King Louis proved indecisive. Everyone wanted him to do different things; Raymond of Antioch wanted the French cavalry, which had not suffered anything like as badly as the infantry, to join his own Antiochene army in an attack on Aleppo; Count Joscelin wanted the French King's aid in recovering Edessa; and Raymond of Tripoli, Louis' cousin, begged him to help recapture the strategic castle of Montferrand. Before the King could make up his mind which of these plans to adopt, an entirely new situation arose. His wife, Queen Eleanor, was Raymond of Antioch's niece and, whether for family reasons or because she thought that his plan was the best of the three, she began to urge Louis to do as Raymond wanted, and to join forces with him against the army of Nur ed-Din. She pleaded her uncle's cause with such warmth however that Louis became jealous. Why was she so partisan? Why did she spend so much time with her uncle? It was all very suspicious. Could it be that the Prince of Antioch's feelings for his niece were warmer than was proper in an uncle? Such questions plagued him, and in the end he worked himself up into such a jaundiced state of mind that he announced his intention of leaving at once for Jerusalem. Queen Eleanor, who had twice his intelligence and more than twice his resolution, was furious. How dare he accuse her of such a thing? If he wanted to go to Jerusalem, by all means let him do so. As for her, however, she would stay in Antioch and divorce him. Louis then removed her by force from Antioch, and carried her off to Jerusalem a virtual prisoner. Raymond of Antioch, her uncle and the unwitting cause of all the trouble, was even more furious than his niece, and from the moment of her enforced departure vowed never to co-operate with Louis again in any way at all. He would not even speak to him.

On arrival in Jerusalem, King Louis discharged his vows as a pilgrim by visiting the holy places, and Conrad III of Germany, who had eventually arrived in a Byzantine ship, accompanied him. Having done their pious duty, the two Princes accepted an invitation by Queen Melisende and the boy King Baldwin III to attend a conference at Acre with all the leading Crusaders in order to decide what to do next. Raymond of Antioch refused to come, and Raymond of Tripoli also declined the invitation; rumour had recently accused him of poisoning the son of Raymond of Toulouse, who had died in agony shortly after arriving in Outremer, and not unnaturally he had taken offence. Whether things would have been different if the two Raymonds had been present, it is impossible to say; certainly Raymond of Antioch had more common-sense in his little finger than the two Kings had in their two heads, but he might not have been able to influence the decision which was eventually taken: a decision of almost unimaginable stupidity. The combined armies of the Crusaders would attack Damascus.

The people of Damascus were the only Moslems anxious to remain on friendly terms with their Christian neighbours, and this for a very good reason: they were as frightened of Nur ed-Din's ambitions as the Franks were themselves. The decision taken at Acre was bound to throw them into the arms of Nur ed-Din, who was by far the most dangerous of the Crusaders' enemies, vastly strengthening him and correspondingly weakening the Christians. It was an act of fatuous ineptitude, and it was made worse by the way in which the resulting campaign against the people of Damascus was hopelessly mishandled.

The army which set out in July 1148 to attack Damascus was the largest the Franks had ever gathered together, and it reached the outskirts of the city on Saturday, 24 July, full of self-confidence. The Moslem governor was taken by surprise, for the last thing he had expected was an attack by the Franks, but he hastily gathered together as many men as he could muster, and sent urgent messages to Nur ed-Din asking him to come to his rescue. Meanwhile, the Crusaders occupied the gardens, orchards and olive groves which surrounded the city. As they approached a village named al-Mizza, the Moslem army, such as it was, tried to stop them, but was decisively beaten and forced to take refuge in the city. If the Crusaders had mounted an immediate attack on the walls, they might have taken Damascus, for inside the city all was confusion and despair; but they were in no hurry, and they lost their opportunity. The next day reinforcements began to arrive in ever increasing numbers, and the Damascenes counter-attacked, driving the Christians back from the walls into the orchards from which they had come. For two more days the fighting continued, and more and more Christians were killed by guerilla

11

fighters who crept up on them under cover of the fruit trees and olives amongst which they were camped. To escape from these hidden attackers, the army moved to an open plain to the east of the city, where there was not enough cover to hide a mouse, let alone a guerilla, and there the Franks hoped to find safety from their enemies. But the choice of the new site was yet another catastrophic blunder by the three supreme commanders, Louis, Conrad and Baldwin; the walls opposite the new position were stronger than anywhere else in the perimeter of Damascus, and there was not a drop of water to be found anywhere near the new camp. So hopeless was their position that, on 28 July, only four days after they had arrived before the city full of confidence and sure of a glorious victory, the Crusaders beat an ignominious retreat. The campaign against Damascus had failed, and the Damascenes had become the allies of Nur ed-Din, whose Turkish cavalry arrived in time to harass the re-treating Christians, pouring arrows into them and ensuring that the road they took was strewn with rotting corpses for months to come.

This fiasco was followed by bitter recriminations between the leading Princes, but exactly who was to blame for it has never been established; probably Conrad and Louis, both of whom were strangers to the politics of Outremer, forced the decision to attack Damascus upon the local Princes, who knew how valuable their alliance with Damascus was but did not dare press their opposition too strongly for fear of losing the support of the two Kings; but this is conjecture. Early in September, Conrad angrily announced his intention of shaking the dust of Outremer from his feet and sailed to Thessalonica, where he renewed his friendship and signed a treaty with the Emperor Manuel, by which the two promised to help each other against the Normans and especially against Roger of Sicily, who had recently ravaged the island of Corfu and sacked the cities of Thebes and Corinth in open acts of war against the Byzantines. To cement the alliance, Conrad's brother Henry of Austria was married to Manuel's niece Theodora. The ceremony was performed with the usual Byzantine magnificence, but the splendour of the occasion did not prevent some of the Byzantines writing to the girl's mother to express their dismay at the spectacle of such a charming and civilised Princess being joined for life to such an obvious barbarian: being 'immolated to the beast of the West', as one court poet put it.

Meanwhile King Louis was unable to make up his mind whether and when to go home. He lingered in Palestine nursing a growing resentment against Conrad and brooding sulkily like a schoolboy about ways to humble him in the future. When he heard of his new alliance with Manuel, he felt both slighted and angry that the German King had stolen a march on him, and his pique spread to embrace the Emperor as well. The news helped him to make up his mind, however, for he decided to change his policy and ally himself with Roger of Sicily, thus spiting both Conrad and Manuel. At Easter 1149 he embarked on a Sicilian ship, taking passage in her to Calabria, and thence he travelled north to Potenza, where Roger welcomed him. The Norman had no difficulty in persuading Louis to help him promote a Crusade against Byzantium; and when eventually the King returned to France, he in his turn had no difficulty in persuading Bernard of Clairvaux to preach as fierily against the Byzantines as he had formerly inveighed against the Moslems. It was an unedifying end to the Second Crusade, with Christians in the West preaching a holy war against Christians in the East, but happily for the time being it came to nothing. Neither the Pope nor King Conrad would have anything to do with an anti-Christian Crusade, and the idea was dropped. Unfortunately for Christendom, however, it was not forgotten.

XIV

♣♣♣

Fate and Change

Fate, Time, Occasion, Chance, and Change?
To these all things are subject.
Shelley, Prometheus Unbound

The principal beneficiary of the Second Crusade was Nur ed-Din. He had
already captured Edessa; he had taken most of the land east of the Orontes
belonging to the principality of Antioch; and although the Damascenes
still feared his ambitions and his power, they were much more friendly to
him after the attack on their city than they had been before. Raymond of
Antioch had been the one man to see clearly that Nur ed-Din was much
the most dangerous enemy confronting the Franks of Outremer, but his
advice had been rejected by his fellow princes; and with the callous
injustice of history he was fated to pay the penalty of their blindness.

In June 1149, not long after King Louis had left the Holy Land, Raymond
marched to the rescue of one of the few castles east of the Orontes which
remained in his hands, and which was being besieged by Nur ed-Din. He
took with him about four thousand knights and a thousand infantry,
and when Nur ed-Din heard of his coming, he hastily lifted the siege and
retreated; he had been told that Raymond's army was much more
numerous than in fact it was, and he believed himself to be outnumbered.
The truth was different, for the Moslem army consisted of six thousand
cavalry, which made it stronger than that of the Christians, and it was not

long before Nur ed-Din was informed of the true state of affairs. As soon as he learned that Raymond was the weaker of the two, he turned about, determined to destroy him. His army surprised the Franks where they were camping for the night in a hollow, and surrounded them before they awoke. Raymond realised that his only chance of survival was to break his way out, but the lie of the land was against him, and a wind blew dust into the eyes of his knights as they urged their horses up the slope towards their enemies. Before noon his army had been virtually annihilated, and Raymond was dead. Nur ed-Din, not to be outdone by the Danishmend Turks who had decapitated Raymond's father-in-law, cut off his head and sent his skull set in a silver case to the Caliph of Baghdad to add to his collection. It is not recorded whether the leader of the Sunni Moslems was edified or not by this latest grisly reminder of the goodness of God to the soldiers of the Prophet, but there is no reason to suppose that he was not delighted with it.

Joscelin of Edessa had not helped Raymond at all; he had made a fragile truce with Nur ed-Din while his fellow Christians were fighting for their lives, but now, with greater justice than in Raymond's case, it was his turn to pay the penalty for his past actions. Six months after the death of Raymond, Nur ed-Din contemptuously broke off relations with Joscelin and attacked him. Surprisingly, at first he had little success, but in the spring of 1150 Joscelin was captured by some Turks in an unlucky moment, when he had become momentarily separated from his escort as he was riding to Antioch. His captors handed him over to Nur ed-Din, who promptly put out his eyes and threw him into prison. There, blinded, unlamented, and almost forgotten, he died nine years later.

The death of Raymond and the capture of Joscelin were followed by the apparently senseless murder of Count Raymond of Tripoli by a band of Assassins. This added Tripoli to the number of states without rulers over which those anxious to succeed plotted and counter-plotted, indulging in the familiar game of dynastic power politics. Baldwin III of Jerusalem, who was still only twenty years old, hurried north to save the city of Antioch from Nur ed-Din, who was forced to be content for the time being with what he had won. A truce was signed, and a breathing space was thus secured in which to find new leaders for the northern states. Joscelin II had had a son, who eventually became titular ruler of Edessa, which had in any case virtually ceased to exist, so it presented less of a problem than the other two. Raymond of Tripoli had also left a son, but he was a twelve-year-old boy, and the reality of power passed into his mother's hands while Baldwin, himself only a few years older, became his guardian. But in the case of Antioch, which was by far the most important of the three even though it had recently lost some territory and many castles, the search for a successor to Raymond was more difficult and prolonged; for his widow, the Princess Constance, persistently and stubbornly refused to marry the various candidates for her hand who were presented to her. After nearly three years of hesitation and equivocation, however, she made up her mind, but the search for a new Prince of Antioch could scarcely have ended more disastrously. She chose for her husband a knight who had come to the Holy Land with Louis VII on the Second Crusade. His name was Reynald of Châtillon, and he was a most obnoxious individual who managed to combine in his single person a larger number of disagreeable characteristics than are usually to be found in one man. If he had a redeeming feature, history knows nothing of it, unless a daredevil brand of recklessness is counted as courage.

The confusion and disarray of the Franks was made worse by a violent quarrel which broke out at this time between Queen Melisende of Jerusalem and her son Baldwin, and which came near to provoking a civil war between them. Over the years, Baldwin had begun to find his mother's control increasingly irksome, and he was determined to cut himself free from her apron strings. Melisende was equally determined to cling to power, whatever her son might do or say, and the kingdom was divided into two camps, one supporting the Queen and the other taking Baldwin's side. But Melisende over-reached herself in the end by trying to exclude her son from Jerusalem; since he was the King, this was so obviously preposterous that her supporters deserted her, and she was forced to retire from politics.

Having at last seized the reality of power in the kingdom of which he had been the nominal ruler since the age of thirteen, Baldwin was eager to prove himself before the watchful eyes of his subjects. He had grown up to be a large young man with a mass of fair hair and a big, bushy beard; he was intelligent, articulate, and well educated, and he had won for himself a reputation for courtesy and good manners, which stood him in good stead. People of all sorts liked him, and he got on well with all sorts and kinds of people; with the more seriously minded of his vassals he took genuine pleasure in discussing serious matters, but he was by no means a dull dog, and he was as happy to throw dice for a wager with a friend or flirt with a pretty girl as he was to talk politics to one of his ministers or religion with a bishop.

Caesarea. The remains of the city wall and fosse built by St Louis in about 1251 after his release from Egypt, when he greatly strengthened the city.

Sonia Halliday

St Louis' coffin being taken aboard ship in the harbour at Tunis; from a manuscript at Châteauroux in France.

Cooper-Bridgeman

Miniature of a King on his throne. It comes from an illuminated *History of the World* produced in Acre in about 1285, which may have been a present to the boy King of Cyprus, Henry II, who was crowned King of Jerusalem in Acre in June 1286 just before the city fell to the Moslems.

British Museum: Add: 15268 16

Marqab Castle. After Krak des Chevaliers, Marqab was the Hospitallers' most formidable stronghold. It commanded the coast road from Tripoli to Lattakieh. It was captured eventually by the Sultan Qalawun, who allowed the small garrison of twenty-five knights to retire on horseback and fully armed; the foot soldiers were allowed to go free but could take nothing with them.

A. F. Kersting

There was little room to prove himself in the north of Outremer, where Nur ed-Din was far too strong to tempt him into a risky military adventure, although he could and did prevent him from taking Damascus for the time being by once more promising help to the Damascenes, who were prepared to forget the recent behaviour of the Franks, so terrified were they of being swallowed up by their over-powerful Moslem neighbour. But the Fatimid Caliphate in Egypt was in even worse disarray than were the Franks, and the weakness of the Egyptians presented Baldwin with certain tempting possibilities. It had been brought about by the appalling behaviour of a long series of corrupt and unscrupulous viziers, each of whom had murdered his predecessor only to be murdered in his turn by his successor, and all of whom the Caliph, a weak and irresolute man, had proved unable to control. There had been bloody riots in Cairo, and at one point two aspirants for the vizierate had fought each other in a full-blooded civil war, until something very like anarchy had replaced law and order everywhere.

All this gave Baldwin the opportunity he sought, for while the Fatimid Caliph was unable to look after his own internal affairs, he was unlikely to be able to do much to help his subjects elsewhere; and Egypt still held Ascalon. The Franks had been casting longing eyes upon this great southern port and coastal city ever since the chance to capture it had been lost by Godfrey of Bouillon and Raymond of Toulouse fifty years earlier, when they had been too concerned with their own quarrel to take the opportunity presented by the Egyptian garrison's willingness to surrender to Raymond. But now, once again, the city was vulnerable, for it could expect no help from Egypt, and Baldwin decided to attack. His first step was to build a formidable castle at Gaza, thus effectively blocking the coastal road from Egypt and isolating the city from outside help except from the sea. Then he assembled the largest army he could muster and, bringing every siege engine he could find with him, he moved up to the city and camped beneath its walls.

Although Ascalon was a much smaller city than places like Antioch or Jerusalem, it was very strong as a fortress, and it could be effectively besieged only by an enemy with control of the sea as well as the land; this Baldwin did not have. The Egyptians had kept its fortifications in good repair; it was well stocked with food and water; and when the Crusaders had been pounding away at its walls for several months with no effect, a large Egyptian fleet unexpectedly appeared and sailed safely into its harbour with some reinforcements and a mass of fresh supplies. The

Franks had not the naval power to interfere. But as the months passed the strain on the defenders increased, and the incessant bombardment of the walls took its toll of shattered nerves as well as of weakened masonry. The most formidable siege weapon was a high wooden tower, taller than the city walls, from the top of which stones, rocks, arrows, flaming faggots and every other kind of lethal missile could be hurled or shot into the streets. One night in July 1153, when the siege had been in progress for seven months, some of the Egyptian garrison stole silently out of the city and set fire to this tower. It burned like a great torch, but unfortunately for the defenders the flames were blown against the wall, where the intense heat of the fire destroyed the mortar between the stones, which fell. By morning there was a breach, and the Knights Templar, stumbling over the hot rubble with their swords in their hands, gained entry into the city streets. However, there were only forty of them, and they would not allow anyone to follow them into the city, so determined were they to take all credit for its capture; although at first the Egyptians believed that all was lost, they soon realised how few men they had to contend with, and they turned on the Templars and killed them. They then piled their bodies in the breach in the wall until it could be repaired, when they hung their corpses contemptuously like washing over the makeshift masonry to stink in the sun.

It was a terrible disappointment. Some people were in favour of lifting the siege and admitting defeat, but the Grand Master of the Hospitallers was against it, and in the end he had his way. The siege went on, and about a month later on 19 August, after enduring yet another heavy and nerve-wracking bombardment, the garrison at last decided that it had had enough. The commander offered to surrender the city to Baldwin if he would spare the lives of himself and his men; Baldwin agreed, and unlike many Crusaders before him he kept his word. The Egyptian soldiers and the citizens of Ascalon marched out of the place unmolested, and Baldwin III of Jerusalem marched in as its conqueror at the age of twenty-three. He had proved himself able to beat his Moslem adversaries in war, and he had also proved that he was able to resist the temptation to massacre them when they were at his mercy; it was a double achievement, and the second was perhaps the greater and certainly the rarer of the two in the annals of warfare between Christians and Moslems in twelfth-century Outremer. Great as was Baldwin's triumph, however, the capture of Ascalon proved to be something of a Pyrrhic victory, for the possession of the city tempted his successors to indulge in military adventures against Egypt, when their real need was to counter the threat to their existence posed by Nur ed-Din and his successors in the north; but that was their fault, and it should not be allowed to detract from Baldwin's twin triumphs, the one a great military victory, the other a victory for humanity.

The fall of Ascalon was destined to be the last great Christian victory in the East, and it was offset by an even greater triumph for Nur ed-Din in the north, where Damascus at last opened its gates to him. The ruler of the city, a man named Mujir, not unnaturally prized his independence. But the citizens of the place had not forgotten the attack on their city by the Franks, and they did not much like Mujir's policy of maintaining a balance of power between the haughty and infidel Crusaders on the one hand and the man whom all Islam regarded as the champion of the Faith on the other. Nur ed-Din's agents in the city fanned the flames of their discontent, and on 23 April 1154, less than a year after the fall of Ascalon, the people of Damascus threw the gates of the place open to him and his army, and greeted him rapturously. He entered Damascus in triumph, and from then on dominated the whole of northern Syria.

Luckily for the Christians, Nur ed-Din fell dangerously ill shortly after his capture of Damascus, and very nearly died. His recovery was slow, and he never fully regained his old energy or his old brilliance, so that his enemies were granted a breathing space, which they could not possibly have predicted. It was prolonged by another unexpected event, for in 1156 the whole of Syria was shaken by an earthquake, which destroyed the fortifications of many of the key cities and strategic castles. Nur ed-Din's men were too busy repairing the walls of Aleppo, Damascus and a dozen other places to wage aggressive war against the Franks, who were similarly employed trying to make good the damage done to their own fortified places, which had suffered less than those in the north, but had nevertheless been extensively damaged. But one man was unaffected by the enforced truce; indeed, it gave him just the kind of opportunity to run amok which he enjoyed. As far as the consequences for other people were concerned, he was uninterested; for as long as his own affairs prospered, he was happy. Reynald of Châtillon, the new Prince of Antioch, stepped onto the stage of history with a flourish, and typically his first action was both irresponsible and barbarous.

He decided to invade and sack the island of Cyprus. Its inhabitants were Christians, but this did not bother him, nor did the fact that it was part of the Byzantine Empire, with which the Franks of Outremer were both allied and at peace. Fifty years earlier, when the men of the First Crusade were starving below the walls of Antioch and later outside Jerusalem, the people of Cyprus had come to their rescue by sending them all the food they could gather together, but their generosity meant nothing to Reynald. The only thing which deterred him from launching an attack on the island was lack of money, and that was soon remedied in his own inimitable way. The Patriarch of Antioch was a man named Aimery; he was exceedingly rich, and Reynald disliked him. He summoned him to his presence, ordered him to hand over a huge sum of money, and when the Archbishop refused to give it to him, he threw him into prison and had him beaten. In the process Aimery's head was wounded, and when Reynald heard of it, he ordered honey to be rubbed into the wound and the Patriarch to be exposed all day in the sunshine, chained and bound, for the insects to persuade him to part with his money. After a day of such torture, the wretched man decided that resistance was useless, and agreed to give Reynald the money he was demanding. Delighted with the success of his little scheme, Reynald pressed ahead with his plans for the invasion of Cyprus.

After being released, the injured Patriarch hurriedly left the city and sought refuge in Jerusalem with King Baldwin, who was horrified by his story. He sent a messenger to the Byzantine governor of Cyprus as quickly as he could to warn him of his danger, but it was too late; Reynald had already landed on the island. He had most of the army of Antioch with him, and he was accompanied by an Armenian Prince, who was already at war with the Byzantine Emperor and therefore had no compunction in taking part in the armed invasion of a Byzantine island. Between them, the forces of Reynald and the Armenian outnumbered the men at the disposal of the island's governor, who were soon either annihilated or captured. Cyprus had been at peace for over a century; it was fat and prosperous, and after the defeat of the local militia it lay at the mercy of Reynald's men. They did not spare it. For three weeks they went on a rampage of murder, arson and pillage almost without parallel in the barbarous records of a barbarous age. Nothing was sacrosanct; churches, monasteries, and convents were robbed; houses were gutted, shops looted, and towns and villages sacked. They burned the crops, destroyed the orchards, stole the animals, and drove the islanders down to the coast like cattle, where they raped the women and the girls and cut the throats of the old, the very young, and all those who resisted them. The savagery went on and on, and it was not until news of the approach of a Byzantine fleet reached the island that the Franks and the Armenians prepared to leave, taking with them most of the leading islanders, until they could ransom themselves; the rest, including some Greek priests whose noses were cut off, were mutilated in various ways and left behind for the Byzantines to find on arrival.

This escapade by the new Prince of Antioch was not calculated to endear him to the Emperor Manuel, and it did not please Baldwin of Jerusalem either. The sheer savagery of Reynald's behaviour was bad enough, but its total irresponsibility was even worse. Manuel was still Emperor of by far the most powerful Christian state in the whole eastern Mediterranean area, and perhaps of the most powerful Christian state in the world, and gratuitously to antagonise him, just at the moment when the forces of Islam had united under Nur ed-Din in a new determination to drive the Christians back into the sea, was insanely irresponsible. As a result, Baldwin decided to seek an alliance with Manuel, and after over a year's negotiations a treaty was signed between the two powers, cemented a little later by the marriage of Baldwin to Manuel's little niece, the Princess Theodora. She was only thirteen years old, and she completely stole Baldwin's heart; even though it was a marriage of political convenience, he fell in love with her the moment he set eyes on her. He had not been exactly promiscuous hitherto, but he had been neither celibate nor ungenerous with his favours; from the moment of his marriage to Theodora, however, he remained completely faithful, and she seems to have loved him in return.

By this treaty Baldwin had agreed to support Manuel against Reynald of Châtillon, and so when, in the autumn of 1158, Manuel marched out of Constantinople at the head of a formidable army intent upon chastising, first the Armenians who had assisted in the rape of Cyprus, and then the execrable Prince of Antioch, he knew that he had nothing to fear from the King of Jerusalem. He moved so quickly that he nearly succeeded in surprising the Armenians, who only just managed to escape his vengeance by flight, and the news of his coming terrified Reynald, as well it might have done. Since he could not hope to stop the Emperor or his army, he decided to submit to him and to crave his forgiveness, even if he had to grovel to him in the process. When Manuel and the Byzantine army reached Antioch early in 1159, Reynald abased himself before him, and eventually received his grudging forgiveness. The Emperor then entered Antioch in state, and Baldwin joined him there. It was the first time that they had met, and Manuel was captivated by the younger man's charm; their meeting was a great success. However, if Baldwin tried to enlist his uncle-in-law's aid in an attack on Aleppo, as has often been suggested, he failed; instead, a week later Manuel signed a truce with Nur ed-Din by the terms of which the Franks of Outremer were protected from further attacks by the Moslem leader, while he himself was left free to fight the Seljuks of Anatolia, who were more dangerous to him than Nur ed-Din.

Having re-established his authority in Syria and shown his ability to intervene effectively there on behalf of his fellow Christians, Manuel returned to Constantinople. Although some of the Franks considered that he had betrayed them by not going on to wage war on Nur ed-Din, most of them realised that the Byzantine Emperor had saved them from him by creating a new balance of power in the area; as long as Nur ed-Din left them alone, Manuel would not interfere; and in return the Franks were happy enough to leave the Syrian alone, especially as this seemed to encourage him to wage war against his rivals, the Seljuk Turks, instead of against themselves. Needless to say, there were a few people who either did not understand the new situation or, if they understood it, cared little or nothing for the common good which was preserved while it lasted, and there is even less need to say that Reynald of Châtillon was one of them. Just over a year after he had knelt humbly in the dust before Manuel and promised to behave himself, he blithely broke both his promise and the new truce with his Moslem neighbours by raiding Nur ed-Din's territory and capturing a vast booty of cattle, camels and horses, which were being taken peaceably to their winter pastures. The results could have been extremely serious, but for once the devil's luck deserted him, and Reynald was captured by some of Nur ed-Din's men before he could reach home. They put him in prison in Aleppo, and since none of his fellow Franks showed any eagerness to ransom him, he remained there for the next sixteen years.

Two years later, Baldwin sickened and died. He was taken ill on a journey as he passed through Tripoli, where he was treated by a Syrian doctor; he grew no better, but insisted on continuing on his way. He got as far as Beirut, where he died on 10 February 1162 at the age of thirty-two. His loss was irreparable, for he had had all the makings of a great and civilised king, and his people mourned him bitterly; even the Moslem peasants of the country through which his body was carried to Jerusalem lined the road to pay their last respects to him, and when someone urged Nur ed-Din to grasp the opportunity presented by his loss to attack the

Franks, he refused; it would have been wrong, he said, to take advantage of a nation mourning for the death of so great a prince.

Baldwin had had no children, and he was succeeded by his younger brother Amalric, who resembled him in many ways. He was tall, although not as tall as Baldwin, and he was fatter than his brother, but in features and colouring they were very much alike; Amalric had the same blond hair and big bushy beard, and his Roman nose was just like his brother's. But the younger man, who was twenty-seven when he came to the throne, lacked his brother's charm and ease of manner; he was taciturn, rather unsociable, and ill at ease in the company of other people, partly at least because he had a slight stammer which embarrassed him. He did not share Baldwin's taste for gambling; instead, he preferred to fill his spare time with amorous affairs, for which he became somewhat notorious, although some serious pursuits attracted him, especially the study of history and law. Finally, he had a healthy respect and a warm affection for money; indeed, some people accused him of avarice. But it was not sheer greed which drove him to make sure that his treasury was always well supplied with money; he realised that without it he would be politically impotent, while with full coffers he could do more or less what he wanted, in both domestic and foreign affairs.

At the time of Amalric's accession, the long shadow of Nur ed-Din lay across all the Frankish principalities from the rump of Edessa in the north through Antioch to Jerusalem in the south, and Amalric realised that only two things stood between him and destruction: the power of Byzantium and the weakness of Egypt. He determined therefore to maintain good relations with the Emperor Manuel at all costs; that was plainly essential; but he also determined to try to gain control of Egypt, for he feared that, if he did not do so, the weakness of the Fatimid Caliphate and the state of virtual anarchy throughout the country might tempt Nur ed-Din to try to seize power there. If that were to happen, the Christians of Outremer would find themselves in a desperately dangerous position, and this Amalric meant to prevent, if he possibly could.

The political situation in Egypt was so bloody and bizarre that it is worth describing in a little detail, although it almost beggars description. At the time of the fall of Ascalon, the Vizier was a man named Abbas, and the Caliph a young man named al-Zafir. The Vizier had a son, Nasr, with whom it seems that the Caliph was having a passionate homosexual affair, and this infuriated Nasr's father, not for moral reasons, but because he was afraid that the Caliph would set his son against him. His suspicions were well founded, for Nasr had just agreed to murder his father. However, someone who was privy to this patricidal plot persuaded the young man Nasr that it might be better to murder the Caliph instead, and seize power; and Nasr agreed. He invited his lover to a nocturnal debauch in his own house, and when he arrived, he stabbed him to death. Nasr's father the Vizier promptly announced that the Caliph had been murdered by his own brothers, whom he arrested and put to death; he then placed the dead man's five-year-old son, a boy named Fa'iz, on the throne in his place. The child had been a witness of his uncles' murder, and not surprisingly suffered from convulsions for the rest of his life. So far all seemed to have gone well for the Vizier and his son, but the murdered Caliph had had four wives, who had not been pleased by their husband's homosexual dalliance with the young man, Nasr, and were not deceived by the official version of events put out by Nasr's father, the Vizier. They organised a military revolt against the seemingly triumphant pair, and the guilty couple fled the country. Luck deserted them, and as they were crossing the Sinai desert they met some Knights Templar, who killed the Vizier Abbas, and made his son Nasr prisoner. The young man offered to become a Christian if they would spare his life, but they received an offer of sixty thousand dinars for him from the late Caliph's four vengeful widows in Cairo, and this they decided to accept. Nasr was duly returned to Egypt and handed over to the tender mercies of the four widows, who personally mutilated him in various painful and ingenious ways, before having him hanged.

Meanwhile, the commander of the military revolt, an Armenian named Ruzzik, took over the vizierate under the nominal authority of the five-year-old Caliph, and things returned to normal for a few years, until the little boy died. He was replaced as Caliph by his nine-year-old cousin, who was forcibly married to Ruzzik's daughter. At this point, one of the ladies of the family took a hand again. The new Caliph's aunt persuaded some of her friends to stab the Vizier Ruzzik as he passed through the hall of the palace; they agreed to do so but, in the event, made a bad job of it, and Ruzzik took some time to die. Before doing so, he invited his murderess to come and see him, and rather foolishly she did so, whereupon the dying Vizier summoned up his last reserves of strength, killed her, and died. His son succeeded him as Vizier, but he lasted no more than fifteen months before being murdered in his turn by the governor of Upper Egypt, a man named Shawar, who held power for eight months before he, too, was ousted by his own major-domo, an Arab named

Dirgham. Shawar escaped with his life, flying the country and seeking sanctuary in Syria at the court of Nur ed-Din, while Dirgham, more thorough than his predecessors, made an exhaustive list of all those people who could possibly pose a threat to his own security; then, having completed it, he had everyone on his list done to death in a glorious orgy of destruction, which left the Egyptian army bereft of all its commanding officers.

This grotesque state of affairs in Egypt could not possibly last for ever, and both Amalric and Nur ed-Din were well aware that, if one of them did not do something about it, the other would. Nur ed-Din was the first to move; in April 1164 he sent an army under the command of a Kurd named Shirkuh, his most reliable general, with orders to reinstate the ex-Vizier Shawar on the understanding that, as soon as Shawar was Vizier once again, he would ensure that the Caliph should become Nur ed-Din's vassal and make Egypt his ally. The Kurdish general Shirkuh took a nephew named Salah ed-Din Yusuf with him, and the man whom the Franks were to know and fear as Saladin thus made his first bow on the stage of history. The Moslem army moved with great speed, by-passing the Franks and catching Dirgham off his guard. By May Dirgham was dead, Shawar was Vizier again, and Shirkuh had achieved everything he had set out to do. This should have been the end of the matter, and if it had been, Nur ed-Din would have succeeded in stealing a march on King Amalric; but it was not the end by any means, for as soon as Shawar found himself back in power, he repudiated his bargain with Nur ed-Din, and ordered Shirkuh to go home. The Kurd refused, and promptly occupied the fortified city of Bilbeis in the delta of the Nile north of Cairo. Shawar appealed to Amalric for help, who was delighted to have the chance to intervene. He marched at the head of the army of Jerusalem to Shawar's aid, and on arrival in Egypt joined him in the siege of Bilbeis. This would almost certainly have been successful in the end, but Nur ed-Din was determined to rescue his Kurdish lieutenant, and to that end attacked the principality of Antioch, forcing Amalric to raise the siege and to hurry home. Shirkuh decided to return too, and Shawar was left in power in Egypt, where the political situation remained as tense and anarchical as ever. Meanwhile, Nur ed-Din was deterred from attacking the city of Antioch itself by his fear of the Byzantines.

Two years later, in 1167, Nur ed-Din ordered Shirkuh to invade Egypt once again; and for the second time the Kurdish general took his nephew Saladin with him. Amalric tried to intercept him, and the Moslem army

12

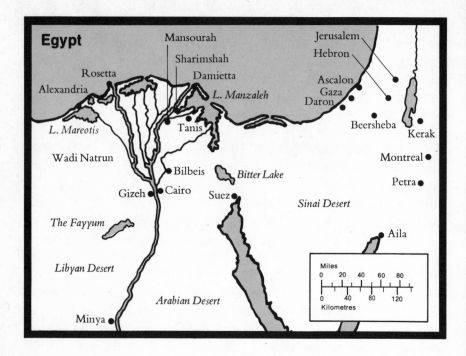

was nearly destroyed by an appalling sand-storm in the Sinai desert, but Shirkuh reached Egypt safely, crossed the Nile, and camped near the Pyramids at Giza on the west bank of the river. Amalric's army arrived a few days later, and took up a position on the east bank near the walls of Cairo, where it was greeted warmly by the Vizier Shawar. An alliance was made between them, and to seal it two of the leading Franks were conducted in great state through the palace to meet the Caliph; staggered by its marbled magnificence and dazzled by the glittering luxury of the place, they were eventually brought face to face with a dark little boy on a golden throne half hidden by a golden veil. To the horror of one of his attendants, one of the Franks insisted on shaking hands with the Caliph after the child had removed the glove he was wearing; it was an unheard of liberty, but the little boy did not seem to mind, and agreed to put his hand in that of this visiting barbarian. The Franks left deeply impressed by the wealth of the Fatimid court.

For a month nothing happened; the two armies glowered at each other across the Nile, and the flies made life intolerable for the soldiers of Christ and the warriors of the Prophet alike. But in March Amalric, whose men outnumbered the Moslems, managed to cross the river and chase

Shirkuh upstream to the town of Minya about a hundred and fifty miles south of Cairo, where at last the two armies fought. The battle was indecisive, for although Shirkuh came off better than the Franks, Amalric's army was still the larger of the two at the end of the day. While the Christians reformed, Shirkuh and Saladin marched north again; they passed Cairo and occupied Alexandria, where Amalric soon followed them and at once besieged the city. But it was a large place, and Shirkuh with most of his army managed to slip out one night, leaving Saladin inside with a small garrison. Something very like stalemate soon developed, and after a few months, when it became clear that neither side could expect to beat the other, Shirkuh sent emissaries to Amalric to suggest peace terms, and Amalric, anxious about affairs in Syria, agreed to them. Saladin played a leading part in negotiating the peace, and it is said that he not only made many friends amongst the Franks at this time, but that he was so much liked and respected that he was knighted by one of the Frankish lords. Even if the story is apocryphal, it is a measure of the high esteem in which Saladin was later held by his adversaries.

If Amalric had been content to leave well alone at this juncture, the history of Outremer might have been very different. When he returned to Jerusalem, he left his own standard flying over the lighthouse at Alexandria; a garrison of his own troops remained in Cairo to keep an eye on his ally Shawar; and the Vizier was bound to pay him a large annual sum for his military support. In effect, Egypt had become a Frankish protectorate. But he was not so content and, having reinforced his alliance with the Byzantines by marrying the Emperor's great niece, the Princess Maria Comnena, he felt strong enough to try once again to conquer Egypt outright. If the Byzantine fleet had blockaded Egypt by sea, he might have succeeded, but he did not bother to wait for naval help from his ally; egged on by the Hospitallers, who could not wait to get at the legendary wealth of the Fatimids, and by some new arrivals from France, who were longing to kill a few Moslems, in October 1168 he marched across the Sinai desert and laid siege to Bilbeis. The town was defended by a mere handful of Egyptian soldiers, and although they fought with a ferocity and courage which surprised Amalric, it was carried after three days of desperate resistance. A bloody and revolting' massacre followed, which shocked even some of the Franks themselves; Amalric did his best to stop the bloodshed, but by the time that he brought his men under control, the damage was done.

Many Egyptians had been prepared to welcome the Franks as deliverers from the anarchical misrule of the Fatimid Caliphate, and the Copts had been especially pleased by the arrival of their fellow Christians; but after the massacre in Bilbeis the whole of Egypt recoiled in horror and revulsion from them, for the killing there had been completely indiscriminate. Moslems and Coptic Christians, women and children, old men and babies in arms had been slaughtered with the same appalling and unselective gusto; and a few days later, when some newly arrived Christians captured the port of Tanis, which happened to be almost entirely inhabited by Copts, there was another holocaust. The Egyptians, who might easily have taken sides with the Franks, were thrown into the arms of Nur ed-Din; the Caliph invited Shirkuh to take possession of Cairo, where he died a few weeks later of over-eating, and the man who was destined to become the scourge of the Franks stepped into his shoes. Saladin became the ruler of Egypt.

XV

♣♣♣

The Wheel of Fortune

The temple is overthrown, the gold has been pillaged, the wheel of fortune has accomplished her revolution, and the sacred ground is again disfigured with thorns and brambles.

Gibbon, *The Decline and Fall of the Roman Empire*

When Saladin became Vizier of Egypt in March 1169 at the age of thirty-one, no one knew much about him. His father was a Kurd named Ayub (or Job), who was one of Nur ed-Din's generals; he had been governor of Baalbek for a time, but had later been moved to the court at Damascus, where Saladin had been brought up and educated in the most famous and illustrious centre of Islamic learning outside Cairo. He grew up to be a devout, even a fanatical, Moslem, but as a young officer he was distinguished most by his skill at polo. His appearance was unimpressive and gave no indication of the remarkable and rare man he was destined to become; he was short, rather red faced, and blind in one eye. He inherited an extremely difficult position as Vizier of Egypt after his uncle's death; the Fatimid court resented his rule, and plotted secretly with Amalric's court in Jerusalem to overthrow him, while some of his fellow officers, who were senior to him in service and even in rank, bitterly resented his elevation to power, and went home to Syria in anger. If the Franks had attacked him soon after his accession to the vizierate, he would have been hard put to defeat them.

But although the Emperor Manuel and King Amalric realised clearly enough that, with Saladin in power in Egypt and in alliance with Nur ed-Din in Syria, the balance of power between the two sides had been rudely upset, Amalric was not ready to attack Egypt. Manuel agreed to send a large Byzantine fleet to blockade the coast and to back up the Frankish army, if Amalric would invade Egypt again; but the Frank's troops had suffered heavily in the last campaign, and time was needed before they could take the field again. It was not until October, six months after Saladin had come to power in Cairo, that the Christian soldiers marched south; the Byzantine fleet, which had been waiting for weeks in Cyprus for the order to sail, guarded their flank, and this large force made straight for the great fortress which guarded the main branch of the Nile, the city of Damietta. Saladin had expected another attack on Bilbeis, and was taken by surprise; but the defenders of Damietta had stretched a great chain across the river, preventing the Byzantine fleet from sailing past in order to stop Egyptian reinforcements reaching the city from the south, and the city walls were so formidable that Amalric hesitated to assault them. Saladin, who dared not leave Cairo for fear of a revolt in the city, ordered as many troops as he could spare to rush to the help of Damietta, and as the days passed the garrison grew stronger and stronger as more and more men came up from the south.

Meanwhile, tension and disagreement grew between the Franks and the Byzantines. The fleet had had to wait so long for the army to be ready that it had consumed much of the food with which it had been victualled before sailing from Constantinople, and Cyprus had been unable to make good the deficiency when at last the ships sailed for Egypt. The sailors were becoming desperately short of food and correspondingly eager to press the attack on the city to a conclusion; but Amalric continued to refuse to risk his men's lives in an assault until he was ready, while sulkily refusing to help his allies by giving them some of his own men's rations. Some of the Franks angrily accused the Byzantines of wanting a share in the spoils of the city at the expense of Frankish lives, but as time went by it became more and more evident that there would be no spoils for anyone; the city was too strong, and the campaign had failed.

In December it began to rain, and the camp became a quagmire. It was time to go home, and after a few days of cold and misery the army burnt its siege equipment and marched north to arrive in Ascalon, tired and depressed, on Christmas Eve. No one had been sorry to say goodbye to the Byzantines, and no one much minded when news arrived of a disaster which had overtaken them. The fleet had been caught off the coast of

Palestine in a terrible storm, and many ships had sunk with heavy loss of life. Throughout the Christmas season the bodies of dead sailors were washed up along the beaches of the Holy Land to be eaten by mangy dogs and fought over by squabbling parties of gulls, but there was little nourishment to be found on them by either dogs or birds; they were too thin.

The failure of the expedition inevitably resulted in recriminations, but the Franks and the Byzantines, needed each other, and the alliance was not broken. Meanwhile, Saladin had completely crushed all opposition to his rule in Egypt, and had established himself there so securely that Nur ed-Din began to grow a little worried about the possible intentions of his over-powerful lieutenant. Saladin made one or two forays against targets in the southern part of Amalric's kingdom, to show his hostility to the common enemy, and in other respects too he behaved with perfect correctness; but Nur ed-Din became more and more suspicious of his ambitions, and relations between the two men deteriorated. He was reassured for a time when Saladin agreed to abolish prayers for the Fatimid Caliph in the mosques of Egypt and to replace them with inter-cessions for the Caliph of Baghdad, and he was pleased when the young Fatimid Caliph died shortly afterwards; the triumph of Sunnite orthodoxy over the heretical Shi'ites had always been close to his heart, and it seemed now to be assured, but it was not long before his suspicions were re-awakened. In 1171 Saladin made one of his forays into Christian territory, and besieged the great castle of Montréal in the hot and stony desert south of the Dead Sea; Nur ed-Din decided to come to his aid and marched south to join him, but as soon as Saladin heard of his coming, he lifted the siege and marched back to Egypt on the pretext of going to the assistance of his brother, who needed his help in Upper Egypt. Nur ed-Din was furious, accusing his subordinate of treachery, and Saladin was alarmed. He called a council of his advisers, many of whom were in favour of defying Nur ed-Din; but Saladin's father, who was staying with him at the time, counselled an immediate apology, and rebuked his son for even thinking of acting disloyally. Saladin accepted his father's advice, and Nur ed-Din allowed himself to be appeased for the time being. But when almost exactly the same thing happened a year later, Saladin hastily retiring to Egypt as soon as Nur ed-Din began to attack the Franks in the north, the older man's fury knew no bounds; he could no longer doubt that his highly independent lieutenant was reluctant to see the destruction of the Franks, who lay conveniently between Syria and Egypt

Anamur Castle on the southern coast of Turkey opposite Cyprus was built by Seljuk Turks in about 1230. It occupies a strategic position dominating the coastal road which runs between the sea and the Taurus mountains. It was such castles as this which forced the Crusaders to use the sea route to Outremer in the latter half of the thirteenth century.

Picturepoint

View of Jerusalem looking east across the old city to the Dome of the Rock and the mosque of al-Aqsa. The Mount of Olives is in the background.

MEPhA

Twelfth-century Norman carvings on capitals in Monreale Cathedral, Sicily. One depicts two foot soldiers with shields, the other a knight mounted on a horse.

Michael Dixon

and thus provided a buffer state between him and his over-demanding master.

Meanwhile, one surprising result of the destruction of the Fatimid Caliphate was to throw the Assassins into the arms of the Franks. This small but formidable Moslem sect, whose headquarters were in the Nosairi mountains between Hama and the coast of Syria, and who practised political murder to further their own ends, had always been nearer to the Shi'ites in doctrine and sympathy than to the orthodox Sunni Moslems of Baghdad, and they were shocked by Saladin's action in Egypt. Their sheikh at this time was a remarkable man named Rashid ed-Din Sinan, who later became known to the Franks as the Old Man of the Mountains, and in 1173 he wrote to Amalric suggesting an alliance between them which should oppose Nur ed-Din and his lieutenant Saladin in Egypt. Delighted to welcome any help in his struggle against increasing odds, Amalric agreed. But the idea of a treaty with the Assassins angered the Templars for a singularly selfish and petty reason; one or two Assassin villages paid them an annual tribute as protection money, and this they would lose if the Assassins became their allies. The Grand Master of the Order therefore determined to wreck Rashid ed-Din's agreement with Amalric, and with a number of other Templars he ambushed Rashid's envoys as they were returning from a meeting with the King in Jerusalem and murdered them. Amalric was so angry that he disregarded the immunity from arrest constitutionally enjoyed by members of the Order and forcibly arrested the man responsible, throwing him into prison. He even contemplated asking the Pope to dissolve the Order of Templars once and for all. He humbly apologised to Rashid ed-Din, assuring him that the culprit had been punished, and Rashid accepted his apology. All was well again. Indeed, the political prospects had not looked so favourable for the Christians for a long time; they had gained a small but much feared Moslem ally in the Assassins, and with Nur ed-Din at odds with Saladin their two principal opponents were too busy with their own quarrels to unite against their Frankish neighbours.

The year 1174, however, brought radical changes to both camps. In the spring Nur ed-Din died. His death was an enormous loss to the Moslems, whom almost single-handed he had united against the Christians in a *jehad* or holy war. He was an austere man, who seldom smiled, and as he grew older be became more and more withdrawn from the world into religious observance; but he was deeply respected by his subjects, who regarded him as something of a saint, and there can be no doubt that he was a great ruler. He was succeeded by his son as-Salih, a boy of eleven, and there was a struggle for the regency which plunged the Moslem world into a disunity and chaos which it had not seen for years. Amalric was not the man to miss such a good opportunity to attack his enemies; he marched against the city of Banyas south of Damascus. Before he could reach it, however, the governor of the place came out to meet him, and offered to make an alliance against Saladin. Amalric could probably have obtained greater concessions, but he was not feeling well, and he signed the proposed treaty as quickly as possible; then he set out for home.

By the time that he reached Jerusalem he was seriously ill with dysentry. Some native physicians were called, and he asked them to bleed him, but they refused; he was not strong enough to stand such treatment, they told him. So he summoned a French doctor, who had no such scruples, and applied leeches to him at once. A few days later, on 11 July 1174, he died. It was the turn of the Franks to be plunged into the divisive quarrels which usually followed the death of a king, and their disunity soon matched that of their Moslem enemies. Amalric, who was thirty-eight when he died, left a daughter aged fourteen, a son a year younger, and a number of daughters younger still. There was no question as to who should succeed him; his thirteen-year-old son was crowned Baldwin IV less than a week after his father's death. But he was too young to assume power, and he was a leper. Plainly a regent had to be appointed, and it was this necessity which plunged the kingdom into factional strife. Meanwhile, an even greater disaster than Amalric's death was about to befall the Christian cause.

In 1176 the Emperor Manuel was forced to turn his attention to the Seljuk Turks of Anatolia. They were ruled by a Sultan of great ambition and considerable ability, whose name was Kilij Arslan. His ambitions had been kept in check while Nur ed-Din was alive, for the great Syrian leader had had no intention of allowing him to become too powerful. But as soon as Nur ed-Din died, Kilij Arslan set about attacking his neighbours one by one, swallowing up their domains; his own brother was one such victim of his aggression, and the Danishmend Turks were another. He soon became by far the most powerful Turkish ruler between Syria and the Bosphorus, and this inevitably brought him into collision with the Byzantines. Fearing for the safety of his lines of communication through Anatolia, the Emperor Manuel, decided to teach him a lesson. He mobilised a very large army, and in September he set out to march against him, taking with him a train of great siege engines with which to reduce any cities which chose to resist him *en route*; this heavy equipment slowed the pace of his march, but he believed that it would be invaluable later in the campaign.

The Emperor marched south from Constantinople until he reached the river Meander, and there he turned inland; marching up the river valley he skirted Lake Egredir to the south, and began the slow ascent of the great mountain range known as the Sultan Dagh near Pisidian Antioch. The road wound its laborious way up to a pass which had once been guarded by a fortress called Myriocephalum, now in ruins, and there the Seljuk army was waiting on the mountainside above the road. The way was narrow, and Manuel's most experienced advisers begged him not to take his cumbersome army over the pass, where the enemy was waiting to pounce on it, but his younger and less reliable advisers regarded such counsel as defeatist and cowardly; thirsting for glory, they urged the Emperor to ignore the dangers and press on. He allowed himself to be persuaded; the vanguard of the great Byzantine army advanced towards the pass, and began to fight its way through the narrow defile; the Turks fell back before them, and it looked as if all was going to be well. But as soon as the main body of the army followed the triumphant vanguard, the Turks wheeled round and charged down on them from the hillside. The Byzantine soldiers were so crowded that they could hardly move, and the huge siege machines made manoeuvre impossible. It is said that the Emperor was the first to panic, but however that may have been, the whole army was soon transformed into a struggling mass of terrified men trying desperately to save themselves as best they could; but very few did so. The Turks went on massacring them until the sun set, and a merciful darkness fell on the bodies and the blood. Manuel escaped with a remnant of his army, and after dark the victorious vanguard joined him; but the great Byzantine army had been as completely destroyed as it had been almost exactly a century earlier at Manzikert, and the disaster at Myriocephalum made the eventual destruction of the Byzantine Empire almost certain.

News of the battle took some time to reach the Franks, and at first they were not entirely displeased by it; they had always disliked and distrusted the Byzantines, and the fact that their haughty Emperor had been humbled tended to amuse rather than dismay them. Syria was ruled by a mere boy, and Nur ed-Din's empire was in total disarray, so they had nothing to fear from that quarter; and Saladin had not yet shown himself to be as formidable as he was later to become. As to Saladin himself, he was probably the one man who realised what an immense change had been wrought in the balance of power. Nur ed-Din's death, followed by that of Amalric, had removed the two greatest obstacles to the realisation of his own ambitions; and the destruction of the Byzantine Empire's military power at Myriocephalum left the Franks at his mercy. Moreover, they were as usual quarrelling with one another and hopelessly disunited. So, in the autumn of 1177, a year after the battle of Myriocephalum, Saladin marched north and headed for Ascalon.

Baldwin IV, Amalric's leprous son, was still only fifteen years old, and he had recently been ill; but on the news of Saladin's approach he hurried to Ascalon with all the troops he could raise, while the Templars concentrated on Gaza. The King reached Ascalon an hour or two before Saladin, who left a small force outside the city to contain Baldwin and his knights while he himself made straight for Jerusalem. The capital was defenceless, but Baldwin somehow managed to send a message to the Templars in Gaza ordering them to join him and, as they approached, he made a desperate bid to break out of the city, even though the odds against him were large. With a courage and an *élan* provoked by the acuteness of the emergency he succeeded and, joining forces with the Knights Templar, he rode north as hard as he could before turning inland to cut across Saladin's path. On 25 November, Saladin's army, safe in the knowledge that no enemies stood between it and its goal, was moving carelessly along the road to Jerusalem near Ramleh when Baldwin and his knights fell on it like a thunderbolt out of the north. The attack was utterly unexpected; some of Saladin's men had gone foraging, and the rest were disorganised and only half armed. They broke and fled under the violent impact of the disciplined charge of steel-clad knights, scattering like a flock of sheep before a tightly-knit pack of wolves. Saladin himself was nearly captured; a few of his best and most seasoned troops stood their ground, but the only reward they received for their courage was to be wiped out almost to a man. On the Christian side, the young King distinguished himself in the thick of the fighting; so did two members of the Ibelin family, which was becoming one of the most powerful clans in Outremer; and at the height of the battle St George took a hand, being seen and identified by several people fighting shoulder to shoulder with his fellow Christians. Saladin escaped with a few of his men, and reached Egypt after a nightmare journey across the Sinai desert, where he and his men were soaked to the skin by incessant winter rain, made miserable by the cold at night, and repeatedly attacked by hostile Bedouin tribesmen.

Baldwin's victory dealt a devastating blow to Saladin's reputation, but it did not change the balance of power, which was heavily weighted in his favour, and it was not long before he had raised another Egyptian army and was on the warpath again. Less than two years after his defeat on the road to Jerusalem, he met and soundly defeated Baldwin in the Jordan valley where the Christians were hunting some Moslem troops who had been raiding the district around Beirut; amongst the prisoners he took on this occasion was the Grand Master of the Temple, who later died a captive. Saladin did not follow up his victory by a general offensive against Baldwin – although he continued to harass him with pinpricks here, there and everywhere when he was least expected – until the late summer of 1180, when a truce was arranged between the two sides. It was to last for two years, and Saladin agreed to it because the whole of Syria was suffering from the effects of a terrible drought earlier in the year; famine was a very real possibility, and it would have been madness to risk the destruction of those meagre crops which had managed to survive the drought by continuing a war in which they would inevitably become a prime target for the opposing side. To Baldwin the truce was a godsend; he desperately needed to seek help, both in western Europe and at the court of the Emperor Manuel, for without new recruits from overseas the fate of Outremer was sealed. But although he sent ambassadors to the West to explain the plight of the Christians in the East, no one responded to his appeal for help; they were too busy with their own affairs, and enthusiasm for the Crusades had waned. Meanwhile, the Byzantines were distracted by troubles of their own as well, and affairs at Constantinople were about to take a turn for the worse.

The Emperor Manuel had been a sick man for some time, and on 24 September 1180 he died. He had always followed a friendly policy towards the West, which he genuinely admired, and his death was a blow to the Franks of Outremer, even though they had not always appreciated his friendship. He was succeeded by his son, a boy of eleven, who took the title of Alexius II Comnenus, while the child's mother, the Empress Maria, automatically assumed the regency. She was the daughter of Raymond of Antioch, whose skull had been set in silver and sent to the Caliph of Baghdad and, as a Latin princess, she was disliked by the people of Constantinople. She had been blamed for her husband's pro-Western policy, which was even more unpopular than she was herself, and her regency was bitterly resented. The people of the city had never forgotten the arrogance of the Crusaders and their acts of brutality as they had passed through the capital of the Byzantine world; the rape of Cyprus was fresh in everyone's memory; and the presence of a small but highly privileged colony of Italian merchants, who had been given special trading concessions and also what amounted to a reserved quarter in the city, was a constant irritant and reminder of the hated western barbarians. They were mostly Genoese, Pisans and Venetians, and they behaved with the offensive arrogance so often displayed by small groups of racially distinct people living in a hostile environment, keeping themselves to themselves and avoiding contact with the native people, whom they openly despised.

As soon as she became regent, the Empress Maria further antagonised the people of Constantinople by making an unpopular member of the Comnenus family, also named Alexius, her principal adviser and some said her lover. After a time, a plot to murder him was uncovered, and the two chief conspirators ran for safety to the Church of the Holy Wisdom, where they sought sanctuary; but their intended victim dragged them from the building and arrested them. It was an extremely foolish thing to do, for it violated the age-old and deeply respected right of all men to take sanctuary in the House of God, and the people of the city were so shocked and angry that Maria was forced to pardon the culprits. More plotting followed, and two years after Manuel's death some conspirators approached yet another member of the family, Andronicus Comnenus, and asked him to rescue the Empire from the hateful Latin Empress, who was supported, they assured him, by no one in the capital but the equally odious Italian merchants. Andronicus was a handsome and amorous Byzantine prince who had profoundly shocked the Franks some years earlier by seducing the Princess Philippa of Antioch. He had been turned out of the city by her enraged brother, Bohemund III, and had then travelled south and laid siege to the young and recently widowed Queen Theodora of Jerusalem, capturing the citadel of her virtue without encountering much resistance from the lady herself; and once again her friends and relations had been furious. Andronicus agreed to lead an armed revolt against the Empress Maria and her son Alexius II, and in the late summer of 1182 he raised an army and marched on Constantinople. The news of his coming spread like wildfire through the city and touched off a violent explosion of hatred against the Italian merchants; for years they had swaggered through the streets with brutal effrontery and overweening pride, while the Byzantines had forced themselves to bottle up their fierce resentment. But their patience was exhausted, and now they turned on these barbarous oafs from Italy, and massacred them almost to a man. The mob in Constantinople did not often take the law into its own hands in this way, but when it did so it could be almost unbelievably savage; some of the things done to the Italians before they died shocked many of the Constantinopolitans themselves, but they were helpless to stop the butchery; and if truth were told, they were probably as pleased as everyone else to see their city cleared at last of the men from Italy, even if they disapproved of the brutal way in which the job was done.

Andronicus entered the city in triumph a few days later, and set about eliminating anyone who might prove to be his rival. The Empress' favourite minister was thrown into prison, where his eyes were put out; the two conspirators whom Maria had pardoned died in mysterious circumstances; and finally the little boy, Alexius II, was forced to sign his own mother's death warrant, and the Empress Maria was quietly strangled. Andronicus was then made co-Emperor with the wretched child whom he had just orphaned, and two months later the boy was murdered. When Andronicus married his twelve-year-old widow, the Princess Agnes of France, he became the undisputed ruler of the Byzantine world. It was not an edifying period of Byzantine history.

Andronicus was sixty-two when he seized power, and he might have remained securely on the throne for years had he not been so terrified of being violently deposed from it; he saw rivals and rebels everywhere, becoming more and more paranoid as time passed and unleashing a virtual reign of terror, not only in the capital, but throughout the length and breadth of the Empire too. People were arrested in great numbers; no one felt safe. Members of the Comnenus family were at desperate risk, even if they had lived in obscurity for years; many of them were executed without trial and without even a pretence of legality, simply because they were Comneni. The plight of one of them eventually became too much for the citizens of Constantinople to bear, and they rose in open and violent revolt; Isaac Angelus, an obscure, elderly and amiable cousin of the Emperor, was arrested, but managed to escape and take refuge in the Church of the Holy Wisdom, where he was granted sanctuary by the clergy. Andronicus ordered his men to arrest him again. This was too much; even his own bodyguard deserted him, and the city rose against him. He was captured by the mob as he tried to escape from the city, and once again the people of Constantinople showed their latent and rarely indulged capacity for savagery; they broke his teeth, tore out his beard and hair, put out an eye and cut off one of his hands before tying him to the back of a mangy camel, when, according to the contemporary Greek historian Nicetas, 'some beat him on the head with sticks; others pushed dung into his nostrils; others again squeezed sponges soaked in excrement over his face. Some thrust at his ribs with spits, some stoned him, and a prostitute fetched a jar of boiling water from a kitchen and emptied it into his face.' He endured all this with incredible courage without making a single complaint, although he prayed continually, 'Lord, have mercy on me! Why do you break a bruised reed?' Finally, he was taken to the Hippodrome and there suspended from a beam by his feet; a spectator ran a sword into his mouth and by a great effort thrust it upwards into his vitals and killed him. He was succeeded as Emperor by the man whose arrest had enfuriated the mob, Isaac Angelus, who turned out to be totally ineffective and incompetent, and Byzantium finally ceased to be a world power. Its collapse was a major political windfall for Saladin, the best bit of luck he had had since the death of Nur ed-Din.

While all this was going on in Byzantium, the petty rulers of the Franks were indulging in some violent squabbles, which at one time threatened to plunge them into civil war. Their affairs were not improved by the release from captivity of the unspeakable Reynald of Châtillon, who had been removed from the political scene for sixteen providential years by his incarceration in a Moslem gaol in Aleppo. The ruler of the city had given him his freedom in a moment of generosity in gratitude for some help he had received from his Frankish neighbours. Reynald's wife, the Princess Constance, had died during his years in prison, and on his return he married the heiress of Oultrejourdain, leaving Antioch in the hands of his stepson, Bohemund III, who had inherited the city on his mother's death. He behaved himself for a time, but to suffer any constraint upon his own personal whims and wishes was contrary to his nature, and he chafed under the restrictions imposed by the truce made with Saladin in 1180. The respite from war might be essential to the common good, even indeed to the survival of his fellow Christians, but such considerations do not seem ever to have occurred to Reynald. One of the terms of the truce ensured that both Christian and Moslem merchants should be able to pass freely through each other's countries without fear of being molested, but the sight of rich Arab caravans moving freely through his territory was too much for Reynald; in 1181 he ambushed a party of merchants on their way to Mecca, and stripped them of everything they owned. In revenge, Saladin captured a large party of Christian pilgrims to the Holy

Land, and told King Baldwin that he would release them when Reynald returned the goods he had stolen. Reynald flatly refused to do anything so foolish, and war inevitably followed.

Despite his superior strength, Saladin failed at first to gain a decisive advantage. Then in December Nur ed-Din's eighteen-year-old son as-Salih died of colic, which many people attributed to poison, and Saladin immediately turned his whole attention to the conquest of Syria instead of the subjugation of the Franks. By June of the following year he had eliminated all rivals for power, and he entered Aleppo in triumph. As Sultan of Syria and Vizier of Egypt, his empire stretched from the sands of the Upper Nile in the south to the plain of the Euphrates in the north, and for the first time the Franks found themselves caught between two hostile fronts which were united under one ruler instead of being bitterly divided between rival Caliphs.

In historical retrospect, it is easy enough to identify some of the landmarks in the decline of Frankish political fortunes as Saladin went from strength to strength; and there is no doubt that the moment when he gained Nur ed-Din's empire was a portentous one for the Christians of Outremer; but it is much more difficult to know how they themselves felt about it. Presumably they went on living their lives, building their houses, ploughing their land, marrying their wives, breeding their children, making their livings, getting drunk and praying against a background of political bickering and occasional outbreaks of war that went almost unnoticed, so used were they to both. There were no mass media of communication, news spread slowly, and there were periods, sometimes of several years, in which nothing much happened on the political stage, and during which people presumably went about their daily lives without giving a thought to the violent possibilities of their age. Yet these times of peace and ordinary living are all too easily ignored by the historian and forgotten by those who read his works, as they were almost entirely disregarded by the chroniclers of the day. Even so, there must have been many ordinary Christian citizens of Outremer who suffered forebodings of the wrath to come when the news that Saladin had unified their Moslem enemies in Egypt and Syria under his own rule reached them.

Reynald of Châtillon, however, was not subject to forebodings of any kind, and the news that Saladin was busy in the north merely encouraged him to stir up trouble in the south. It is doubtful whether anyone else could have thought of something so likely to enrage the enemies of the Franks as the plan he now put into action. He built a number of small

13

ships and transported them in pieces on the backs of camels and other pack animals to the head of the Gulf of Aqaba, where he attacked and captured the port of Aila from its Moslem garrison, although a fortress on an offshore island nearby held out against him. Having assembled his ships, he launched them and sent them south with orders to pillage the coastal towns, capture all the merchant ships they encountered, rob the caravans of pilgrims on the way to Mecca and, finally, to attack the holy city itself. He himself remained behind to blockade the island fortress. The progress of this piratical expedition was marked by the sacking of peaceful little towns, attacks on defenceless pilgrims, the burning of ships in harbour and the sinking of others at sea. As news of these events spread, it shocked the entire Moslem world, and the governor of Egypt took prompt action to avenge this brutal and impudent affront to Islam. He ordered the Egyptian navy to punish the men responsible for it, and an admiral named (somewhat incongruously to Western ears) Lulu, set out in pursuit of them. He recaptured the port of Aila and then chased the Christian fleet and destroyed it. Reynald escaped, but nearly all his men were captured; some were taken to Mecca to be publicly executed there, while the rest were beheaded in Cairo. Saladin swore a solemn oath that one day he would make Reynald pay the penalty of his crimes.

It was not until the late summer of 1183 that Saladin made his next move; he assembled a large army near Damascus and then marched south-wards, invading Galilee in strength. The Franks were caught at a disadvantage. King Baldwin's health had become so much worse that he was forced to watch his own body slowly decaying; 'his leprosy so enfeebled him,' wrote William of Tyre, 'that his body could no longer aid him. Sight left his eyes, and his hands and feet began to shred away. So he could no longer govern the kingdom and attend to its needs.' As a result he decided to delegate his authority to his brother-in-law, a noble Frenchman named Guy of Lusignan. It was a bad choice. As Saladin approached the Franks called every fighting man in the country to arms, including some visitors from Europe who happened to be there at the time, and set out under the command of Guy to meet him. But when the two armies did meet, Guy proved so inept and indecisive that he was widely accused of cowardice, and deposed from his new position. Despite his desperate ill health Baldwin assumed command again, naming his six-year-old nephew, yet another Baldwin, as his eventual heir, and these political moves were approved by the leading lords of the kingdom.

Reynald of Châtillon played no part in all this, however, for he was occupied elsewhere. The lady whom he had married after returning from his long period of captivity in Aleppo, the heiress of Oultrejourdain, had been married twice before; and at the time of Saladin's invasion she was preparing for the marriage of her eldest son by her first husband, a boy of seventeen named Humphrey of Toron, to the little Princess Isabella of Jerusalem, who was only eleven. Since Humphrey was the eventual heir to the lordship of Oultrejourdain, the marriage was to be solemnised in the great castle of Kerak in the desert east of the Dead Sea. This was the family seat and the stronghold from which Reynald raided the Moslem caravans which travelled between Egypt and Syria, even when they were covered by a truce; for truces meant little to him. There he and his wife were preparing to entertain the wedding guests with the greatest possible splendour, and all through November the feudal aristocracy of Outremer, together with a few Byzantine princes and some visiting nobles from Europe, began to arrive at the castle; so did a host of minstrels and entertainers of various kinds. But before the wedding could take place, there was a sudden alarm. Saladin and his army were approaching from the north.

The guests had no time to leave; Reynald himself only just succeeded in reaching the safety of the castle before the Moslem host burst round it like a wave around a rock. The men and women of crusading days may have been capable of great brutality, but they also had a marvellous sense of occasion; and when they wished they could behave with a kind of sublime panache and mad courage which takes the breath away. On this occasion they reacted to the sight of Saladin's camp fires around the castle and the sound of missiles from his siege engines pounding its wall with a show of just such indomitable spirit and splendid *insouciance*. They continued to make preparations for the wedding as though nothing of any consequence had happened; the sound of music and singing could be heard every night by the Moslem soldiers encamped in the desert around Kerak, as the wedding guests feasted and danced until the small hours of the morning. The mother of the bridegroom, the lady heiress of Oultrejourdain, personally sent dishes from her own table to Saladin with a message to say that, if she had known he was coming, she would have prepared something more special for so noble a guest. Not to be outdone, Saladin, who was by nature a chivalrous man and a courteous one, enquired which part of the castle was occupied by the bridal couple, and gave orders that it should not be bombarded; but his mangonels continued to hurl great rocks at the other parts. The siege lasted until 4 December, when Baldwin IV, despite his leprosy, was carried in a litter at the head of the army of Jerusalem to the relief of his fellow Christians in Kerak, and Saladin was forced to retire.

The siege and relief of Kerak illustrate the importance of castles in the warfare of the day. The first Crusaders were skilled castle builders, but they were not so skilled as the Byzantines, and as the years went by the Franks of Outremer learned a great deal about the art of fortification from the military engineers of Byzantium. Individual castles varied very much in both size and strength, ranging from enormous fortresses like Krak des Chevaliers to places less than a tenth its size. Krak des Chevaliers, in the northern part of the county of Tripoli overlooking Moslem territory, was the headquarters of the Hospitallers. The Arabs called it Hisn al-Akrad which the Franks corrupted, first, to Le Crat and, later, by some analogy with Kerak, which meant fortress, into Krak, and, because of its tenure by the Knights of the Hospital, Krak des Chevaliers. The Oxford scholar and art historian, T. S. R. Boase, has said that 'as the Parthenon is to Greek temples and Chartres to Gothic cathedrals, so is Krak des Chevaliers to medieval castles, the supreme example, one of the great buildings of all time.' Its site illustrates the motives of the castle-builders of the day; it is set on a steep hillside at a height of 2,300 feet, looking out over a wide stretch of what was enemy country in the days of the Knights, and this it completely dominated. 'What think you of a town,' wrote the Moslem traveller Ibn Jubayr when he visited Homs, 'that is only a few miles away from Hisn al-Akrad, the stronghold of the enemy, where you can see their fires, and whence each day the enemy may raid you on horseback?' Another Moslem, the historian Ibn al-Athir, called it 'a bone in the throat of the Moslems,' while the Christian Andrew of Hungary described it as 'the key of the Christian lands.' It could hold a thousand horses and five thousand men, and although it eventually surrendered to the Mameluk Sultan Baibars, it was never taken by storm; it was too strong. No invader, knowing that an army could retire into the safety of its impregnable walls and towers, would dare to press on into hostile territory and leave such a force behind him; and although Krak was the greatest of all the Crusader castles, the whole of Outremer was studded with them. They gripped the heights of the land from the borders of Syria in the north to the deserts south of the Dead Sea; some were no more than strongly fortified villages; others were fortified towns like Tyre; others again were small baronial castles, and some were almost as vast and formidable as Krak itself. They were seldom farther apart than a day's ride; and many

of them, standing like sentries on high crests or craggy hill tops, could
signal to each other at night. They were provided with cisterns for the
storage of water or covered ways going down to hidden springs or
reservoirs hewn from the rock, and many of them could stand a siege
lasting a year or more; the great castle of Montréal in the northern fringe
of the Arabian desert and even farther south than Kerak, did not fall
until it had been besieged for a year and a half, and half its men had gone
blind from lack of salt, or so it was said at the time. These castles provided
a system of defence in depth which has seldom been equalled for strength
or completeness, and which made it possible for the Franks, vastly outnumbered as they were by the surrounding Moslems, to survive for two
centuries.

After Saladin had raised the siege of Kerak, the fighting became
sporadic and rather half-hearted; there were raids and counter-raids, and
when Saladin tried to take Kerak again the following autumn, it again
proved too strong for him. Then, in the spring of 1185, Baldwin at last
died; he was twenty-four, and there was little left of him to bury, so
thoroughly had his leprosy done its wasting work. His subjects were
suffering, too, from the beginnings of a famine; the winter rains had failed,
and it was essential for the Christians to make peace. Fortunately, Saladin
had troubles of his own; both in Egypt and in Syria there were rumblings
of jealousy amongst some of his subjects, and the Emir of Mosul was
threatening rebellion. So he agreed to a four-years' truce with the Franks,
and for their part they thankfully made peace with him.

Slowly prosperity returned to Outremer, and the threatened famine
was averted as food flowed in from Moslem countries, whose merchants
were only too eager to renew their trade with their Christian neighbours
and through them with Europe. It even looked for a few halcyon days as
if the peace might become permanent, for Saladin was taken desperately
ill and it was thought that he would die; but the luck of the Franks was
out, and he recovered. In contrast, Baldwin IV was succeeded by his eight-
year-old nephew in the spring of 1185, and the little boy was duly
crowned as Baldwin V; but before he had been on the throne for more
than a few months he died in the summer of 1186. With the depressing
inevitability of night following day, violent dissension between the leading Frankish lords followed the death of the little King, and once again
civil war nearly engulfed the realm. Fortunately for everyone concerned,
the truce with Saladin held; he did nothing to break it and when, after
much bitterness, Baldwin IV's sister, Sibylla, was crowned Queen of

Jerusalem, and her unpopular husband, Guy of Lusignan, was crowned as King Guy with her, the new monarchs were determined to do nothing to jeopardise the peace. But they counted without Reynald of Châtillon.

Trade had begun again between Egypt and Syria, and Moslem merchants were moving freely once again through Frankish territory, protected by the terms of the truce; but the sight of such wealth passing freely through the land was too much for the lord of Oultrejourdain. Early in 1187 he attacked a huge caravan, which was travelling from Cairo to Damascus with only a small escort of Egyptian soldiers to defend it from Bedouin raiders; the soldiers were quickly and easily killed, and Reynald took the merchants together with their women and children back to his castle at Kerak, where he held them to ransom. The loot from the caravan was enormous, and he was delighted with it. When Saladin was told what had happened, he sent envoys to Kerak to demand the release of the prisoners and proper compensation for the losses they had suffered; but Reynald would not even receive these messengers, and they were forced to go on to Jerusalem and lay their complaints before King Guy. The King tried to make Reynald do as Saladin asked, but Reynald took as little notice of him as he had of Saladin's envoys, and Guy, who was an irresolute man, did not force the issue. Saladin could do no more, and war inevitably followed.

It could not have come at a worse moment for the Christians, who were violently disunited and hopelessly outnumbered by their enemies. The Prince of Antioch and the Count of Tripoli were so appalled by Reynald's irresponsibility that at first they refused to have anything to do with the war provoked by his breach of the truce, and the Kingdom of Jerusalem was left to face alone the assembled might of the Moslem world; but later they changed their minds. However, even when the Christians had mobilised every available man, assembling an army eighteen thousand strong, they were weaker than Saladin; for although their army was almost as large as his, where they could put no more than twelve hundred heavily armoured knights and about four thousand light cavalry into the field, Saladin had twelve thousand horsemen under his command, many of them Kurds like himself.

This Moslem host crossed the Jordan on 1 July 1187 at a point just south of the Sea of Galilee, and attacked the town of Tiberias. It fell almost at once, but the citadel held out, defended by a small garrison, and in it was the Countess of Tripoli, the wife of Raymond of Tripoli, who was with the army at Acre. Before the news of Saladin's capture of the town reached Acre, however, there was a heated argument between the leaders who were assembled there. Count Raymond was strongly in favour of a passive and defensive role for the Christian forces, on the grounds that in the extreme heat of summer the army which did the marching and attacking would be at a disadvantage; therefore, all the Franks had to do was to wait until Saladin was forced to retreat by lack of water and other supplies; he would not be able to maintain so huge an army in the field for long in the heat and dust of a Palestine summer. Most people agreed with Raymond, but Reynald of Châtillon accused him of cowardice, and he was supported by the Grand Master of the Temple; they should march out to meet the Moslems, they argued, and not sit supinely on the defensive. King Guy, who disliked Raymond, agreed, and the necessary orders were given. By the following evening, 2 July, the army reached Sephoria half-way to Tiberias, and camped there. There was plenty of water, and their position was a strong one; if Saladin should attack them there, they would almost certainly have the best of the ensuing battle. But at this point a message arrived from the Countess of Tripoli with news of the events at Tiberias. Once again there was a heated argument, and once again Raymond argued strongly in favour of staying where they were; to march through the waterless hills of Galilee in the heat of July would be to play straight into the hands of Saladin, and that would do no one any good, least of all his wife. As before, most people agreed with Raymond, and it was decided to remain on the defensive at Sephoria; but after dark the Grand Master of the Temple talked privately to the ever-irresolute King and persuaded him to change his mind.

The next day was hot and airless. The Christians set out before dawn, but long before mid-day both men and horses began to suffer terribly from heat and thirst; the sky was like brass, there was no shade on the barren hills of Galilee, whose rocks were too hot to touch; and dust kicked up by the men's feet choked and enveloped everyone except those in the vanguard. Meanwhile, Moslem skirmishers continually poured arrows into the Christians ranks, riding off again before their victims could retaliate. By late afternoon the army had reached a rocky hill with twin peaks known as the Horns of Hattin, and there Guy decided that it, should camp for the night. Some of the knights begged him to press on to the lake a few miles away, but he refused. When Raymond heard of his decision, he exclaimed, 'Ah, my God! The battle is already lost; we are dead men.' The well around which the army camped proved to be

Captions for following pages

A sixteenth-century miniature of a battle between Turks and Christians. The Hospitallers defended the city of Rhodes against Suleiman the Magnificent in 1522 with such courage that, when at last they admitted defeat, the Sultan allowed them to go free, even supplying them with shipping. This picture may be intended to depict that battle.

Snark

The Wilderness of Judaea. The country between Jerusalem and the Dead Sea becomes increasingly barren and deserted, and it is only in places like Jericho, which is fed by its own spring, that water is found in abundance.

Ronald Sheridan

A formalised painting of Jerusalem being attacked by Moslems, while Christian soldiers defend it. Christ himself is seen in the city above the main gate.

Scala

dry, and of the night which followed a Moslem chronicler later said that 'the angels of death kept watch that night'.

When the Christians awoke in the morning, they found themselves entirely surrounded by Saladin's army. Some of the Moslems had set fire to the dry scrub on the stony hillside, and the wind was blowing the smoke into the eyes of the Franks, half-blinding and choking them. Their one thought was of water, and they charged their enemies in an attempt to break through their ranks and reach the lake, which they could see far away below them, sparkling and shimmering in the blue distance five miles away; but they were driven back by Saladin's soldiers and by the flames, and many of them were killed. As usual, the knights fought with almost incredible courage, throwing back charge after charge by the enemy cavalry and inflicting heavy losses on the Kurdish horsemen; but as the fighting went on and on throughout the morning with hardly a moment's respite, the sun climbed higher and higher into the blue and fiery mid-summer sky of Palestine, beating down on to their heavy armour until the steel became too hot to touch, and they were exhausted by the heat. Many of the infantry had already been killed or captured; the ground was littered with bodies, and the wounded lay with swollen tongues and lips turning black with thirst, praying that they might die; it was obvious that there was not much time left in which to turn the tide of battle, if indeed it could be turned at all. The King therefore ordered Raymond of Tripoli to lead his knights in one last attempt to break out, and they thundered down the hill like the vengance of God in a terrible charge, and the enemy gave way before them, opening their ranks and letting them through; but as soon as they had passed, the Moslems closed ranks again, and the knights found themselves unable to rejoin their fellow Christians. There was nothing they could do but ride unhappily away from the battle. Another group of knights broke out a little later, but they were the last to escape; for the rest the end was near.

When it came, Saladin's soldiers found King Guy at the summit of the hill on one of the Horns of Hattin surrounded by those of his knights who had not broken out with Raymond of Tripoli or been killed; the great majority of them were lying on the ground, motionless and prone. Some were dead, some wounded, the rest were too tired to move. The King and his leading nobles, including Reynald of Châtillon and the Grand Master of the Temple, were led away to a tent which was being erected on the battlefield for Saladin, and there he received them with his accustomed courtesy. He invited King Guy to sit next to him and, seeing his thirst, he handed him a beaker of cold water; gratefully Guy drank from it, but as he was about to hand it to Reynald of Châtillon, Saladin said quickly to his interpreter, 'Remind the King that it was not I but he who gave that man a drink'; for by custom to share food or drink with a prisoner was to spare his life. A moment or two later, he turned to Reynald and taxed him with his many crimes; but Reynald was unabashed, replying loudly and insolently, and this was too much for Saladin; he drew his sword, and cut off his head. An Arab chronicler has described what followed; King Guy, expecting to be the next to die, 'shook in all his limbs. But the Sultan calmed his fears. "Kings," he said, "are not in the habit of killing kings, but that man had gone too far." '

The battle of Hattin was a disaster on an unprecedented scale for the Christians in Outremer. Their army was annihilated, the only fighting men left were scattered over the country in garrisons in towns and castles. After the battle Saladin began to mop them up methodically and at his leisure; in the process he captured so many Frankish prisoners that they became a glut on the slave markets of the Moslem world, their commercial value falling to a record low level; one man even exchanged a slave for a pair of sandals. One after another, the towns and cities of Outremer surrendered to the victorious Sultan; Tiberias had been the first, but now it was followed by Acre, Nablus and Jaffa. Tyre, where most of those who had survived at Hattin had taken refuge, withstood his first attack on its massive walls, and he did not think it worth wasting lives to subdue it; instead he passed on to Sidon, which surrendered at once. Beirut soon followed, but the Christians of Jerusalem would not open the gates of the city where Christ had died to the infidel, and Saladin was forced to besiege it; it took just under a fortnight, until 2 October 1187, for his troops to reduce and occupy the city. There was no massacre, for Saladin himself had given strict orders that Christians should not be molested, and he was obeyed. They were allowed to ransom themselves by paying a comparatively small sum of money to their captors: ten dinars for a man, five for a woman, and one for a child, although even that proved too much for some of the poor to pay. But Saladin showed himself a generous victor, and many who could not afford to buy their freedom were released for nothing.

When at last the autumn rains came, and Saladin disbanded his army, sending the men back to their farms and homes, the East was Moslem once again. He had avenged the appalling defeats inflicted on Islam by the Crusaders, and by always behaving with justice, humanity and generosity he had won a moral victory, which was perhaps more important even than his military triumph; for Islam had been demoralised for centuries by graft, selfishness, lies and the kind of murderous misrule which had destroyed the Fatimids of Egypt. Now it had a leader who had proved himself to be completely reliable: a man who had never been known to break his word to friend or foe, and this was so unusual by the standards of the day as to be nearly incredible, winning him enormous respect both amongst his fellow Moslems and amongst his Christian opponents. But if he had won the admiration of the world and reclaimed the old Moslem lands for Islam, he had not finally won the war against the Franks, for they managed to cling on in three towns and five great castles; Tyre, Antioch, and Tripoli held out against him, and so did Beaufort, Chastel Blanc, Marqab, Tortosa and Krak des Chevaliers. They provided the Christians with little more than a toe-hold or two on the land, and Saladin probably considered them unimportant: he would be able to deal with them later, when he chose to do so. But history was to prove him wrong.

XVI

♣♣♣

The Trade of Kings

War is the trade of Kings.
Dryden, *King Arthur*

When news of the disaster in the Holy Land reached Europe, it was
greeted with horror. The King of Sicily dressed himself in sackcloth as a
sign of mourning; Pope Urban III, who was already a sick man, died of
shock, and everywhere people crowded into churches and cathedrals to
pray that God's anger should be turned away; no doubt his people had
sinned against him, but now they would show him how sorry they were.
But their horror was tinged with incredulity; they could hardly believe
that such an appalling calamity could have befallen the entire Christian
community in Outremer with such suddenness. At one moment travellers
were returning with stories of the strength and splendour of the Kingdom of Jerusalem and of what luxurious lives its citizens were enjoying,
and at the next they were told that the Holy City itself had fallen to the
infidel, and the true Cross had been lost. It was impossible to believe that
the whole edifice built so painfully and laboriously over the years by the
Crusaders had been smashed in a few disastrous days, and that only a few
refugees in Tyre and elsewhere had somehow managed to survive.

Pope Urban was succeeded by Gregory VIII, an amiable monk, who
immediately issued an appeal for a new Crusade, promising all those who

took the Cross that their sins would be forgiven and that they would go to heaven if they were killed. He died less than two months later, while trying to make peace between the Pisans and the Genoese in order that the two cities might be free to join the Crusade. Clement III, a conciliatory man who had been born in Rome, was elected to take his place, and no one had ever needed a conciliatory nature more than he, for the Pisans and the Genoese were not the only people in Europe fighting one another; wherever you looked, people were at odds, and until they could be persuaded to make peace it was not much use trying to persuade them to go to the aid of the beleaguered Christians of Outremer, or what was left of it. The King of Sicily was at war with the Byzantines, but this was of little importance compared with the plight of England and France, for Henry II of England was almost permanently at war with Philip Augustus of France. As head of the Plantagenet family, Henry ruled a larger part of France than King Philip Augustus did himself; he was Duke of Normandy, Brittany and Aquitaine, and Count of Anjou, Maine, Poitou, La Manche and Auvergne, and this alone made the relationship between the two men extremely difficult. Even in the rare intervals of peace between them, they watched each other with deep suspicion, for each knew that the other would invade his land at a moment's notice, if he was given the smallest excuse to do so, and neither would have been surprised if his rival had taken the offensive without any excuse at all. Matters were made worse by Henry's two sons, Richard and John, whose loyalties were, to say the least, less than predictable; Richard especially was prone to change sides and fight with fine impartiality, first with his father against the French King and then, when it suited him, with Philip Augustus against his father. It was not until after the death of Henry II in 1189 that the Kings of England and France were ready to join a new Crusade.

The German Emperor Frederick Barbarossa was ready sooner. In his late sixties, he had been on the throne for over thirty years, and although he had by no means had a peaceful reign, by the time of Saladin's triumph in the East he had overcome his enemies at home and abroad. The Welf family, headed by his great rival Henry the Lion, Duke of Saxony and Bavaria, had been tamed; the Lombard cities, which had revolted against him, had been pacified; and Pope Alexander III, with whom he had long been at odds, had died. Both as the elder statesman of Europe and as a man Frederick was enormously respected. As a young man he had dazzled his contemporaries, for he had seemed to be endowed with all the virtues; he was brave to the point of fearlessness, intelligent, decisive and possessed of untiring energy, while physically he was well-built, attractive, with a fair skin, curly reddish hair and beard and a face which was perpetually smiling. Although by the time of the Third Crusade he was nearly seventy, he had lost nothing of his charm, and he was still as vigorous as many men half his age. More than any other western European monarch since Charlemagne, he embodied the idea and the ideal of medieval kingship; and when he took the Cross in the spring of 1188 a great wave of enthusiasm swept over Europe. An Englishman, William of Newburgh, was so carried away that he referred to him as 'our Emperor'.

Frederick made his preparations for the Crusade with care. He wrote letters to the King of Hungary, the Byzantine Emperor and the Seljuk Sultan, through whose lands he intended to march, and he received polite replies from them all; he also wrote to Saladin, who replied equally politely but made it crystal clear that he was not intimidated by the approach of the German Emperor. When he set out on 11 May 1189, his contemporaries spoke with awe of the might of his army, which numbered, they believed, between a hundred and a hundred and fifty thousand men. Although these were exaggerations, it was by far the largest single crusading army ever to leave Europe, consisting of about twenty thousand knights, at least as many infantrymen and perhaps as many as six or seven thousand camp followers. Moreover, it was not only large but well equipped and well disciplined. The march through Hungary was uneventful, but as soon as the army entered Byzantine territory, there was trouble; in the absence of a strong ruler in Constantinople, the Serbian countryside was infested with bandits and brigands, who attacked the Crusaders whenever they got the chance. They did little damage, although they killed a few stragglers, but the Germans blamed the Byzantines, and hostility towards them soon appeared. The Emperor Isaac Angelus was a weak and foolish man, and when he was told that the Emperor was marching towards the capital at the head of a huge army, which rumour made out to be even larger than it really was, he fell into a panic, which was made worse when Frederick occupied Philippopolis. So, when the German Emperor sent ambassadors to him to make arrangements for the army to cross the Bosphorus into Asia, Isaac threw them into prison.

It was an extraordinarily stupid thing to do, for it simply confirmed Frederick's belief that the Emperor was his enemy; he decided to summon a fleet from Germany, to launch a combined attack from sea and land on Constantinople and to ask for the blessing of the Pope on a Crusade against the Byzantines. When Isaac heard of these plans, he became even more terrified, and after some hesitation he released the ambassadors and made his peace with Frederick. But by this time the autumn was so well advanced that Frederick decided that it would be rash to attempt to march across Anatolia until the spring; the icy, snow-laden winds which blew down from Russia in winter across its treeless steppes and barren hills were too dangerous. So he took up winter quarters at Adrianople and waited for the spring.

In March 1190 the army crossed the Dardanelles into Asia from a point near Gallipoli, thus avoiding the Bosphorus, where there might have been trouble with the citizens of Constantinople. Frederick then marched south to Philadelphia and thence to Laodicea before turning inland into country held by the Seljuk Sultan, who had promised him and his army safe conduct across his domain. The men soon began to suffer the same hardships of hunger and thirst as had been endured by all previous Crusaders, and it was not long before they discovered that the Sultan's promise of free and unhindered passage across his land was worthless; for soon after passing the site of the battle of Myriocephalum, still littered with the bones of those who had died there, mounted Turkish archers appeared and began to inflict casualties on the marching men. In fact, the Sultan was not to blame, although naturally enough he was held responsible by the angry Germans; it was his son Qutb ad-Din, who happened also to be Saladin's son-in-law, who had authorised the attacks; and the deeper the Christians moved into his father's territory, the more he harried them and the more they suffered. On 18 May 1190, the two armies met just outside Iconium (the modern Konya), and a pitched battle followed. Qutb ad-Din's regular troops had been rein-forced by hordes of Turcoman nomads mounted on tough little Asiatic horses, but his combined forces were no match for the disciplined German soldiers, and Frederick won a brilliant victory. When the Sultan was told, he hurried to apologise for his son and to make his peace with Frederick, and the rest of the Crusaders' journey through his domain was uneventful. When they entered the territory controlled by the Christian Armenians, it seemed that their troubles were over; but they were not.

At the beginning of June the Crusaders began the long descent of the Taurus mountains onto the coastal plain of Seleucia, and Frederick rode ahead of the army with a small group of friends and guards, reaching the banks of the river Saleph before the others. No one knows for certain what happened next; it may be that the old Emperor was thrown from his horse into the river and was stunned, or he may have been swept away by the current as he tried to drink the water, the weight of his armour preventing him from swimming to safety; all that is known for sure is that he was drowned. His death was a shattering blow to his followers. 'At this point,' wrote a man from Cologne in despair, 'and at this sad news our pen is stilled, and our story finished.' The great Crusade was finished too. With their leader dead, the Germans were like sheep without a shepherd; some went home by the way they had come; others sailed to Palestine, where a few of them later formed the nucleus of the Order of Teutonic Knights; and Frederick's son tried to lead what was left of the army to Syria, but he caught a fever in the hot and swampy plain of eastern Cilicia, and had to be left behind, while the army began to disintegrate into an undisciplined rabble. Pathetically clinging to the mortal remains of their dead King, they carried Frederick's body pickled in vinegar with them, but it brought them little luck; they were attacked and savagely mauled by the Turks as they crossed the mountains into Syria, and when the survivors reached Antioch in mid-June, it was difficult to believe that they had once been part of the finest crusading army ever to leave Europe. Their demoralisation, which was already far advanced, was soon completed in the brothels of Antioch. Meanwhile, despite the vinegar the Emperor's body had begun to fall apart and stink; it was hastily buried in the cathedral, while Saladin gave thanks to God for his death as a miraculous delivery from a most powerful enemy, and the Christians in Tyre tried to hide their bitter disappointment at the frustration of their hopes.

Fortunately for them, by the time that the great German Crusade had collapsed, the French and English Kings were on their way. Philip Augustus was twenty-four at the time, a dull and rather unimpressive young man who was blind in one eye and personally untidy; he had no love of war, was timid rather than brave, hated ostentation, had no taste for the arts, and led a simple and unpretentious life; but as a politician he was both wiser and more cunning than his English rival. Richard, who was thirty-two years old, was his antithesis. The most gifted member of a gifted family, fortune and heredity had combined to endow him with a superb physique and a galaxy of talents; with the figure of a Greek god, he was tall, immensely strong, fair-haired and so handsome that he fascinated both his friends and his enemies, while at the same time captivating everyone by his charm of manner and courage. He was a good

14

general, had unbounded energy, loved the pomp and panache of his kingly office, and was a genuine lover of poetry and music; but he was also a man of some psychological instability, tending to fly from one emotional extreme to the other. Some people have suggested that he may have been homosexual, although the nearest the most eminent modern historian of the period has come to suggesting such a thing has been to say that Richard's 'tastes did not lie in the direction of marriage', which does not necessarily imply the same thing; and, of course, he did marry Berengaria. His gravest fault was a temper which drove him occasionally to do violent and cruel things with a callousness which was in contrast to his normal generosity and gallantry. But even if he had his faults, both during his lifetime and long afterwards he was a favourite hero of poets and troubadours, and men of all nationalities – English, French, German, Turkish, and Arab – have looked back on him as the man who came nearest to 'embodying the romantic ideal of medieval chivalry, while Saladin personified all that was most noble and generous in the faith of Islam; and there is some truth in this popular view of the two men.

Philip of France and Richard of England, having made peace after the death of Henry II, agreed to go on a joint Crusade together. They did so largely because neither trusted the other to keep the peace or to refrain from invading his rival's kingdom if one of them were to go east while the other stayed at home. So they set out together from Vézélay on 4 July 1190 to march to Lyons, where their ways parted; Philip then took the road to Genoa, where the Italians had agreed to transport his army by ship to the Holy Land, while Richard marched south to Marseilles, where the English fleet had orders to meet him. King William of Sicily, who was married to Richard's sister Joanna, had invited them both to assemble their forces in the island, and despite the fact that William had recently died, Philip and Richard decided to meet in Messina, as they had originally planned. Meanwhile, because William had had no children by his wife Joanna, he had been succeeded by a cousin named Tancred, an ill-favoured little man, who soon found that his inheritance was no sinecure.

Philip arrived in the island first, landing at Messina in early September and making his way unostentatiously to a palace which Tancred had put at his disposal. Richard arrived a few days later in a thoroughly bad temper after a tiresome journey, coming ashore at Messina in marked contrast to Philip in flamboyant style and being conducted to another palace outside the walls of the city, where his sister Joanna joined him. He was devoted to her, but her arrival served only to increase his bad temper, for the story she told him made him furious. Since her husband's death, she said, she had been abominably badly treated by Tancred: she had been shut up in her room like a prisoner, and Tancred had quietly stolen her dowry instead of returning it to her; he had also appropriated a number of things which the late King William had left to his father-in-law, Henry II of England, and which therefore Richard naturally regarded as belonging to him now that his father was dead.

While Richard was working himself up into a rage over Tancred's various sins of commission and omission, his English soldiers were behaving thoroughly badly in the town, molesting the women and fighting anyone who dared to object, and the situation there was becoming explosive. On 3 October, while Richard was still in a black and angry mood, brooding over the insults to his sister, there was an anti-English riot during which a group of infuriated Sicilians were heard making some highly uncomplimentary remarks about Richard himself; these were reported to him, and did not improve his temper. His patience was exhausted, and he ordered his troops to attack the city, which they took, in the words of an Anglo-Norman poet named Ambroise, 'in less time than it takes a priest to sing mattins'. It was a piece of sheer piracy, and it troubled King Philip, but it cowed Tancred, who promptly agreed to hand over Joanna's dowry and a large sum in gold in place of the legacy owing to Henry II, at the same time offering to sign a treaty with the English King. Richard, who liked gold, agreed, and a treaty was duly signed.

With peace restored and Richard in a better temper, the two kings decided to spend the winter in Sicily; they did not sail for Outremer until the spring of 1191, Philip leaving at the end of March and Richard ten days later. The French King had an uneventful voyage, reaching Tyre in mid-April, where his arrival delighted everyone, and put new heart into them all; they had had to wait a very long time for help to reach them, and the German fiasco after the death of Frederick Barbarossa had been a dreadful disappointment, but at last help on the scale they had all prayed for had arrived. Knowing that Richard was also on his way to join them, people began to believe that perhaps fortune had at last decided to smile on them again.

But Richard's voyage was far from uneventful, and lasted longer than anyone had expected. After the fleet had sailed past southern Greece, violent storms made life extremely uncomfortable for a few days, and

Richard, who was a bad sailor, was horribly sea-sick. One of his ships foundered, while others were blown off course to Cyprus; and on board one of these were Richard's sister Joanna and the daughter of the King of Navarre, Princess Berengaria, whom he intended to marry. Cyprus was ruled by a pretender to the Byzantine throne, Isaac Comnenus, who was in rebellion against the legitimate Emperor Isaac Angelus, and who had somehow managed to establish himself in the island despite a few rather feeble attempts by the government in Constantinople to subdue him. When news arrived of the approach of large numbers of ships, he became thoroughly alarmed; and when some of Richard's men were wrecked on the island, he threw them into prison. The vessel carrying Queen Joanna and the Princess Berengaria was not wrecked, but it ran for shelter in Limassol Bay, where the captain sent ashore to ask for water and supplies; Isaac Comnenus peremptorily refused to give him any help at all, and forbade anyone from the ship to land.

When Richard arrived a few days later, he was furious; his natural tendency to violence, which was never more than dormant, erupted in a great burst of angry aggression. He led his men ashore and attacked Limassol, which surrendered at once. Isaac fled to a place of safety, from which he offered to come to terms with Richard. The two men duly met, and Isaac agreed to everything Richard demanded; but he repudiated his agreement as soon as he had left the English camp. He had hardly departed when Richard's hand was greatly strengthened by the arrival of a large party of knights from Outremer, who had come to bid the English King welcome, together with the rest of the English fleet. Sure now of his superiority, he was in no hurry to chastise Isaac; and it was not until he had married Berengaria with as much pomp as the circumstances allowed, and she had been crowned Queen, that he set about conquering the island. Isaac put up some resistance, but it did him little good, and by the end of May he was a prisoner of the English King. It does not seem to have occurred to Richard that Cyprus was an integral part of the Byzantine Empire, or that its inhabitants were Christians and, having extorted an enormous booty from them, he installed two Englishmen as governors of the island until he should decide how to dispose of it; to him it was simply conquered territory.

So it was seven weeks after Philip Augustus of France, at the beginning of June, that Richard arrived off the coast of Outremer to find the combined armies of the Franks besieging Acre. It was nearly four years since the battle of Hattin, but somehow the survivors of that disaster had succeeded in hanging on in Tyre until help came. They had been magnificently led by a cousin of the French King, Conrad of Montferrat, whose arrival in the city at the time of Saladin's great triumph had been providential. He was an immensely able man, ruthless and determined. When Saladin, who had captured his father at Hattin, paraded the old man below the walls of Acre, threatening to kill him if Conrad did not surrender the city, he replied that his father had lived long enough; it was probably time for him to die in any case. Conrad had been joined by a number of newcomers from the West, who had not waited for the kings to stop fighting amongst themselves before setting out to aid their hardpressed fellow Christians. Before his death, King William of Sicily had sent help to the men besieged by Saladin in Tyre; later some Danes, some Italians and some men from Flanders had sailed into the harbour there to offer their services as soldiers of the Cross, and they had been followed in 1189 by a contingent of Englishmen. As the years had gone by, Saladin had released some of his more illustrious captives on payment of various kinds of ransom, and they too had strengthened the small but belligerent remnant of the Christian army which had not been destroyed on the Horns of Hattin.

Meanwhile, in the summer of 1188, Saladin had set free King Guy of Jerusalem and some of the lords of his kingdom on condition that he should leave the country; Guy had duly promised to go home to France, but as soon as he was at liberty he had asked the Church to release him from his vow and, since it had been made to a Moslem and not to a Christian, the Church had obligingly and unhesitatingly done so. But when Guy presented himself at the gates of Tyre, Conrad of Montferrat, who had saved the city and had been acclaimed ever since as its leader, had refused him entry; indeed, he had gone further, and had refused to recognise him as King. An immediate and lasting feud between the two men had been the result, and from that moment the surviving Christian community had been split into two bitterly hostile factions devoted more to destroying each other than to fighting their common enemy, Saladin. It was a disastrous development, and even Guy, who was neither the most intelligent nor the wisest of men, realised after a time that to sit below the walls of Tyre in helpless and frustrated anger was not helping the Christian cause. He had mobilised his supporters and made a sudden and most surprising march on Acre, which he had tried to take by assault. He had failed, but that had not deterred him, and he had camped below the city walls and begun to lay siege to it. Surprisingly, Saladin had failed to dislodge him, whereupon the Moslem army had invested the besieging Franks instead. As time had gone by, Guy had been joined by reinforcements, even Conrad of Montferrat coming to help him in the battle for the city. The arrival of King Philip Augustus of France had greatly strengthened the Christian army there, and the arrival of Richard by sea with twenty-five ships was greeted with rejoicing by the Crusaders and alarm by the Moslems, who saw the vessels arriving full of men, while on shore everyone blew trumpets and horns, beat drums, and lit bonfires in welcome.

Philip Augustus had had a number of enormous and highly efficient siege weapons built, two of which had been nicknamed by the soldiers God's Own Sling and The Wicked Neighbour; but he was not an aggressive man, and his presence had done little to inspire the troops. Richard had not been there for twenty-four hours before he had put new heart into everyone by his mere presence amongst them. Unfortunately, both he and Philip fell ill soon after his arrival, and Richard was forced to keep to his bed for some time, his mouth and throat covered with sores; but he continued to direct operations from his tent. He had assumed command of the Christian army on reaching Acre, and no one had questioned his right to do so; during his illness it became evident that it had been wise to accept his command, for he pursued hostilities with far more vigour from his sick-bed than Philip Augustus had ever done when in full health. Day and night siege engines creaked and groaned as they hurled great rocks at the walls and over them into the town; and the thudding of their impact was followed by the crash of falling masonry and the sight of clouds of dust billowing lazily into the air like great yellow flowers unfolding. Saladin's men did their best to interfere with this bombardment, and Ambroise made a note of some of the encounters which resulted; it was a very personal war. 'It happened,' he wrote, describing one vivid little incident, 'that a knight was down in the fosse outside the camp on an affair of his own that no one can do without. As he placed himself so, a Turk in one of the enemy's outposts, to which he was paying no attention, separated from his companions and raced his horse forward. It was villainous and discourteous to seek to surprise the knight while so occupied. The Turk was already far from his own people, and was approaching the knight with lance to slay him, when our men shouted, "Run, Sir, run!" He had barely time to get up. The Turk came up at full gallop, believing that he would be able to turn his horse and wheel back, if he needed to do so, but by God's grace, he did not succeed.

The knight cast himself to one side, and took up two stones in his hands; but listen to how God takes vengeance! As the Turk checked his horse to turn back on him, the knight saw him clearly, and as he drew near, struck him with one of the stones upon the temple. The Turk fell dead, and the knight took his horse and led it off by the rein.'

While incidents like this were happening daily, there were occasions when a different spirit prevailed. The Moslem chronicler, Baha ed-Din, relates how 'the two sides were so accustomed to the sight of each other that the Moslem soldiers and the Frankish soldiers sometimes ceased fighting to talk. The two throngs mingled, singing and dancing together, after which they returned to fighting. Once they said, "We have been fighting for a long time, let us stop awhile and allow the boys of the camps to show us what they can do." So they matched two parties of boys, who struggled together with great eagerness. One of the young Moslems, seizing a young infidel, lifted him off the ground and threw him down, making him a prisoner. A Frank who was watching came forward and redeemed the captive for two gold pieces. "He was your prisoner," the Frank said to the victorious youth.' But after such rare interludes the bombardment continued, and whenever a breach was made in the wall, however small, a handful of Crusaders would try to rush into the city; but signals from the defenders always brought immediate reprisals from Saladin, who would launch a diversionary attack on the Christians' rear, and the attempt on the walls would have to be abandoned. Towards the end of June, while Richard was still too ill to take part in the attack, the French made just such an assault, concentrating on a large breach made by the mangonels, but the defenders fought like fiends, and a signal was made to Saladin, who attacked the Christian camp, and by evening the French were forced to retreat, carrying their dead and wounded with them. At about this time, a kind of bitter desperation began to possess both sides; they fought now without giving or expecting mercy. Some newcomers who had arrived with Robert, Earl of Leicester, and Andrew of Chavigny burnt a Moslem prisoner alive within sight of the wall, and the garrison immediately took their revenge by burning a captive Crusader at the stake.

But the plight of the six thousand Moslems cooped up in Acre grew worse daily, for with the coming of the English fleet they were completely blockaded from the sea, and food was getting so short that the last of the carrier pigeons with which they had been used to send messages to Saladin had been eaten by the end of June. Their courage was undiminished, but it was becoming obvious that courage alone could not save them; the odds against them were too great. There was talk inside the city of surrender, and although it amounted to nothing for the time being, it did the morale of the defenders no good. During the course of yet another attack on the city on 2 July, Saladin counter-attacked with every man he could muster, and his nephew Taki ad-Din made a furious attempt to break through the Christian lines, but he failed. A few days later the English, thirsty for glory and hungry for loot, tried to carry the place while the French were otherwise occupied; they too failed, but they came so close to success that the weary defenders decided that they had had enough. A man volunteered to swim out of the harbour and along the coast, until he was free of the Christian lines, and thence to take a message to Saladin, telling him that they could hold out no longer. On 12 July they offered to surrender on terms: their lives were to be spared, and in return they would hand over the city intact to the Crusaders, pay them a large sum in gold, release fifteen hundred prisoners including a number of lords, and return the True Cross, which had been captured on the Horns of Hattin; when all these conditions had been met, they themselves were to be set free. Richard agreed at once, and the siege was over.

Saladin was appalled. When the swimmer reached him, he read his message and told the man to return to the city and tell the defenders that he could not agree to the terms they had offered; but almost as he was speaking, he was dismayed by the sight of bonfires on the city wall and the banners and crosses of the Franks being run up over its towers and ramparts. Acre had already fallen, and any further help from Saladin would come too late. Being the man he was, he decided to honour the agreement made by his lieutenants, even though he did not like it, and for once the Christians honoured their side of the agreement too. The Moslems were allowed to leave the city unmolested; indeed, the victors watched them go with some emotion, as they marched out of the place into captivity, for their courage had been so dauntless that they had won the respect and even something like the affection of their enemies. They were thin, unkempt, half-starved, dirty, and in rags, but they were un-bowed; and this was something the Crusaders could admire.

As always, as soon as the Crusaders had won the battle, they began to quarrel amongst themselves. They squabbled over precedence and over who should live where; they took sides against each other, Richard supporting King Guy, and Philip backing Conrad of Montferrat; as the senior German, the Duke of Austria wanted to be treated on a par with the French and English Kings, and ran his standard up next to Richard's, whereupon some English soldiers promptly hauled it down and threw it ignominiously into the ditch below the wall: an insult which the German never forgave nor forgot; and the merchants who had owned property in Acre before the city had fallen to the Moslems did everything they could to gain possession of it again at the expense of the newcomers who had fought shoulder to shoulder with them during the siege. Things became a little easier when the problem of the kingship of Jerusalem was solved by confirming Guy in the office during his lifetime, but promising it to Conrad of Montferrat at Guy's death. They were further eased when the Duke of Austria, still sulking angrily and nursing his injured pride, decided to go home, and was followed by the French King. Philip Augustus did not like war, did not like Richard, and did not like the Holy Land, where he had been ill almost continuously since his arrival; he had done his duty as a Christian, and that was enough. Richard, who was afraid of what Philip might do to the English lands in France when he got home, tried to persuade him to stay; but he was adamant. On 31 July he sailed out of Acre on the first stage of his journey to Brindisi.

After Philip's departure, Richard was without a rival. His first task was to ensure that Saladin should keep the promises made in his name by the commander of the garrison in Acre, and this the Sultan was prepared to do; he was not a man who broke his word. Richard sent ambassadors to his camp, where Saladin greeted them courteously; some of the Frankish prisoners were released, a first instalment of the promised gold was paid, and the ambassadors were shown the True Cross as an earnest of its eventual return when all the other terms of the surrender had been honoured. But Richard complained that the released prisoners did not include any of the lords whom the Moslem governor of Acre had promised should be freed, and he demanded that Saladin should set them at liberty at once, refusing to release any of the Moslem prisoners in return, until he had done so. Saladin, who did not trust him, refused. Treating this as a breach of the terms of surrender, Richard coldly ordered the execution of the Moslem prisoners. Two and a half thousand men, together with their wives and children, were led out onto the plain by the city into a kind of enclosure of blankets hung on cords, and there they were butchered in full view of their fellow countrymen in Saladin's outposts. Some were hanged, others were killed by the sword, while the Moslem cavalry attacked in a frenzy of anger, trying to break through to the scene of the execution; but they failed. When the massacre was complete, the English soldiers left the bodies of the dead on the blood-stained ground for the Moslems to bury. Looking back on the day, Ambroise thanked God for the slaughter.

Having rid himself of the Moslem prisoners, at the end of August Richard led his men out against Saladin. With the English fleet guarding his right flank, he marched south, while the enemy harrassed him as best they could on the left. The weather was extremely hot, and some of the English soldiers fell out or fainted, only to be killed at once by the Moslem cavalry. From time to time someone would cry out in prayer, '*Sanctum sepulchrum adjuva!*' – 'Help us, Holy sepulchre!' – and the others would take it up, the prayer rising up in a great gust of sound rippling back along the marching column. They passed Haifa and Mount Carmel, and trudged on through the summer heat to Caesarea. Camping early and sometimes resting for a whole day, it took them a fortnight to reach Arsuf, even though it was only about sixty miles from their starting point at Acre; and there they found Saladin's army blocking their way. The Moslems were drawn up across the coastal plain; they had many more cavalrymen than the Christians, but they were lightly armed and mounted on fast little Arab ponies, while the Christian knights, though they were fewer, were heavily armoured and mounted on horses with limbs like tree trunks: the ancestors of the great shire horses of England and the *percherons* of France. Richard arranged his men in a tight formation, close together and bristling with lances and pikes like a giant steel hedgehog; most of the knights were in the centre with the English bowmen in front of them, while the Hospitallers were on the extreme left and the Templars on the right by the sea. Philip Augustus had left the greater part of the French army of Crusaders behind him when he had sailed for France, and most of it was with Richard under the command of Hugh of Burgundy; King Guy of Jerusalem was there too, and so were many Normans, Bretons and men from Flanders. When everyone was in place, Richard rode along the line with the Duke of Burgundy to steady the men and encourage them to stand firm; no one was to break ranks or charge until the order was given.

Formidable and motionless, the Christian army waited for the enemy to attack, as the sun climbed up into a golden sky and the dew of early morning turned into steam in its heat. Aware of the battle which was about to engulf them all, the men of both armies were silent, and the only noises to be heard were the barking of dogs in the distance and the occasional neighing of a restive horse. Then, quite suddenly, at nine o'clock, the stillness of the morning air was splintered by the yelling and baying of the Moslem infantry, as they rushed forward to discharge a barrage of darts and arrows at the waiting Christians. The attack was fierce, and the men on foot, who bore the brunt of it, were thrown into confusion for a moment; but the mounted knights behind them were unmoved, the darts and arrows of the enemy bouncing off their armour, in the words of a chronicler who was present, with the noise of steel hammers striking an anvil. The attacks were delivered in waves, but after a time the Bedouin and Egyptian infantrymen suddenly spread out to allow the Turkish cavalry to charge through their ranks, their swords and axes flashing in the sun as they galloped up and hurled themselves against the steel mass of Christians. The Hospitallers, who took the main weight of the attack, were hard pressed, but the left of the Christian line was not turned, and after each Turkish charge the English bowmen reformed and took a heavy toll of the enemy horsemen, the arrows from their long bows penetrating the Moslems' light armour as though it were egg shell. The pace was too great to last, and as the day grew hotter the Turkish cavalry began to tire; but still Richard did not give the order to charge. One after another, his subordinate commanders begged him to do so, the Grand Master of the Temple returning again and again to implore him to give the word, and again and again Richard told him to wait. But there is a limit to human patience and restraint, and two knights of the Temple, who had reached that limit, took matters into their own hands; without waiting for the command from Richard, they charged the enemy on the spur of the moment, and immediately all the Templars galloped after them. Imagining that the order to charge must have been given, all the other knights on the field of battle moved forward to the attack, gathering speed in a cloud of dust. Seeing that he could not stop his men, Richard spurred his horse into a gallop and joined them, taking command at the centre of the attack. The sheer weight and momentum of a thousand or more steel-clad knights, each with a lance almost the size of a telegraph pole, and each mounted on a huge, snorting, steel-clad horse weighing more than a ton is difficult to recreate in the imagination, and it proved too much for the tired and frightened Moslems. Some simply fled before the avalanche of steel, bone and sweat could crash into them, while those who stood firm were crushed and broken, and in a matter of minutes the Moslem army was in flight. The field was Richard's, and so was the day.

It was a timely victory for the Christians but not a decisive one, for by nightfall Saladin had rallied most of his men again, and their casualties proved to have been fewer than he had feared. The Christians too had suffered only small losses, and the balance of military power between the two sides had not been much changed by the battle. But its moral effect was enormous, for it was the first time that a Christian army had met Saladin since the Horns of Hattin, and the legend of his invincibility was shattered once and for all, while Richard's reputation had never stood so high; he even won for himself a place in Moslem folklore as the great and fierce Malik Ric. The morale of the Christians was immeasurably strengthened, while that of Saladin's troops suffered, and so did their confidence in the Sultan.

After the battle, Richard marched south from Arsuf to Jaffa, where he repaired the fortifications and made sure of a strong base on the coast where his fleet would be safe. Saladin who had expected him to make a dash for Jerusalem, led his men to Ramleh on the road to the capital, and waited there to dispute the way with him, while ordering his engineers to strengthen the defences of the city before Richard could reach it. When he heard that the Christians had taken Jaffa, he rushed some troops to Ascalon, determined that it should not also fall into Frankish hands again, and demolished the city stone by stone, despite the agonised pleas of the inhabitants. 'I take God to witness,' Saladin is reported to have said, 'that I would rather lose all my children than cast a stone from its walls, but it is necessary.' So he pressed the work of demolishing one of the most prosperous cities in the country, for he was afraid that Richard would march south and attack him before he could complete the work of demolition.

But Richard had worries of his own; his men were tired, and it would have taxed even his authority and powers of leadership to persuade them to follow him if he had tried to make them take the field again so soon after their recent exertions; they were revelling in the comforts and amenities of Jaffa, where food and drink were plentiful and prostitutes had been imported from Acre, and they made it very clear that they looked upon an extended holiday in the city as no more than the due reward of their labours. Moreover, there was political trouble in Cyprus and in Tyre, where Conrad of Montferrat was growing too strong for Richard's liking. It was time to make peace. He sent envoys to Saladin, who agreed to discuss the possibility of a truce, and authorised his brother, al-Adil, to speak for him.

The negotiations which followed were protracted and devious; they lasted for a year, and they were conducted with great courtesy in an atmosphere at times more suited to comic opera than to what the Germans call *real-politik*. Richard and al-Adil became quite fond of each other during the course of their long discussions, and at one time Richard even suggested that Saladin's brother should marry his sister, the widowed Queen Joanna of Sicily, although he had not taken the trouble to inform the lady herself of this project before mooting the idea; when she heard of it, she was horrified, and promptly told her brother that nothing would induce her to marry a Moslem. Saladin seems to have treated the proposal as a joke, and his brother, when asked if he would consider becoming a Christian in order to marry Joanna, replied with his usual urbanity that he would find it difficult to become a good Christian; but to show that there was no ill feeling, he entertained Richard to dinner at Lydda with great lavishness and splendour. At the end of the evening, the Christian King and the Moslem Prince parted with protestations of affection and mutual esteem, which must have seemed exceedingly odd to any ghosts of the First Crusaders, who might have been hovering, restless and unseen, in al-Adil's banqueting hall. But from Richard's point of view these friendly contacts were marred by the discovery that al-Adil was also conducting separate peace negotiations with Conrad of Montferrat, who had not bothered to tell the English King what he was doing, while Saladin's brother, like the highly skilled diplomat that he was, had also kept his meetings with Conrad secret.

While these various conversations dragged on, the winter rains came, and Saladin disbanded half his army. Richard refused to be defeated by the weather, however, and in November he marched on Jerusalem; but it did him little good, for after his men had suffered miseries of discomfort in wet and icy weather, he recognised his mistake and reluctantly marched his men back to the coast again, where he set them to rebuild Ascalon. During this time, the political rivalries between the various dynastic factions in Acre became so bad that the Pisans and the Genoese actually went to war with each other, the Pisans taking King Guy's side against Conrad of Montferrat, and the Genoese championing Conrad. It became increasingly urgent that the quarrel between the two men should be settled, especially since Richard received news from home at about this time that his brother John Lackland was engaged in treasonable negotiations with the King of France, and he knew that he could not stay much longer in Outremer if he wished to keep his crown in England. To his surprise he discovered that support for Conrad was widespread; Guy's wife Sybilla was dead, while Conrad had married her younger sister

Isabella, and now had a better claim to the throne than Guy. Richard had always backed Guy in the past but he now decided to press Conrad's claims instead; to compensate Guy, he offered him the kingship of Cyprus, although he had to buy it from the Templars to whom Richard had previously sold it. Everyone was delighted by this solution to the problem which had divided them for so long, and preparations for Conrad's coronation were pressed forward in an atmosphere of relief and rejoicing; but this public happiness was destined to be short-lived.

According to the chronicler Ernoul, on 28 April 1192 Conrad's wife Isabella was late for dinner, having lain rather too long in her bath, and Conrad decided to dine with his friend the Bishop of Beauvais. But when he arrived, the Bishop had finished dinner, and although he offered to have a meal prepared for his unexpected visitor, Conrad would not hear of it; he did not want to be a nuisance, and he was perfectly happy to walk home again. On his way back, however, as he turned a corner, he was accosted by two men, and while one of them held his attention, the other stabbed him, and he was carried to his palace a dying man. The murderers were Assassins, whom Conrad had offended in some way in the past, and his killing had been ordered by the Old Man of the Mountains, Sheikh Sinan; one of the guilty pair was killed on the spot, and the other was arrested. He confessed that he was an Assassin and guilty of the crime, but some people refused to believe him, blaming Richard instead. The subject has been exhaustively discussed by historians, a few of whom have continued to accuse Richard of the murder; but such a thing would have been wholly untypical of him, and there is no reason to doubt his innocence.

As the daughter of King Amalric I Conrad's widow, the Princess Isabella, was heiress of the kingdom. Despite the fact that she had been married twice, she was still only twenty-one years of age, and by all accounts she was ravishingly beautiful. For obvious political reasons it was important that she should choose another husband as soon as possible, and within a week of Conrad's death she was married to Henry of Troyes, Count of Champagne, a young man of many parts and great charm who was the nephew of both the King of England and the King of France. Although it was a marriage of political convenience, it proved to be a very happy one; Henry fell passionately in love with his wife, and Isabella found him a welcome change after her late husband, who had been both middle-aged and somewhat formidable.

Although Henry never took the title of King, his marriage to Isabella solved the problem which had vexed the kingdom for so long, and Richard felt free to return to the one thing he really enjoyed: warfare. At the end of May, he captured the town of Daron south of Gaza in a lightning stroke which caught the Moslem garrison off their guard, and a fortnight later, on 7 June, he set out from Ascalon at the head of his army to march on Jerusalem again. Five days later he reached Beit-Nuba, the point at which he had turned back the previous winter, and there once more he halted. To have advanced further would have been highly dangerous; water was known to be short, the city was strongly garrisoned, and Saladin was there in person. Even if Richard had advanced on the place, and captured it, it was very doubtful whether the Franks of Outremer would have been able to hold it after he himself had returned to England. So the army stayed where it was, and contented itself with sending out patrols to harass any Moslem soldiers they might meet in the country between Beit-Nuba and Jerusalem. On one of these expeditions, as Richard's horse topped a hill near Emmaus, there away to the south-east across a marble landscape dappled with olive trees and pomegranates lay Jerusalem in the distance, its domes and towers shimmering in the sun. It was the nearest he was destined ever to get to the Holy City, and as if he knew it, he covered his face so as not to gaze on a sight so long desired and yet so unattainable.

For three weeks the army lay at Beit-Nuba without doing much, and many people longed to advance on Jerusalem whatever the dangers might be; but Richard was too good a soldier not to realise that an attack on the city would do little more than satisfy the romantic longing in every man's heart without serving any useful military purpose, and he refused to give the order to advance. But this frustrating inactivity ended on 20 June, when news was brought to the camp of the approach of an enormous caravan bringing supplies to Saladin from Egypt; it was winding its slow northward way through the difficult desert country south of Hebron, where the stony hills of Judea run down to the Dead Sea in a barren desolation of rock and dust. According to Baha ed-Din, who later heard the stories of the survivors of the caravan, 'when this was reported by some Arabs to the King of England he did not believe it, but mounted and set out with the Arabs and a small escort. When he came up to the caravan, he disguised himself as an Arab and went all round it. When he saw that quiet reigned in the camp and that everyone was fast asleep, he returned and ordered his men into the saddle.' Another authority relates that Richard was challenged by some of the Moslem sentries guarding the camp, but that one of his Bedouin companions, motioning him to be silent, answered the man in Arabic without checking his horse, and the little party was soon swallowed up in the darkness. When Richard returned with the army, the caravan with its small escort of Egyptian soldiers was no match for the Crusaders, who vastly outnumbered them, and everyone and everything in it was captured; soldiers, merchants and their wares, Saladin's supplies of food and war material, over a thousand horses and almost as many camels, all fell into the Crusaders' hands. The sheer quantity of the loot did something to cheer the men up and make them less bitterly disappointed when, on returning to Beit-Nuba laden with booty, Richard finally abandoned any idea of attacking Jerusalem and ordered the army to retreat to Jaffa.

After his abortive expedition against Jerusalem, Richard resumed negotiations for peace once more, but the future of the city of Ascalon, which Saladin had demolished and Richard had rebuilt, proved to be an insuperable obstacle to agreement; Saladin was prepared to agree to many things but not to the inclusion of Ascalon in Outremer. The argument was prolonged, and Richard prepared to sail for home as soon as he could reach agreement with the Sultan, moving to Acre in readiness. But on 27 July, Saladin, who was smarting from the loss of Daron and from his recent defeats at Acre and at Arsuf, saw an opportunity for revenge and, moving quickly down to the coast from Jerusalem, he launched a sudden attack on Jaffa. The garrison was taken completely by surprise, and although the Christian soldiers fought with their accustomed bravery the odds against them were too heavy, and after three days they surrendered. When Richard heard the news, he reacted with a mixture of speed, calculation and inspired boldness which was typical of him at his best. With the help of the Genoese and the Pisans he sailed at once from Acre, while his army marched south by land as fast as it could. He arrived four days later, and at the sight of his ships the Christian garrison grabbed their arms again, and launched a violent attack on Saladin's men, who fought back angrily; they outnumbered the Franks, and it began to look as though they were bound to prevail once again. But at this juncture a priest leapt from the city wall and, running down the beach into the sea, swam out to Richard's galley. It was easily recognisable, for it was painted bright red, and it had a prow carved in the shape of a dragon's head; on reaching it, the swimmer climbed aboard, and told the King that the battle in the city was going badly for the Christians. It was the first that Richard had heard of any battle in the city, and he decided immediately to go to their aid in spite of the fact that he had only a handful of knights and a few hundred infantrymen with him. To the horror of the sailors he ordered them to row their ships inshore and beach them, and as soon as he felt the keel of his own galley grate on the sand, he leapt into the water and waded ashore at the head of his men. The Moslems were taken by surprise, and Richard attacked with such impetuosity and dash, fighting in person at the spearhead of his attack, that Saladin's men were routed, spilling out of the city in panic and fleeing for their lives. They did not stop until they were five miles away inland.

The recapture of Jaffa was almost the last of Richard's exploits in Outremer, but Saladin forced one more battle on him, and it proved to be a memorable one. After his men had fled in confusion from Jaffa, Saladin had soon learned how small a force Richard had had at his disposal during the battle; since the main Crusader army had still not passed Caesarea, Saladin decided to attack the English King before these reinforcements could reach him. On the night of 4 August he led the Moslem army as quietly as possible to within striking distance of the Christians' camp just outside the walls of Jaffa, and there drew them up for an attack at dawn the next day. But luckily a Genoese who had strolled out of the camp just before sunrise heard the sound of horses neighing and men moving nearby, and as the sky began to lighten in the east, he saw a glint of steel and heard the chinking of metal on metal a field's length away. Running back to the camp he raised the alarm, so that as the sun came up and Saladin moved up to the attack, he found the English, French and Italians waiting for him.

Richard had only fifty-four knights with him, and they had only fifteen horses between them; he also had about two thousand infantrymen, including some Italians and a contingent of English archers with both long bows and cross bows, but that was all. He drew the infantry up in a tight half-circle, the men in pairs with an archer between each pair, and he told them to plant their shields in the ground in front of them as an improvised steel fence; tent pegs were driven into the earth in front of this fence in a swathe of spikes to upset Saladin's horses; and finally each man drove the shaft of his spear into the ground at an angle with its point towards the enemy, so that the whole Christian front bristled with steel.

The battle began with the Sultan's cavalry attacking in waves of a thousand horsemen, but the Christian line held firm; again and again they charged, and again and again they were driven back. The fighting lasted all morning, and by afternoon the Moslems seemed to be tiring.

As they charged yet again, Richard ordered the English archers, whom he had held in reserve, to move through the weary infantrymen and loose a volley of arrows at the enemy. Under this hail of missiles the Moslems were stopped in their tracks, the horses rearing and bucking in a confusion of hoofs, limbs, fallen riders and corpses, while the air was rent by the screams of the wounded. Ordering the archers back, Richard on one of the only available horses then led his men in a sudden charge against the dis-ordered enemy, while Saladin watched in grudging admiration and wonder at the sheer courage of his opponent; indeed, so moved was he by Richard's dauntless spirit that, when the English king's mount was killed under him, he ordered one of his grooms to lead a pair of horses through the battle under a flag of truce and to give them to Richard with his compliments. It was a gesture as immortal in its way as Richard's valour. A little later, under cover of the confusion of battle some of Saladin's men managed to steal round the Christians' flank and reach the town, where some Genoese marines turned tail and sought the shelter of their ships; but before they could exploit their success, Richard galloped up with a handful of knights and rallied the town's defenders. By evening, Saladin's men had had enough; they could do no more, and the Sultan gave the order to retire. Leaving their dead on the field, they marched wearily back to Jerusalem, convinced that the terrible golden-haired Malik Ric was invincible.

Shortly after the battle Richard fell ill, lying in his tent in a high fever, fretting over plans for his return home, where his brother's plotting with the French made his presence urgently necessary. When Saladin offered the same terms as those proposed before the battle outside Jaffa, Richard could not afford another long period of haggling, and on 2 September he signed a treaty of peace which was to last for five years; the Christians were to have the coastal cities as far south as Jaffa, but not Ascalon, which was to be demolished once more; and pilgrims were to be allowed free access to the holy places in Jerusalem, Bethlehem, and Nazareth. The war was over, and after recovering from his illness Richard sailed from Acre on 9 October 1192. His ship was wrecked near Aquileia at the head of the Adriatic in Venetian territory. In an attempt to escape the notice of the bitterly hostile Duke Leopold he travelled through Austria in disguise, but he was recognised as he passed through Vienna and made captive. He remained a prisoner, first of Leopold V of Austria and later of the German Emperor Henry VI, until the spring of 1194, when he returned to England after paying a vast ransom. He did not stay there long, but soon crossed to France to defend his feudal lands. For five years he did so with his customary skill and gallantry until, in March 1199, he was wounded by an arrow in a minor skirmish with a rebel vassal; the wound festered and became gangrenous, and on 11 April Richard died. Saladin had died before him, at Damascus on 3 March 1193, at the age of fifty-four and soon after Richard had left the Holy Land. With his passing Islam lost its greatest champion and Christendom its most noble adversary.

XVII

♣♣♣

So Fine a Place

All those who had never seen Constantinople before gazed very intently at the city, having never imagined there could be so fine a place in all the world.

Villehardouin, *La Conquête de Constantinople*

The Fourth Crusade was the brain-child of Pope Innocent III, who was elected Pope in 1198 at the age of thirty-seven. He was the son of a certain Trasimondo de Conti, Count of Segni, and his mother was a member of an old Roman family, the Scotti, so he brought to the papacy the advantages of a noble birth; but that was not all, for he had a brilliant intellect, a gift for politics and an exalted doctrine of his own office. His greatest ambition was to make the whole world recognise the supremacy of the See of Rome, not only in religious matters, but in secular affairs too; for, as he wrote to the Patriarch of Constantinople, 'the Lord left to Peter the governance not only of the Church but of the whole wide world'. In order that kings themselves might be under no delusion about the superiority of his office to theirs, he wrote to King John of England telling him that God had set 'one over all, whom he appointed his Vicar on earth', namely himself, while he reminded Philip Augustus of France that 'to princes power is given on earth, but to priests it is also attributed in heaven'. He himself was 'the Vicar of Him whose is the earth and the fulness thereof, the whole wide world and all that dwell therein'. In person he was a small man, slight and handsome, although his grey eyes were set a little too close together and his features were a trifle sharp. His movements were quick, and gave the impression that he was always in a hurry; he was an eloquent and persuasive speaker; and he had been trained as both a philosopher and a lawyer.

He had not been Pope for more than a week or two before he spoke of the need for a new Crusade. Part of his motive was a real desire to help the Christians in the East, but part was less altruistic, for he wanted to rebuild the Latin Kingdom and Church of Jerusalem in order that the authority of Rome should be asserted there once again. Moreover, there was no doubt in his mind that the new Crusade must be under his authority and his alone; in his view, the kings of Europe should have nothing to do with it. The only really successful Crusade had been the First, and no king had taken part in that; kings had led both the Second and Third Crusades, and very little had come of them. There had been an even more recent example of the futility of Crusades led by royalty, for after King Richard's departure from Outremer, Henry VI of Germany had mounted a Crusade of his own, which had reached the Holy Land in the early summer of 1197 only to collapse in September when Henry had died suddenly; admittedly, the Germans had captured Tyre and Sidon before their army disintegrated when they received the news of Henry's death, but this had done little to change the new Pope's poor opinion of Crusades sponsored by kings.

So the fact that the crowned heads of Europe were squabbling again suited Innocent admirably, for it meant that they were too busy to take much interest in his call for a new Crusade. In England King John, who had succeeded his brother Richard on the throne, had inherited his quarrels with Philip Augustus of France, while in Germany Philip of Swabia was fighting a civil war against Otto of Brunswick of the House of Welf for the imperial crown. The way was thus clear for the Pope to recruit the kind of men whom he wanted for his expedition to the East, and he sent preachers into France and Germany to persuade the barons to take the Cross. They were successful, but it took a long time to recruit sufficient numbers of men to make a crusade possible, and even when an army had been raised, there were some problems to be solved; in the absence of the kings money was short, and money was badly needed to pay for ships to transport the new army to Outremer, for, owing to the decline of Byzantine power, the old road across Anatolia was no longer open. Since even the greatest of the lords who took the Cross did not possess a fleet of ships, the Crusaders were forced to look to Venice; and although the

Venetians were prepared to provide the necessary shipping, they wanted a great deal of money in return. No one knew quite where to raise it, but since there was no alternative, a bargain was struck with them, and during the summer of 1202, nine years after the death of Saladin, the new Crusading army began to assemble in Venice on the island of San Niccolo in the Lagoon between Murano and the Lido.

There had been a good deal of argument over the objective of the Crusade, some people urging yet another expedition to reinforce the Franks in Acre, while others wanted the army to attack Egypt. After Saladin's death his sons, of whom there were seventeen, had begun fighting over the inheritance, and the old Sultan's empire had quickly disintegrated; the unity of Islam, which he had done so much to forge, did not survive him. Egypt was considered the weakest point in the enemy defences, and in the end it was agreed that an attempt should be made on the land of the Nile. But the Venetians were not at all keen to attack Egypt, where their ambassadors were currently trying to negotiate a trading treaty with the Sultan, while the Doge, Enrico Dandolo, was haggling with the Crusaders over the cost of the journey; although naturally he did not tell them that his emissaries were in Cairo. He was a cunning old man, however, and when the Crusaders told him that they were very sorry, but they could not raise the full amount of money which they had promised, he saw his opportunity; he pretended to be extremely displeased, saying that he would not provide any ships at all until he had been paid in full, and he threatened to cut off supplies to the army on San Niccolo. The Crusaders were helpless, and the Doge could dictate his own terms; he would provide the ships as he had promised, he told them, on condition that before sailing to Egypt the army would help him capture the port of Zara on the way down the Adriatic. The Venetians had been at war with the King of Hungary, in whose territory Zara lay at the time, for some years, and having recently lost the town to the Hungarians, they wanted it back again. But Hungary was a Catholic country, and when Innocent heard of the project, he forbade it. This was extremely awkward for the Crusaders, but they were in no position to argue with the Doge, and so, reluctantly ignoring the Pope's command, they agreed to do as they were asked.

The fleet sailed on 8 November 1202, and an attack on Zara was launched two days later. The Hungarian garrison was outnumbered, and the city fell after four days of fierce fighting, only to be sacked by the triumphant Crusaders. By the time that they had finished pillaging the place, it was too late in the year to venture to sea on a long voyage, and the army settled down to spend the winter in the captured city. When Innocent heard of what had happened, he was shocked and appalled at the open disobedience of the men of his own Crusade, and immediately excommunicated them all; a little later, when he was told that the Crusaders had had little choice in the matter, he forgave them, leaving only the Venetians under sentence.

During the course of the winter, Philip of Swabia sent envoys to the Doge with a suggestion. In 1197, Philip had married the daughter of the Byzantine Emperor Isaac Angelus, the Princess Irene, who had a brother, Alexius. The Emperor Isaac Angelus had proved to be so hopelessly effete and ineffectual that, after the Byzantines had tolerated him for ten years, they had not been too unhappy when his own brother, also named Alexius, had unseated him and usurped the throne. Isaac Angelus had been thrown into prison and blinded, and his son had fled from Constantinople to seek refuge with his sister Irene. Philip of Swabia asked the Doge whether he would be willing, before going to Egypt, to make a detour with the Crusading army by way of Constantinople, and there put his brother-in-law, the Byzantine Prince Alexius, onto the throne in place of the usurper. Alexius, he said, would not be ungrateful, if Enrico Dandolo would do this for him; indeed, as soon as he became Emperor in the usurper's place, he would pay the Venetians the money owed to them by the Crusaders, supply them with everything they needed for their campaign against Egypt, and put a huge contingent of Byzantine troops at their disposal for the great expedition against the Moslems. He assured the Doge too that the usurping Emperor was so unpopular with the people of Constantinople that they would rise in revolt against him as one man, as soon as they heard of the arrival of the rightful heir to the throne, Isaac Angelus' son, Alexius.

Dandolo, who loved money, and hated the Byzantines, was delighted by the idea; but some of the Crusaders were far from happy at the thought of interfering by force in the affairs of another Christian nation, and a few of them refused to go any further with the main body of the Crusade, making their own way eastward to Outremer. However, the vast majority had been taught to believe that the Byzantines were treacherous and untrustworthy creatures, who had obstructed other Crusaders in the past, and to regard them as only doubtfully Christian, since they refused to recognise the supreme authority of the Pope. Indeed, ever since the time of the First Crusade, dislike of the Byzantines had been growing in the West; it had been nourished by envy of their riches, resentment at the way in which they obviously despised all western Christians as barbarians, and the sort of angry scorn felt by country bumpkins for supercilious and unmanly city dwellers. Dislike had matured into hatred; misunderstanding and mutual distrust had bred even more hatred. Besides, the idea of an attack on Constantinople was not a new one; Frederick Barbrossa had thought of assaulting the city, and quite recently Henry VI of Germany had planned an attack on the place, but had been dissuaded by the Pope. So, with all this backlog of hatred to aid them, it did not take long for the Doge and the other leaders of the Crusade who were in favour of adopting Philip of Swabia's suggestion, to persuade most of the rank and file to fall in with the new plan.

It was more difficult to persuade Innocent to give his approval, but he was told only that the Crusaders were going to put Alexius, the rightful heir, onto the throne in Constantinople, and that the young man had promised to end the schism between the Orthodox Church and the Church of Rome as soon as he became Emperor. This sounded all right; the Pope could hardly object to such a programme; but it seems that he had his suspicions that there might be more to the expedition to Constantinople than met the eye, for he let it be known that he would not countenance any attack on Christians. The Crusaders' plans were now complete and, when Alexius joined them in Zara in late April 1203, the order was given to embark on the ships of the Venetian fleet, and the great armada set sail.

They travelled by way of Corfu round Cape Malea at the southern tip of Greece and up through the Aegean to land on the island of Andros, which they sacked; thence they made their way north to the Dardanelles, where they landed at Abydos on the Asiatic shore. They stayed there for a week, partly to allow the stragglers to catch up, and partly in order to steal the harvest as it was reaped and thus replenish their ships' holds with food for the coming weeks. Geoffrey of Villehardouin, the great chronicler of the Fourth Crusade, described the departure of the fleet at the end of the week:

> The Straits of St George to eastward, with the full array of warships, galleys and transports, seemed as it were in flower. It was indeed a marvellous experience to see so lovely a sight. The ships sailed onwards up the straits, until, on the Eve of St John the Baptists's Day, they came alongside St Stephen's, an abbey some four or five miles

distant from Constantinople, and from which all on board the ships had a full view of the city. Here the fleet came into port and the ships cast anchor. I can assure you that all those who had never seen Constantinople before gazed very intently at the city, having never imagined there could be so fine a place in all the world. They noted the high walls and lofty towers encircling it, and its rich palaces and tall churches, of which there were so many that no one would have believed it to be true if he had not seen it with his own eyes, and viewed the length and breadth of that city which reigns supreme over all others. There was indeed no man so brave and daring that his flesh did not shudder at the sight. Nor was this to be wondered at, for never before had so grand an enterprise been carried out by any people since the creation of the world.

The fleet dropped anchor off Chalcedon on 24 June, where many of the knights went ashore and occupied one of the Emperor's palaces, while some set up tents in its grounds, and a little later others landed at Chrysopolis. But the citizens of Constantinople across the water showed no signs of coming out *en masse* to welcome Alexius as their rightful sovereign or of turning against his uncle, the usurper, as Alexius had led everyone to believe that they would; on the contrary, there were obvious signs of military preparations on the European shore, and hopes of a peaceful entry into the city diminished. So, after a few days delay and preparation, the Crusaders attacked Galata on 17 July, and captured it without much difficulty; they hauled in the boom across the mouth of the Golden Horn, and their fleet then sailed in and anchored under the walls of Constantinople. The usurping Emperor decided that a quiet life was more to his taste than a heroic resistance, and slipped away quietly with his favourite daughter and as much portable wealth as he could carry; eventually he sought political asylum at the court of the Seljuk Sultan of Rum. Bereft of their Emperor, the palace officials retrieved the blind and doddery ex-Emperor Isaac Angelus from his dungeon and set him on the throne again; as soon as he was firmly reinstated on it, they sent a message to his son Alexius to tell him that he could therefore stop fighting. Alexius was taken completely by surprise and did not know what to do; the Crusaders, however, did. They replied that they would stop fighting as soon as Alexius was made co-Emperor with his father, but not before; and the Byzantines, who were in no position to argue, perforce agreed. On 1 August, the young man was duly crowned as Alexius IV Angelus in the Church of the Holy Wisdom, while the leading Crusaders looked on.

Since they had now done what ostensibly they had come to do, they might have sailed away at this point, had it not been for the promises which Alexius had made to them. To give him his due, he tried to honour them, but he soon discovered that keeping his word was much more difficult than giving it. He ordered the clergy to acknowledge the supreme authority of the Pope, but when they refused, there was no way of forcing them to obey; he tried to raise the money which he had promised to the Venetians, but there was not enough in the imperial treasury to discharge his debt, and he was forced to ask the Doge for time to pay, while he raised the money by extra taxation; and as for the army of Byzantine soldiers, which he had promised to supply for the invasion of Egypt, even if he could have found enough trained men at a moment's notice, their loyalty would have been so very uncertain that the Crusaders would have been mad to take them along. Naturally enough, however, his failure to keep his promises did little to endear Alexius to the Crusaders, who became progressively irritated by him. But their irritation was nothing to the hatred he inspired in the people of Constantinople, to whom his advocacy of the Pope, together with his generally pro-western policy and his oppressive new taxes made him anathema. Their detestation of the new Emperor was only exceeded by their loathing for the Crusaders, who were camped just outside the city; parties of swaggering Venetians and drunken Frenchmen made it almost impossible for the women of Constantinople to venture out into the streets, and there was not a shop or a market-place which was safe from their thieving hands. In an access of religious xenophobia, some Crusaders burnt down a mosque, which had been built for the use of visiting Moslems, and when the flames got out of control, a whole quarter of the city was destroyed. Tension in the city mounted dangerously high, and in February the people rose in violent revolt; they deposed the wretched Alexius, and strangled him, and the throne was seized by one of their leaders, a nobleman named Murzuphlus, who was known to be anti-western in his sympathies. The old Emperor Isaac Angelus saved the rebels the trouble of murdering him by conveniently dying of grief in the dungeon into which once again he had been thrown.

It was obvious to everyone that the revolt had been aimed not only at Alexius but also at the Crusaders, who had brought him to the city and put him on the throne by force; it had been an anti-Latin, anti-western, anti-papal revolt, and the Crusaders had no intention of allowing it to succeed. There had been talk for some time of the desirability of putting one of their own number on the imperial throne and of dividing the Byzantine Empire between them, and after the deposition and murder of Alexius such a course seemed not only desirable but necessary. They had not come all this way merely to see their plans frustrated by a palace revolution backed by a city mob, and they decided to attack the place in force. Geoffrey of Villehardouin described the attack:

> On the Thursday after mid-Lent Sunday [5 April 1204], all the troops embarked on the warships...It was, I can assure you, a marvellous sight to see the fleet drawn up in battle formation in a line extending well over half a French league. On the Friday morning the warships, galleys and other vessels approached the city in due order, and began to deliver a fierce and determined assault. In many places the Crusaders landed and advanced right up to the walls; in many others the scaling ladders on the ships came so close to the battlements that those on the walls and the towers crossed lances hand to hand with their assailants. The assault continued, fast and furious, in more than a hundred places, till round about three o'clock in the afternoon. But, for our sins, our troops were repulsed in that attack, and those that had landed from the galleys and transports were forcibly driven back on board. I must admit that on that day our army lost more than the Greeks, and the latter were greatly delighted.

It was a serious reverse, but the Crusaders' losses were not so heavy as to preclude another attack, and six days later they returned to the charge once more. Their objective was to breach the sea wall where it came down to the water's edge at the head of the Golden Horn near the quarter of the city known as Blachernae, and the Byzantines soon realised what they were trying to do. 'The citizens of Constantinople,' wrote Villehardouin, 'were now much less afraid of our troops than at the time of our first assault. They were, in fact, in such a confident mood that all along the walls and towers there was nothing to be seen but people. Then began a fierce and magnificent assault, as each ship steered a straight course forward. The shouts that rose from the battle created such a din that it seemed as if the whole earth were crumbling to pieces.'

The Crusaders did not have things all their own way; the Byzantines launched their own sharp-prowed galleys, and fought to prevent them reaching the walls. But fate and the wind were against the defenders.

The assault had been going on for a considerable time [continued

Villehardouin], when our Lord raised for us a wind called Boreas, which drove the ships still farther onto the shore. Two of the ships which were tied together, the one called the *Pilgrim* and the other the *Paradise*, approached so close to a tower, one of them on one side and one on the other, as God and the wind drove them onwards, that the ladder of the *Pilgrim* made contact with it. Immediately a Venetian, in company with a French knight named Andrew Durboise, forced their way in. Other men began to follow them, and in the end the defenders were routed and driven out. The moment the knights aboard the transports saw this happen, they landed and, raising ladders against the wall, climbed to the top, and took four more towers. Then all the rest of the troops started to leap out of warships, galleys and transports, helter-skelter as fast as they could. They broke down about three of the gates and entered the city.

The army poured in and, although there was some fighting in the streets and squares, once the outer walls had been breached the resistance of the Byzantines collapsed; by evening Constantinople was in the hands of the Crusaders; Murzuphlus and the other Greek leaders had fled, and the French and Venetians had triumphed.

The next day a massacre began, and it beggars description. For three days twenty thousand armed men roved the city in bands, often drunk and always totally out of control, raping, murdering, robbing and looting as they went. The destruction was immense; for centuries works of art from all over the world had been brought to Constantinople and treasured there, and visitors had gasped at the splendour of the place. During this sack of the city, many of its crowning glories were stolen by the Venetians, and more were destroyed by the French who were in the mood for destruction and violence. Priests robbed the churches; a Cistercian abbott named Martin from Pairis in Alsace threatened to kill a Greek priest in the Church of the Pantocrator, unless he showed him where the church's sacred relics were hidden. When he had been directed to them, he girded up his loins and filled the skirt of his cassock with a piece of the True Cross, a trace of the Blood of Christ, a large part of St John's arm, an entire arm of St James, a foot of St Cosmas, a tooth of St Lawrence, and bits and pieces of twenty-eight male and eight female saints, all of which he carried away in triumph laughing with delight. In the great Church of the Holy Wisdom soldiers tore down the silk curtains, ripped the silver from the iconostasis, got roaring drunk on liquor which they drank from the sacred vessels of the altar, and installed a whore on the Patriarch's throne, where she sang bawdy French songs while others led in horses and mules to urinate and defecate all over the floor. In the streets no one was spared; nuns were stripped and violated, women and girls were subjected to unspeakable obscenities, and children had their heads cracked like egg-shells against the walls as soldiers swung them by the heels. Fires, which were started in various parts of the city, raged uncontrollably sweeping through whole districts and leaving them blackened, smoking, and in ruins. The Byzantine chronicler Nicetas, whose life was saved by a Venetian friend, wrote a lament on the fall of the city, in which he complained bitterly that even the Moslems would have been more merciful than these men from the West, who called themselves Christians. But Villehardouin finishes his description of the capture and sack of the city with perfect sincerity by describing how delighted everyone was by the victory and by the riches they had all acquired. 'They all rejoiced and gave thanks to our Lord for the honour and the victory He had granted them,' he wrote, 'so that those who had been poor now lived in wealth and luxury. Thus they celebrated Palm Sunday and the Easter Day following with hearts full of joy for the benefits our Lord and Saviour had bestowed on them.'

It remained only to carve up the carcase of the Byzantine Empire and divide it between the victors. The Venetians, who were more subtle and craftier than the French, secured the lion's share, but a Frenchman named Baldwin of Flanders was elected Emperor; he was crowned in the Church of the Holy Wisdom according to the Latin rite on 16 May 1204, but his coronation endowed him with a mere shadow of the power enjoyed by his Byzantine predecessors. Most of Greece and the other European lands of Byzantium fell to the Venetians or the French nobles, who ruled them in virtual independence of the new Emperor, although he was allowed to keep Thrace under his own personal authority, while the greater part of Anatolia was already in Seljuk hands. Moreover, although the Byzantines had lost Constantinople, they held out against the Crusaders in two centres of resistance in the East; at Trebizond, Alexius Comnenus and his brother, who were grandsons of the amorous and unfortunate Emperor Andronicus, established themselves on the southern shore of the Black Sea, where they founded a dynasty which lasted three times as long as the precarious Latin Empire set up by the Crusaders in the capital; while at Nicaea the daughter of Alexius III, the usurping uncle of the Crusaders' *protégé*, together with her husband set up a court to which all the leading

Byzantines rallied, regarding it as the true centre of the Empire until Constantinople should be liberated.

When the news of the Crusaders' victory reached the West, everyone went mad with delight. Even Innocent, who had excommunicated the Venetians for their attack on Zara, heard of the fall of the capital of the Byzantine world with gratification, for it meant the extension of his own divine authority as the successor of St Peter over the whole of the schismatic eastern Church. He wrote an enthusiastic letter of congratulation to the new Emperor Baldwin, in which he gave unqualified approval to everything that had been done. When the Byzantines heard of the Pope's approbation, their bitterness knew no bounds. To be fair to Innocent, when, later, details of the sack of the city and the brutality of the Crusaders reached him, he was horrified; but by this time the damage was done, and few if any Byzantines heard of the Pope's second thoughts.

The Byzantines had always disliked and despised the Franks as barbarians, capable of almost any brutality or vile action; it was widely believed, for example, that they 'christened their infants with saliva, ate the flesh of wolves, drank their own urine, and washed their dirty trousers in their cooking pots.' But when they came to believe that the Pope had given his blessing to the rape of their city and the massacre of its inhabitants, their hatred for the West took on a new dimension, which was to have consequences which lasted for centuries.

XVIII

♣♣♣

Children of the Lord

Do no sinful action, speak no angry word;
Ye belong to Jesus, children of the Lord.
                                          C. F. Alexander

The cynical perversion of the Fourth Crusade might have been expected
to bring the whole crusading movement into disrepute or even to kill it,
but it did no such thing. In the early thirteenth century Crusades or, at
any rate, armed expeditions which were called Crusades, were mounted
against the Moors of Spain and against the Albigensian heretics of
Languedoc in France; and although the war against the Albigensians
degenerated into an overtly political struggle, it was preached with such
religious fanaticism that if anything the crusading ideal began to inspire
more people at this time than ever before. Indeed, it was a time of
immense religious enthusiasm everywhere, but the nature of people's
enthusiasm was subtly different from that which had excited the men of
earlier crusading days. The First Crusaders had dreamed of becoming the
soldiers of Christ, and had believed themselves to be called by God to
liberate the holy places from the oppressive rule of the infidel by force
of arms; they had marched eastwards trusting in the power of the Lord
God of hosts to make them mighty in battle. When Innocent III purposely
excluded the crowned heads of western Christendom from the ranks of
his own Crusade, emphasising the fact that there could be no other

leader of the Crusade but himself, he did so because he believed that the spiritual authority of his office would be a more powerful weapon to wield against the Moslems than the secular power of the European kings. Others took Innocent's idea even farther, preaching the power of the poor, the pure in spirit, the gentle and the meek. Had not Christ said that the meek would inherit the earth? And had not that great soldier of Christ, St Paul, said that God's strength was made perfect in weakness? Was it possible, therefore, that the former Crusades had failed because they had relied on the strong men of this world and not on the weak and the poor, who alone were filled with the authentic power of God? Such speculation fascinated a great many people, and created an atmosphere in which the extraordinary idea of a children's Crusade could not only grow, but be taken seriously.

There had been precedents of a sort. After Chartres Cathedral had been burnt down during the night of 10 June 1194, an astonishing wave of religious enthusiasm had swept the people of France; everyone had been determined to build an even more glorious house for the celebrated Virgin of Chartres, and amongst those who had flocked to the city to help accomplish the enormous task as quickly as possible there had been groups of children led by young boys claiming to possess special gifts of God. In most penitential movements, too, groups of children had taken part, many of them youths who were believed to be miracle workers. So when, in the spring of 1212, a shepherd boy of about twelve years of age named Stephen, who came from the little town of Cloyes some thirty miles south of Chartres, turned up with a large group of children at the Abbey of Saint-Denis, where King Philip Augustus was holding his court, claiming to have a letter from Christ himself ordering him to preach a new Crusade, no one was particularly surprised. They were not very impressed either, and Philip Augustus told them all to be good and go home; but Stephen was not to be diverted from his God-given task, and he began preaching outside the gates of the Abbey to the children of the town.

From Saint-Denis, Stephen travelled round France preaching as he went, and promising to lead the children of Christ to the Holy Land. The seas would dry up before them, as they had when Moses had led the children of Israel out of the land of Egypt; and God would deliver Jerusalem into their hands, for had not Christ said that unless people became as little children, they could be no means enter into the kingdom of heaven? Plainly therefore it was only to children that the gates of the heavenly city would be opened. Let them all trust in God and follow him, and he would lead them to victory in the power of the Holy Spirit. He must have been endowed with an extraordinary power of speech, for the children of France followed him in droves, and many adults were profoundly impressed by him, although the Church was sceptical. He inspired other children to go out and preach the Crusade also, and he arranged to meet them all at Vendôme at the end of June. When he did so, people spoke in wonder of thirty thousand children converging on the town; probably there were less than half that number, but even if there were no more than ten thousand, that is still a lot of children.

From Vendôme Stephen led his juvenile Crusaders to Marseilles. Most of the children were under twelve years old, the journey was long and hot, they had to beg for food, and some died on the way, while others were so disheartened by the hardships of the journey that they thought better of the whole thing and turned back; not all succeeded in finding their way home. When Stephen and the others reached Marseilles, the people of the town were kind to them, and their spirits revived; all was going to be well after all. In high excitement the next morning they hurried down to the harbour, expecting the sea immediately to divide before them; when it did not, their disappointment was intense. Some blamed Stephen for betraying them, but the majority settled down to wait for God to change his mind; it was unthinkable that he would not do so. But the miracle which they awaited was slow to materialise, and when two local merchants offered to provide seven ships to carry them free of charge to the Holy Land, the children gratefully accepted their offer and thanked God for this less spectacular but, in a hard commercial world, hardly less surprising miracle. Tradition has it that the merchants' names were Hugh the Iron and William the Pig. The children were duly embarked, the ships set sail, and thereafter nothing was heard of them for eighteen years.

Stephen's enthusiasm was infectious. Not long after he had set sail from Marseilles, a German boy from the Rhineland followed his example, and began to preach a Crusade to the children of Germany. His name was Nicholas and, like Stephen, he was astonishingly successful in persuading others of his own age to follow him; like Stephen too, he promised them that the sea would dry up before them, and that God would lead them to the Holy Land in triumph, not by winning miraculous military victories over the Moslems but by converting them to Christianity. Other children were fired by his oratory and went off on their own to preach in other parts of the country, and in a few weeks a mass of young people gathered in Cologne. Once again, the chroniclers speak of thirty thousand children or more, and once again it is impossible to say how many there were, although there were certainly a great many. Splitting into two groups, they took different roads. Nicholas led the larger group, which was believed at the time to number twenty thousand children, through Switzerland to northern Italy by way of the Mont Cenis pass. It was a ghastly journey, and two out of every three children fell by the wayside, either dying or suffering some other fate of which there is no record; those who reached Genoa were treated kindly enough, and when the sea once again refused to divide miraculously before them, many of them decided to accept the offer of the civic authorities to receive them as Genoese citizens. Nicholas refused to admit defeat, however, plodding on with the rest of his followers to Pisa, where the sea proved equally unco-operative, and thence to Rome, where the Pope welcomed them gently, and told them to go home. They tried to obey him, but very few succeeded, and it is said that one of those who did not survive the journey was Nicholas. His father was dragged away by some of the parents of the other children who had perished; they accused him of encouraging his son in his madness and thus of being a party to the deaths of their own children. The man was arrested and hanged.

The second group of German children suffered similar hardships and disappointments. They crossed the Alps by way of the St Gotthard pass. and marched to Ancona, where once again the obstinate sea did not divide. Discouraged but undaunted, they walked on to Brindisi, where the miracle once more failed to come to their aid; this was too much for them, and although a few took ship to the Holy Land, most began the long journey home. The fate of those who sailed to Outremer is unknown, and so is that of the great majority of the children who tried to return to their native villages. Pitifully few succeeded in reaching their homes.

But the fate of the French children was, if anything, even worse than that of the Germans. In 1230 a priest arrived in France with a terrible story. As a young man, he told the fascinated but appalled people of France, he had been one of a small number of young priests who had felt it their duty to accompany the children when they sailed from Marseilles. They had not gone far when a gale blew up off the coast of Sardinia, and two of the ships had been wrecked; everyone on board had been lost. The other five ships had weathered the storm and sailed on, only to find themselves surrounded a day or two later by some warships from Africa manned by Saracens, who had been warned by the two kindly merchants of

Marseilles, Hugh the Iron and William the Pig, to expect them. The French ships had then been escorted into an Algerian port, where many of the children had been sold in the slave market, and spent the rest of their lives in servitude; others had been carried to Egypt, where they had fetched better prices, and a few had even reached Baghdad, where eighteen of them had refused to renounce their Christian faith, and had been martyred. The man who told this story had escaped the fate of the children because, as a priest, he was an educated man, and the Moslem governor of Egypt had taken him and a few others like him into his household as interpreters and teachers; they had even been allowed to practise their own religion, and eventually for some reason this one man had been allowed to return to his native land to tell the tale of the lost children. It is unlikely that William the Pig or Hugh the Iron were ever found and brought to trial, although a later legend identified them with two men who were hanged for a different crime.

XIX

♣♣♣

Into Egypt

The men that set their faces to go into Egypt to sojourn there;
they shall die by the sword, by the famine, and by the pestilence.

Jeremiah, 42, 17

While the children were making their own pathetic attempt, Pope
Innocent was planning yet another great armed expedition to the Holy
Land, but he did not live to see his plans completed; he died at Perugia on
16 July 1216. He was succeeded by Honorius III, who was as dedicated
to the idea of a new Crusade as Innocent himself, and did everything he
could to rouse the enthusiasm of western Christendom for another great
military effort in the East. It soon became evident, however, that not much
help could be expected from France, where the war against the Albigensian heretics was still occupying most people; but fortunately the response
to the call for a Crusade in Hungary and Austria was enough to make
up for the tepid reaction of the French. The Hungarian King took the
Cross, and his example was followed by Duke Leopold VI of Austria, who
promised to join the Crusade with a large army when the time came. But
as usual it proved difficult to find enough ships to transport the new
expeditionary force to its destination; Venice, Genoa and Pisa were so
suspicious of one another that they refused to take part in any joint
venture lest one city should steal a march on the others in the process. In
the end, Leopold found his own transport, arriving in Outremer in

September 1217, and King Andrew of Hungary followed him with a much reduced force in the few ships which were willing to carry him to Acre, which he reached shortly after Leopold. They were joined by King Hugh of Cyprus, a boy of nineteen, who was the son of Amalric II of Jerusalem and had succeeded Guy, who had died childless. The three men brought with them only a small army, which probably did not number more than about five thousand men in all.

The Franks of Outremer were neither very much impressed nor particularly pleased to see them. Since the death of Saladin, the Moslems had been too busy to wage war, either bickering amongst themselves for the control of his empire, or trading with their Christian neighbours. Both sides had become prosperous as a result, and neither was eager to throw away the blessings of peace, which they had been enjoying for some years, in exchange for the dubious glories of war. As usual, however, the newcomers were deeply shocked by the mere idea of living in peace with infidels, and were impatient to go out and kill a few of them as soon as they could. They were shocked too by the luxury and wealth which the Franks of Outremer were enjoying almost as a matter of course and by their oriental clothes and manners; it was intolerable that Christians, who had taken the Cross and vowed to liberate the holy places from the yoke of the unbeliever, should have become so corrupted and decadent that they could live in idleness and dissipation side by side with the enemies of Christ without lifting a finger against them.

Nothing is more confusing than an attempt to unravel the tangled family relationships of the various royal houses of Outremer; it is made no easier by the way in which people in succeeding generations were given the same names, so that in each period of crusading history men named Hugh, Bohemund, Conrad, Raymond or Baldwin seem to have married women called Maria, Eschiva, Isabella or Alice. At the time of the Fifth Crusade, the King of Jerusalem was an old man named John of Brienne, who wore the crown by virtue of his marriage some years previously to a seventeen-year-old girl called Maria, who was Queen by hereditary right; she was the daughter of Queen Isabella of Jerusalem by her second marriage to Conrad of Montferrat, and she had died at the age of twenty-one shortly after marrying John, who was thus left to reign alone. When Andrew of Hungary, Leopold of Austria and Hugh of Cyprus landed at Acre, John welcomed them to Outremer. Indeed, Hugh was his step-brother-in-law, since his father Amalric II had been Queen Isabella's fourth and last husband. And, since there was nothing he could do to dissuade them from dashing off to slaughter a few Saracens, he suggested a united campaign under his own command as King of Jerusalem.

Although the newcomers were not so numerous as they would have been had they not been forced to leave some of their number behind for want of ships in which to make the long voyage from Europe, the army which took the field in the autumn of 1217 under John of Brienne's command was more formidable than anything mustered by the Christians since the days of the Third Crusade, and al-Adil, Saladin's brother, who was in command of their opponents, retired tactfully before them. Denied the chance of a decisive battle, John's army achieved very little. It had set out without any particular idea of what it was going to do; it was undisciplined, each section of it looking to its own commander and taking very little notice of John himself; and, having taken and sacked the city of Beisan, it wandered northward around the Sea of Galilee without achieving anything, and eventually returned to Acre. The one and only concrete result of this futile campaign, apart from breaking the truce with al-Adil, was the capture of a large earthenware jar, which was believed to be one of the waterpots which had been used at the marriage at Cana of Galilee, when Christ had miraculously turned the water it held into wine. King Andrew, who acquired this relic, was as delighted with it as if he had captured Jerusalem itself.

Two more abortive raids into Moslem held country were undertaken during the course of the winter, and neither succeeded in doing anything worth while. The King of Hungary, who was getting more and more bored with life in Acre, welcomed the news that Bohemund IV of Antioch was planning to marry the half-sister of Hugh of Cyprus in Tripoli, and went off happily to join the wedding party there; but the festivities were cut short just after the New Year by the sudden and unexpected death of Hugh, and this was too much for King Andrew. He returned to Acre, gathered his men together and, having made arrangements with the Seljuk Sultan of Rum for safe passage through his land, he marched them home again through Anatolia. Leopold decided to stay in Outremer, but even with his help the Franks were not strong enough to mount another offensive against the Moslems, and they spent the winter strengthening the fortifications of Caesarea, while the Templars built an almost impregnable castle at Athlit on the coast where it was able to guard the main pilgrim route. It was not until the arrival in April and May 1218 of another large batch of Crusaders, most of whom were

Dutchmen or Germans with a sprinkling of Scandinavians, in a fleet of Frisian ships, that a new military venture could be planned.

Egypt was the next objective. It was now the citadel of Moslem power; if it could be captured, the whole of southern Palestine, including Jerusalem, would fall into Christian hands almost without a struggle, and their enemies would be forced to withdraw to their strongholds in the north, Damascus and Aleppo. The plan was to attack and take the port of Damietta in the delta of the Nile, and there to await reinforcements from Europe, where it was believed that a large army of Frenchmen was already assembling; with their added strength, the crusading army would then invade the whole of the delta and capture Cairo, while their fleet controlled the Nile. Leopold of Austria, the Hungarian captains who had not gone home with King Andrew, and the Grand Masters of the Military Orders all put themselves under the command of John of Brienne, both as King of Jerusalem and as an old and experienced soldier; and on Ascension Day the army embarked on the Frisian ships and sailed out of the harbour at Acre.

The fleet was split up during the voyage, and a few ships reached the mouth of the Nile two days ahead of the rest; but by 29 May, five days after setting sail from their home port, the whole fleet had arrived and was anchored just off shore, and the army landed on the west bank of the Nile. As in the days of King Amalric's attack on the city fifty years earlier, a great chain had been stretched across the Nile just below the town to prevent the ships reaching the city walls, and behind this chain was a bridge of boats; the whole thing was protected by a small but strongly fortified tower on a little island near the west bank. When their preparations were complete, the Crusaders attacked this tower; but they were repeatedly driven back until they launched a floating castle, which they had built on two galleys lashed together. The castle itself was covered in copper sheets and great leather hides to protect it from attack by Greek fire, and at the top it had a drawbridge, which could be let down onto the enemy ramparts when the galleys were rowed near enough to their walls. It had been designed by a German school-master named Oliver, who later became one of the chief historians of the Crusade, and it proved to be highly effective. The Egyptians defended the tower with great tenacity, spraying their enemies with jets of flame as soon as they got within range, but after a fierce fight two Flemish soldiers beat them back with their long lances, the bridge was lowered and the two men got a footing on the tower; they were two against many, but they laid about the Egyptians with iron flails with such terrible ferocity that no one could stand up to them. They were soon joined by a swarm of other soldiers, and the defenders were driven off the top of the tower; they fought hard to prevent the Crusaders from descending the stairs into the fort, but their casualties were heavy and, when only a handful of them were left alive, they surrendered. The tower unexpectedly yielded a huge booty, and as soon as it had been captured the great chain across the river was dragged ashore; the way was clear for the Frisian ships to sail right up to the walls of Damietta.

The news of this Christian victory horrified the Moslem world. The Sultan al-Adil, Saladin's brother, who was in his mid-seventies, died of shock, and all Islam expected to hear of the fall of Damietta at any minute; Allah seemed to have deserted his warriors. But the Franks decided not to press an immediate attack on the city, for they knew that reinforcements were on the way, and they did not want to risk a rebuff so soon after their first great victory for years; failure at this juncture would have done enormous harm to the morale of the troops, and caution seemed to be the wisest policy. Almost certainly, the Crusaders made the wrong decision; for if they had captured the city, they might well have gone on to conquer the whole of Egypt while their enemies were still shocked by their defeat and unready to meet another attack; and for a time the city was vulnerable. But they missed their opportunity, and the moment passed.

As they settled down instead to besiege the place, some of them decided that they had done their duty; there was a steady trickle of men leaving Egypt to make their own way home, while boredom spread amongst those who remained. As the weeks passed, dysentry broke out in the camp and took its usual toll, and with the coming of winter with its rain, life became progressively more uncomfortable; the morale of the men sank lower and lower. It revived for a time when a new Papal army arrived to swell the Christian ranks, but unfortunately this was commanded by an intransigent fanatic of a man, Cardinal Pelagius, to whom the Pope had granted plenipotentiary powers. It was not long before he had managed to set everyone by the ears, quarrelling with King John, dividing the army into two hostile factions and insisting on taking command of military operations, although he had no qualifications as a military man. Despite his total lack of experience and his growing unpopularity with the other leaders, he was lucky, and when Saladin's nephew the Sultan al-Kamil attacked the Crusaders' camp, the Moslem troops were beaten off with heavy losses, largely owing to the alertness of John of Brienne. After Christmas, Pelagius decided that the morale of the men could only be restored by action, and so in February he ordered them to attack the Sultan's troops, who were spending almost as miserable a winter as their enemies; but before they could do so, news arrived that al-Kamil had suddenly fled with his army. It seems that he had heard of a conspiracy against him by some leading Emirs, and that he had succumbed to panic and moved away in search of safety. The Crusaders immediately occupied his camp, captured a large booty, and completed the isolation of Damietta, which was now totally cut off from all supplies.

By the time that al-Kamil had dealt with the conspirators and was ready to resume the offensive against the Christians, they were so well entrenched that the fate of Damietta seemed sealed. From the Moslem point of view it began to look as if peace would have to be sought. Meanwhile, as the fighting continued and winter passed into a short-lived spring, the miseries of cold and wet weather were soon replaced by the discomforts and diseases of a scorching Egyptian summer. It was at this time that the Crusaders entertained a somewhat surprising visitor to their camp. Francis of Assisi was the first of many Franciscans to travel to the East in an attempt to win the minds of men, by preaching and the example of his own poverty, to a vision of God seldom imparted by Christians with swords in their hands. He asked permission to visit the Sultan and, after some hesitation, Pelagius gave him leave to do so; he was sent across the lines under a flag of truce to the Moslem camp. There, in the words of Steven Runciman, 'the Moslem guards were suspicious at first but soon decided that anyone so simple, so gentle, and so dirty must be mad, and treated him with the respect due to a man who had been touched by God.' Al-Kamil received him with the greatest courtesy, but despite the Saint's appeal to him to become a Christian he did not for a moment contemplate doing so; instead he listened politely to what his guest had to say, offered him some splendid gifts and, when these were refused, returned him to the Christian camp with a guard of honour.

The Nile flood failed that year, and by the end of the summer Egypt faced famine unless food could be imported from elsewhere; this prospect forced the Sultan to sue for peace, and in September he did so. He offered to cede Jerusalem, Palestine and Galilee, and to return the True Cross, if the Christians would evacuate Egypt. On the face of it, it was a marvellous offer, and many of the Franks were in favour of accepting it at once; but Pelagius refused even to consider it. He disapproved on principle of coming to terms with Moslems, and he seems also to have been influenced by some spurious 'prophecies' which were being passed from mouth to mouth, foretelling the triumph of the Crusade and the collapse of Islam. He was supported by the Military Orders, who were convinced that neither Palestine nor Galilee could be successfully defended unless the castles east of the Jordan were also handed over, and this al-Kamil was unwilling to do; for he had to keep the road between Egypt and Syria open, and this passed through Oultrejourdain. So the offer was rejected, and the opportunity was missed. If some of the Crusaders were bitterly disappointed, they soon forgot their resentment, for two or three days later, on 5 November 1219, Damietta at last fell; it succumbed without a struggle, for the garrison was so exhausted that the defenders simply stopped manning the walls, and the Franks walked in. It was a terrible blow to the Egyptians, and it raised the hopes of Pelagius to such a height that he became even more sure that the days of Islam were numbered and that the forces of anti-Christ were about to collapse.

However, they did no such thing. Instead, the Egyptians withdrew up the Nile to Mansourah, while Pelagius and his men settled down in Damietta. As had been the case so often in the past, after the victory the Crusaders fell out amongst themselves, and the whole of 1220 was wasted in bickering and dissension. John of Brienne had a row with Pelagius over the future of the captured city, and sailed home to Acre in a rage; and the jealousies between the various national groups became so acute that they were restrained only with difficulty from fighting one another rather than the enemy. After eighteen months of this kind of thing, the morale of the Crusaders, which had sunk to vanishing point, was slightly revived by the arrival of some Germans under Duke Louis of Bavaria, and in July 1221 he and Pelagius decided to attack the enemy at last. They led the army out of Damietta and marched towards the Egyptians full of confidence; but the Nile was in flood at the time, and Pelagius blithely placed his men in a position where the Moslems had only to open the sluices to swamp their enemies. Pelagius was forced to sue for peace or die, and peace was granted only on the Sultan's terms; the Franks were to abandon Damietta in return for an eight years' truce and the return of the True Cross. In the event the True Cross could not be found, and the Fifth Crusade ended with the damp and ignominious retreat of the Crusaders to Acre, having achieved precisely nothing.

There was a sequel however. A most notable absentee during the whole campaign in Egypt had been the Emperor Frederick II of Hohenstaufen, whose coming had often been expected but repeatedly postponed. He was a remarkable man; half German and half Norman, he had been brought up in the Norman kingdom of Sicily, an island half Arab and half Greek both in culture and ethos. At the time of the defeat of the Fifth Crusade, he was thirty years old, neither tall nor short, already running to fat, red-haired and beginning to go slightly bald, with a full and sensual mouth and cold green eyes. One Moslem said drily that he would have gone dirt cheap in the slave market. But if he was physically unimpressive, he was intellectually brilliant; he spoke French, German, Italian, Latin, Greek and Arabic fluently, and he had a good knowledge of a number of subjects which ranged from philosophy to medicine. He was a lecher, a schemer, an autocrat, a treacherous friend, a dangerous enemy and, if not an agnostic in religion, a sceptic who shocked his devout contemporaries by his unconventional disregard for the religious proprieties and his obvious lack of the kind of blind unquestioning faith which most of them equated with virtue. Pope Innocent had been his guardian, Pope Honorius his tutor; yet he fell out with Pope after Pope, for he did not disguise his lack of respect for their spiritual authority.

He was awaited by the Franks of Outremer because they knew that he had taken the Cross as long ago as 1215, and no one could understand why he should keep making excuses not to honour his vow; the campaign in Egypt came and went, and still Frederick did not sail east. But in 1225 their hopes of seeing him were greatly raised, when he married the fourteen-year-old daughter of John of Brienne, Queen Yolanda of Jerusalem. His former wife, a Spanish princess, had died two years previously, and this new alliance was politically most expedient from everyone's point of view; the Kingdom of Jerusalem was immensely strengthened by it, while Frederick added another crown to those he already possessed. The fact that little Yolanda hated the whole thing was neither here nor there; when she told her father, weeping, that her new husband had seduced one of her cousins on their honeymoon, there was nothing he or anyone else could do about it. She spent the rest of her short life in Palermo, where Frederick sent her as soon as she was pregnant, and there she died a few days after giving birth to a son. She had served her brief purpose, and her death does not seem to have mattered very much to Frederick, except that it weakened his claim to the throne of Jerusalem; while she had lived, his right to the Kingdom had been beyond question, but after her death he could claim authority only as regent for the infant son she had borne him, since the child was the rightful heir.

The end of Frederick's seemingly endless reluctance to honour his vow as a Crusader came shortly after the death of Yolanda, when he embarked at Brindisi with a large army bound for the Holy Land; but the fleet had hardly left port before a fever broke out on board, and one of the Emperor's subordinate commanders, the Landgrave of Thuringia, fell ill and died. Frederick was the next to succumb to the sickness, and while ordering the fleet to sail on without him, he landed at Otranto and took to his bed. It was an entirely reasonable thing to do, but when his departure from the fleet was reported to Pope Gregory IX, the Roman pontiff was so sure that the whole thing was just another trick on Frederick's part to evade keeping his vow as a Crusader that he excommunicated him.

While this put the Emperor in an extremely awkward position, by his reaction he showed himself to be a formidable adversary. He issued a statement which gave a true account of the facts, making it clear to everyone that the Pope had perverted the truth in order to find an excuse to humble him, and he followed up this verbal salvo by proceeding on his way to the Holy Land as soon as he had recovered his health, despite the fact that no excommunicated person could legally go on a Crusade, thus pointedly ignoring both the Pope's authority and the sentence imposed on him. Gregory was astonished and extremely angry, but there was nothing more he could do; he had already used his ultimate weapon.

Frederick landed at Acre on 7 September 1228. The lords of Outremer welcomed him with mixed feelings; some were pleased to see him for the additional military strength which he brought to the Kingdom, but the Templars, the Hospitallers and the clergy would have as little as possible to do with him, for he was an excommunicated man; and they were not alone in their religious scruples. But the common people greeted him warmly, and a poet named Freidank even went so far as to suggest that the Pope had been wrong to ban him from the sacrament. But popularity was no substitute for trained troops; without the Military Orders the Emperor could rely on no more than eleven thousand men, and this was not enough for an offensive against the Moslems. If he was to achieve any results, it would have to be by diplomacy rather than force of arms.

Fortunately, the Moslems, who had united to defeat the Fifth Crusade, were once more quarrelling amongst themselves. As a result, the Sultan was as eager to come to terms with Frederick as he was keen to achieve something spectacular with which to confound and infuriate the Pope.

This state of affairs was a measure of the change which had come over the crusading movement since its early days; the idea of an excommunicated Emperor treating in a friendly way with the rulers of Islam, while the Pope back in Rome prayed for the failure of his efforts, would have been as unthinkable in Godfrey of Bouillon's day as the idea of the Devil asking for baptism. But diplomacy suited Frederick better than war, and although the bargaining position of the two sides was about equal, as the months of careful negotiation passed the quarrels in the Islamic world grew worse, weakening the Sultan's hand and giving the advantage to Frederick. As a result, in February 1229, al-Kamil offered peace terms, which the Emperor accepted; the Kingdom of Jerusalem was once again to receive the city of Jerusalem itself, as well as Bethlehem, Nazareth and much of Galilee and the country round Sidon, which still remained in Moslem hands; but the Dome of the Rock and the Mosque of al-Aqsa in Jerusalem were to become a Moslem enclave in the Christian Kingdom, and Moslem pilgrims were to be allowed free access to them. All prisoners of war were to be sent home to their own lands, and the peace was to last for ten years.

It was a triumph for Frederick. He had been excommunicated, and the Pope had prayed for the failure of his mission, but he had succeeded in winning back the holy places of Christendom where many others, in the full odour of sanctity and with the blessing of the Pope, had signally failed; moreover, he had done so without shedding a drop of blood, either Christian or Moslem. Predictably, however, far from being grateful to him, religious people on both sides deeply disapproved of the treaty; fanatical Moslems accused the Sultan of betraying Islam, while fervent Christians were appalled to learn that the two great Moslem shrines in Jerusalem were to be left in the hands of the supporters of anti-Christ. More reasonably, the military also disapproved, pointing to the impossibility of holding the newly-won territory, whose frontiers they rightly considered to be indefensible. This disapproval became almost universal when Frederick announced that he intended to go up to Jerusalem, and to be crowned King there, for he was not the King but only the Regent and father of the rightful King, and an excommunicated man. The Patriarch of Jerusalem threatened to put the city under an interdict if it received the insufferable German blasphemer, and sent the Archbishop of Caesarea to Jerusalem to see that his orders were obeyed; but when the Archbishop arrived, he found that Frederick had already been in the city for two days and, in the absence of a priest willing to perform the ceremony, had crowned himself King of Jerusalem in the Church of the Holy Sepulchre by placing the crown on his own head.

It was almost, though not quite, the final outrage. After his self-coronation Frederick entertained the men of his entourage to a banquet, to which he also invited many of the leading Moslems who had remained in the city, talking to them in fluent Arabic and evidently enjoying himself greatly. After the meal he insisted on visiting the Moslem sanctuaries, and the Kadi of Jerusalem led him by way of the Via Dolorosa to the old Temple area, where he admired both the Dome of the Rock and al-Aqsa Mosque. Not wishing to offend his illustrious Christian visitor, the Kadi had told the Muezzin of al-Aqsa not to call the faithful to prayer while the Emperor was in Jerusalem; but at sunset Frederick asked why the minarets were silent. When told the reason, he protested that his chief purpose in coming to the city had been to hear the Moslem summons to prayer and they must not change their customs for his sake. As if to underline his respect for them, when he saw that a Christian priest had followed him into the Moslem sanctuary, he turned on him angrily and warned him never to trespass there again; in future such an offence would be punished by death. The astonished Moslems listened in silence; Frederick was a kind of Christian strange to them, and they did not admire him, despite his compliments. Being themselves faithful and convinced Moslems, they could understand and admire a faithful and convinced Christian; but they neither understood nor trusted this fat little German Emperor with his cold eyes, who disparaged his own religion and flirted with theirs without being committed to it. He was neither one thing nor the other, and what was the use of that?

News soon arrived that a Papal army had invaded Frederick's domain in Italy, and he decided to go home. On 1 May 1229 he left the Holy Land for good, moving down to the harbour at Acre before dawn in order to avoid the unwelcome attentions of the people of the city, who had learned to loathe him by this time; but someone had spread the news of his departure around the town, and the Street of the Butchers, through which he had to pass, was crowded with booing people, who pelted him with lumps of dung and pieces of offal. Some of the barons, hearing what they took to be a riot, hurried down to the scene to restore order; but Frederick knew that behind their bland faces and polite smiles they too hated him, and when they bade him a courteous farewell, he cursed them to their faces.

His achievements in Outremer proved ephemeral, but when he reached

17

Italy he had the satisfaction of routing the Papal army and forcing peace on the Pope on virtually his own terms; he was tactful enough to allow Gregory to save his face, however, and the wording of the Treaty of San Germano, which they both signed, was studiously respectful of the Papal dignity. In return, Gregory lifted his sentence of excommunication, and the brilliant, eccentric and somewhat unsavoury little German autocrat, who had been execrated by the Church for delivering Jerusalem from the yoke of the Moslems, was welcomed back into her ample bosom once more as her 'beloved son'. Frederick celebrated his restoration to a state of grace by arranging a great service of thanksgiving in Bitonto Cathedral; the sermon was preached by a certain Nicholas of Bari, who glorified the Emperor's majesty as divine and expressed the opinion that he should be treated as being on something very like equality with God. The evidence seems to show that, by and large, Frederick agreed with him.

XX

♣♣♣

The Noise of Horsemen

The whole city shall flee for the noise of the horsemen and the bowmen; they shall go into thickets, and climb up upon the rocks.

Jeremiah, 4, 29

At the time when Saladin's star was in the ascendant over Islam, another star was about to rise six thousand miles away over one of the remotest and most desolate landscapes of central Asia; it was a star whose baleful light was destined to increase in brightness until it both dominated and terrified the nations of the world from the China Sea to the Atlantic Ocean. In the year 1167, the wife of a petty Mongol chieftain named Yesugai gave birth to a boy in a tent pitched somewhere on the banks of the river Onon east of Lake Baikal and north of the Gobi desert. His father was away at the time fighting a tribe of Tartars, whose chief was named Temuchin. Having won the fight and killed his adversary, he returned in triumph to be told of the birth of his son; when he was taken to see him, the child was gripping a clot of blood in his hand, and for some obscure reason Yesugai saw in this a symbolic confirmation of his victory over the Tartar, and he decided to call the boy Temuchin after the dead man. At least, that is the traditional story. The child grew up in the austere world of the nomadic shepherds of the Asiatic steppes, where poverty, hardship and tribal warfare were commonplace, and the survival of the fittest was a fact of life. When he was nine years old, his father was poisoned, but thanks to the protection of his mother he survived until he was of an age to look after himself; this he proceeded to do with such savage and remorseless efficiency that in a few years he had achieved hegemony over most of the Mongol tribes, subduing them one at a time in a series of lightning wars. By the time that he was twenty-seven he was elected Khan of all the Mongols, and took the name of Jenghiz.

Jenghiz Khan has been called the Napoleon of the steppes. Physically he was a tall man, and it is said that he had eyes like those of a cat. He was a soldier of genius and a brilliant administrator; he was endowed with apparently limitless energy and great powers of endurance, and he had the kind of power to fascinate and dominate the men of his time which was also possessed by Alexander of Macedon and a handful of other individuals down the centuries: individuals who, perhaps fortunately for the rest of us, have always been rare. The measure of his achievement is that he created one of the largest empires the world has ever seen, and he did so during the course of only twenty-one years. It would have been an extraordinary feat for the ruler of a highly organised state with a long history of military prowess, but the Mongols were nomadic barbarians with no central government or organisation and a long history of petty tribal jealousy. Their one quality was toughness for, like the Huns before them, their way of life was hard; mounted on small horses as hardy as themselves, they led their flocks of sheep and goats, upon which they depended for their livelihood, to their traditional pastures, north in summer and south in winter, crossing deserts and mountains on the way and with very little food or rest and less comfort to sustain them. Having united these Mongol tribes into one nation under his rule, Jenghiz then used them to conquer the other nomadic tribes and clans around him, most of whom were Turkish, such as the Keraits, the Naimans and the Uighurs; those who resisted were either annihilated or conquered and enslaved, but those who submitted were allowed to retain their own hereditary tribal organisation under their own chiefs, subject only to the authority of the Great Khan himself, as Jenghiz came to be called.

At its peak his army was enormous. Historians used to speak of half or even three-quarters of a million men, but most scholars today regard such figures as exaggerated; even so, there were probably as many as three or four hundred thousand Mongolian and Turkish tribesmen, mounted on fast little horses and armed with bows and lances. They were organised in multiples of ten, a group of ten thousand forming a unit which could operate independently, and, with their mobility and speed, their complete disregard of danger, their indifference to death and their utter ruthlessness, a horde of Mongols on the march was both terrifying and, for years, virtually invincible. 'Even today,' one New Zealand historian, J. J. Saunders, has written, 'after a lapse of seven hundred years, there is something terrifying and awe-inspiring about this most frightful of all nomad assaults on civilised society...A vast drama was played out against an appalling background of blood and ruin such as the world had not seen since the days of the Assyrian massacres, and was not to see again until the Nazi exponents of genocide killed their millions in our own sombre age.' This is no exaggeration. In June 1222, the large and populous city of Herat in Afghanistan, which had revolted against its Mongol over-lords, was reduced after a siege, and its entire population of several hundreds of thousands of men, women and children was systematically slaughtered as a warning to other potential rebels; the killing lasted a week. Jenghiz Khan did not call himself 'the flail of God' for nothing; his ruthlessness was part of a deliberate policy of spreading terror before him, so that people whom he attacked were cowed by the mere mention of his name and ready to submit before he attacked them.

Having consolidated his rule over virtually all the nomadic tribes of eastern Asia, Jenghiz turned his attention to northern China; by 1215 he had conquered the Chin Empire with its capital at Pekin and, in the following years, he subjugated the other provinces and petty states of eastern Asia. In 1219 he turned westwards, invading the huge Moslem Empire of the Khwarismian Turks, which stretched from the river Indus to the Persian Gulf and northwards to Kurdistan and southern Russia; and despite the fact that the Moslem prince Mohammed Shah could put four hundred thousand men into the field, Jenghiz totally defeated him. The fall of these two great Empires sent a shiver of fear through the world, especially the Islamic world; for if such states as these, which everyone had regarded as all-powerful, were unable to defend themselves, what hope was there for smaller and weaker peoples? Christians tried to reassure themselves that they had nothing to fear, for it was widely believed that the Mongols were, if not Christians themselves, at least very favourably disposed towards Christians; but when they invaded the Christian kingdom of Georgia early in the new year of 1221, and utterly defeated it, Christians became as fearful as their Moslem enemies. Before he died, Jenghiz sent his army on a huge aggressive raid deep into southern Russia, where it destroyed a large Russian army on the banks of the river

Kalka and pillaged much of the Ukraine and the Crimea before retiring. Once again people tried to reassure themselves that this was only an isolated raid, which would not be repeated; and when news of Jenghiz' death in 1227 followed soon after it, they felt sure that the worst was over. They were wrong.

After two years of dynastic rivalry over the succession, one of Jenghiz' sons, Ogodai, became Great Khan in his father's place. It soon became clear to everyone that he meant to adopt the same policy of imperial expansion as that of his father, and that he would allow no liberties to be taken with his authority; some Chinese rebels were quickly chastised, and the Khwarismian Turks, who had taken the opportunity provided by Jenghiz' death to revolt, were brutally suppressed. In 1237 Mongol hordes invaded southern Russia once more, and a few years later they swept through the Ukraine and Poland, killing, looting and laying the country waste; they reached Liegnitz in Silesia sixty-five miles west of Breslau, where they routed the combined forces of the King of Poland and the Teutonic Knights of eastern Germany. Nothing lay between them and the countries of western Europe; but the Mongols turned southwards and devastated Moravia, Hungary and Croatia as far as the Adriatic coast, where news of the sudden death of Ogodai saved the rest of Europe from a similar fate. When the terrible invasion ebbed at last, and the noise of the Mongol horsemen receded into Asia, southern Russia was left under the domination of the Golden Horde as a reminder to the rest of Europe of the fate which it had so narrowly escaped.

The official religion of the Mongols was primitive; they were Shamanists, who believed that the world was peopled by a large number of good and evil spirits which could be magically controlled by the shamans or priests. But Nestorian Christians had spread widely throughout Asia during the preceding centuries, and many of them had acquired positions of importance in the Mongol Empire. Nestorianism had been condemned as a heresy in the fifth century for proclaiming the doctrine that in Christ there had been two persons, one human and one divine, while orthodox churchmen asserted that Christ was a single person with two natures; one might be forgiven for thinking that this theological difference between the early Nestorians and their orthodox opponents was more a matter of verbal definition than of grave religious substance, but no one thought so at the time, and the Nestorians were severely persecuted. In Asia, however, they had found sanctuary from their tormentors, and the Nestorian Church had flourished. Jenghiz himself had been inclined to favour these Nestorian Christians, and some of his sons had married Nestorian princesses from a Turkish tribe, the Keraits, who had been converted to Christianity two hundred years earlier. The ruler of the Keraits in Jenghiz' day was a man named Toghrul, who seems at one time to have taken the title Ong Khan, and it may have been a corruption of this to Johann that gave rise to the legend of Prester John, a great and powerful eastern king who was a Christian, and who would march westwards to the aid of his fellow Christians in their struggle against Islam.

The influence of the Prester John legend can hardly be exaggerated. Perhaps because it was just what Christians in the West wanted to believe, hardly anyone doubted that somewhere in the vast and unknown depths of Asia there was a Christian Emperor who would help them destroy Islam. A bishop of Acre wrote to the Pope at the time of the defeat of the Khwarismian Turks to tell him that the war in central Asia was being waged by 'him whom the people call Prester John'. As the years passed, the idea that this legendary hero might have died was gradually accepted, but the belief in the continuing reality of a great Christian power in Asia remained as firm as ever. Indeed, it was so strong that it was one of the main causes of the next Crusade, which was undertaken at least partly in order not to miss the opportunity of attacking Islam while such a powerful ally in Asia was available to help in its destruction. Since Louis IX of France was not only ready and willing to take the Cross but eager to do so as an act of thanksgiving for his recovery from a serious illness, the time seemed doubly ripe, and in August 1248 he sailed from Aigues-Mortes west of the Camargues, while his army of between fifteen and twenty thousand men embarked in the old harbour at Marseilles singing the old Crusader hymn *Veni Creator Spiritus*.

Nearly twenty years had passed since the Emperor Frederick Hohenstaufen had left the Holy Land to the jeers and insults of the people of Acre; they had been years of what has been called 'legalised anarchy', during which the ten years of peace ensured by Frederick's treaty with the Sultan were wasted in civil war, after which war had again broken out between the Franks of Outremer and their Moslem neighbours, reinforced by a large army of Khwarismian Turks who had escaped destruction by the Mongols. In the summer of 1244, ten thousand Turkish horsemen had swept down through Galilee and attacked Jerusalem, which had fallen to them after a short struggle, and which they had then mercilessly sacked. The loss of Jerusalem had been followed by a disastrous

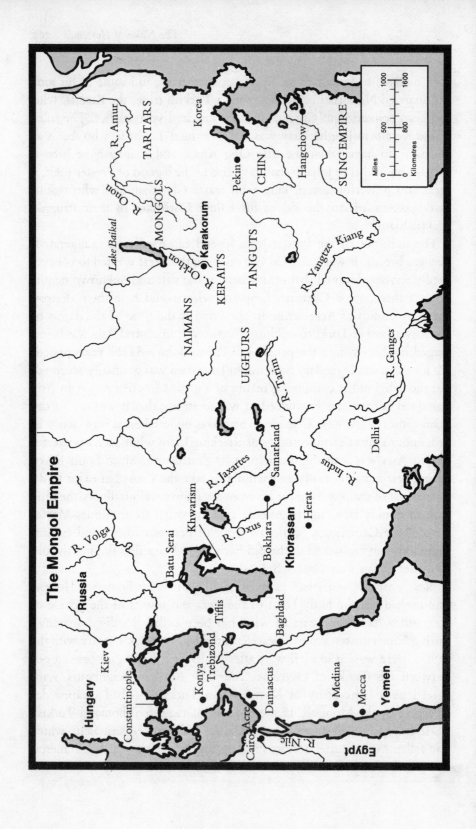

The Mongol Empire

battle at Gaza, when the Christian army had been badly defeated by a large force of Egyptians and Khwarismians; fortunately the victors had had troubles of their own, and bitter dissension in the Moslem camp had saved the Christians from complete annihilation. They had retired into their fortified coastal cities, where they had been able to hold out while their enemies turned from the attack to fight each other.

Louis IX was the son of Louis VIII and the grandson of King Philip Augustus; his father died when he was twelve years old, and his mother, Queen Blanche of Castille, whom he adored, became Regent during his minority. He grew up to be a deeply and genuinely religious man; even Voltaire considered that his subsequent canonisation was fully justified. He was thirty-four when he sailed for the East, a very tall young man, thin, fair-haired and slightly anaemic, but both physically strong and of immense strength of character. He has been described as the ideal king of the middle ages: an accomplished knight, fearless in battle, heroic in adversity, unbending when sure of the justice of his cause and as ascetic and devoted to the service of God as the most dedicated of monks or hermits. He fasted regularly, loved sermons, heard two masses a day and all the offices, getting up at midnight each night and dressing for Mattins in his chapel, and surrounded himself at all times, even when travelling on horseback, with priests chanting the hours. In manner he was gentle, charming to his friends and readily approachable by all men, but with all his virtues there was another side to his character, which is less appealing; occasionally, he gave vent to terrible outbursts of anger, and he could be severe to the point of intolerance with those whom he considered to be evil-doers. Moreover, he was an autocratic father to his children and a repressive husband to his high-spirited and rather jolly wife, Margaret of Provence.

Perhaps she had too much sense of humour for Louis. John of Joinville, the chief chronicler of the Sixth Crusade, tells a story which suggests as much.

You must know that the Queen had heard that I had been on a pilgrimage and had brought back some relics. I sent her by one of my knights four pieces of camlet [soft cloth of silk and camel's hair] which I had bought for her. But when the knight entered her apartment, she threw herself on her knees before the camlets which were wrapped in a piece of white linen. The knight, seeing the Queen do this, flung himself on his knees also. 'Rise up, my good knight,' the Queen said to him, 'it is not fitting for you to kneel when you are the bearer of relics.' 'Madam,' replied the knight, 'these are not relics, but pieces of camlet sent you by my lord.' On hearing this the Queen and her ladies burst out laughing. 'The devil take your lord for making me kneel to a parcel of camlets,' the Queen cried.

But Margaret's sense of humour was not the only thing which made her marriage to Louis difficult; the queen mother, Queen Blanche, was an impossible mother-in-law, if John of Joinville is to be believed.

Queen Blanche treated Queen Margaret so harshly that, in as far as she could help it, she would not allow her son to be in his wife's company...The palace in which the young King and his wife most liked to live was at Pontoise, because there the King's room was on an upper floor and the Queen's room just below it. They had so arranged matters that whenever the ushers saw Queen Blanche approaching they would knock on the Queen's door with their rods, and the King would run quickly up to his room so that his mother would find him there...The King was once by his wife's side, at a time when she was in great danger of dying from injuries she had suffered in childbirth. Queen Blanche came to her room, and taking the King by the hand, said to him, 'Come away, you're doing no good here.' Queen Margaret, seeing that the Queen Blanche was taking him away, cried out, 'Alas! Whether I live or die, you will not let me see my husband.'

Louis and the French fleet sailed to Cyprus, which they reached in mid-September. The King had laid his plans with care, and great quantities of wine and grain had been collected in the island to await his arrival and that of the army of Outremer which came to meet him there. It did not take Louis and the leading lords long to decided that their military objective should be the conquest of Egypt; it was the weakest link in the Moslem chain of defence as well as being a prize rich enough to tempt any conqueror. Louis wanted to invade at once, but he was persuaded not to risk putting to sea while there was still a possibility of winter storms, and the whole expedition settled down to spend the next few months in Cyprus. Just before Christmas, everyone was immensely excited by the arrival of two envoys from the Mongolian commander in Mosul with a letter full of compliments and expressions of support for the Christian Crusade against the Moslems. It was not the first time that contact had been made with the Mongols; Innocent IV, who had become Pope in 1243, had sent an embassy led by a Franciscan friar, John of Pian del

Carpine, to the court of the Great Khan in order to convert him to the true Catholic faith. After an adventurous journey across Russia and the steppes of Asia, he had reached Karakoram, where he had been courteously welcomed by the great man himself; but as soon as the contents of the Pope's letter were revealed, John was curtly dismissed with a message to the Pope ordering him to acknowledge the Great Khan as his suzerain and telling him to come and do him homage. Undaunted by this discouraging precedent, Louis greeted the Mongolian ambassadors warmly, and promptly sent an embassy of his own to the court of the Great Khan with instructions to seek a military alliance with him. A Dominican monk named Andrew of Longjumeau, who spoke fluent Arabic, was appointed as chief ambassador; and he duly set off on the enormous journey of over four thousand miles to the Gobi desert. But he had no greater success than John of Pian del Carpine; he was greeted kindly, his gifts were graciously accepted, and he returned with a letter suggesting that Louis might like to send a similar tribute to the Great Khan annually. The King was deeply disappointed, but he did not give up all hope of enlisting the aid of the Mongols in a war against Islam in the future. Meanwhile it was time for him to leave Cyprus and sail to Egypt.

This was easier said than done, for as usual there was a shortage of shipping; but by mid-May 1249 enough vessels had been collected to transport the army to the mouth of the Nile. A storm scattered them during the course of the voyage, and the King arrived with a few companions before the fleet could be gathered together again. They were expected, and the beach was defended by Moslem soldiers, but Louis refused to await the arrival of the main body before attempting to land; he disembarked with the men he had with him, and waded ashore to engage the enemy. There was a battle on the beach, but although the Franks fought at a disadvantage, some still floundering knee-deep in the sea, the first furious onslaught of the Egyptian cavalry was driven back, and they managed to establish a beach-head. Louis wanted to lead an immediate counter-attack, but cooler heads dissuaded him from running into unnecessary danger, and events soon proved their advice right. Fakhr ad-Din Ibn as-Shaikh, the Moslem commander, had been a friend of the Emperor Frederick II, and was getting a little old for military command in the field; seeing the failure of his cavalry charges, he ordered his men to withdraw into the safety of the walls of Damietta. But when he reached the city he found the citizens in a panic and, instead of rallying them, he decided to abandon them and the city to their fate. Seeing him march away the people of the place concluded that all was lost and streamed after him, carrying as many of their belongings as they could and leaving the bridge of boats over the Nile intact. When the Franks arrived a few hours later, they found the city deserted and the gates wide open; they could hardly believe their eyes; the Fifth Crusaders had taken fourteen long costly months to take Damietta, and all they had to do was to march across the bridge and take possession of it. It is not surprising that their first action on entering the place was to sing a *Te Deum* of thanksgiving for their victory

Louis had been lucky, and he had no intention of making Pelagius' mistake of invading Egypt while the Nile was in flood, so he settled down in Damietta to wait for the river to subside. It was the right decision, but it left the army at the mercy of idleness and the Egyptian summer, and neither did the Crusaders any good; food ran short, disease took its toll, and morale suffered. It was a relief when the waters of the river began to sink, and an even greater relief when the order was given half way through November to advance on Cairo. Reinforcements had recently arrived, amongst whom there was a small body of English Crusaders under the Earl of Salisbury and a larger number of Frenchmen under the King's younger brother, Alfonso of Poitou, and everyone was in high spirits as the army marched out of Damietta. As if once again to prove the partiality of God, the aged Sultan died three days later. He was a descendant of Saladin with the family name of Ayub, an unlovable man but a capable ruler, and his loss would have been a disaster for the Egyptians had it not been for the prompt action of his widow. The Sultana was much younger than her late husband; she had been born an Armenian slave, and her name was Shajar ad-Durr, which means Branch of Pearl. With the connivance of some of the palace staff and the ministers of state, including Fakhr ad-Din, she concealed the fact that the Sultan was dead; the Mameluks still came and went, edicts were signed, petitions were answered, the day-to-day business of government was discharged as though he were still alive, and no one outside the Sultana's small inner circle of friends guessed that old Ayub was in his tomb. When at last Shajar ad-Durr's secret was discovered, she and Fakhr ad-Din were too firmly in power to be dislodged, and the crisis which would have been caused by the Sultan's death had been avoided. Even so, when the Crusaders heard that Ayub was dead, they saw the hand of God in the demise of the commander of the hosts of Satan.

Louis' advance was cautious, for his way was criss-crossed by canals, and he did not mean to be caught off his guard as the army crossed one after another of these waterways. The enemy was entrenched behind the greatest of them, the Bahr as-Saghir, which was a branch of the Nile itself, and when the Franks reached it just before Christmas, Louis ordered them to make camp on its banks opposite the town of Mansourah. For six weeks the Crusaders tried to build a mole out into the river, by which they would be able eventually to cross it, but the Egyptians bombarded them with great stones and Greek fire as they worked, and although they retaliated in kind little progress was made. The Greek fire particularly terrified them. John of Joinville described it flying through the air 'like a great keg with a tail as long as a spear. The noise it made was like thunder, and it looked like a dragon...At night it gave so great a light that we could see objects in our camp as clearly as in the day.' This Greek fire wrought such havoc with the wooden siege engines and inflicted so many casualties that in the end the attempt to build the mole across the river had to be abandoned; another way to attack the enemy must be found.

It was provided by an Egyptian, who came to the camp and offered to show the Crusaders a ford across the Bahr as-Saghir if they would pay him five hundred bezants in advance. The man was as good as his word, and at dawn on Shrove Tuesday, 8 February 1250, Louis led the greater part of his army across the river, while the Duke of Burgundy guarded the camp. The crossing was slow, and although strict orders had been given that no one should attack the enemy until the whole army was across, one of Louis' brothers, Robert of Artois, decided to ignore them. Hoping to take the enemy by surprise, he led a charge of about fourteen hundred knights against the Egyptian camp, while the rest of the Crusaders were still fording the canal. At first, the attack was brilliantly successful. The Egyptians were taken completely off their guard; some were still asleep, others were half-dressed, and Fakhr ad-Din was having his beard dyed with henna after his morning bath, when the chivalry of France with the Knights Templar and the Earl of Salisbury and his men erupted at full gallop into their midst. Fakhr ad-Din was killed on the spot, and those who escaped the same fate fled in a panic towards the safety of Mansourah.

If Robert of Artois had waited for his brother Louis to join him at this point, as both the Grand Master of the Temple and William of Salisbury urged him to do, the history of the whole Crusade might have been different; but he refused to do so. Instead, having accused them both of cowardice, he galloped off after the fleeing Egyptians, and Salisbury and the Templars reluctantly followed him. It was a disastrous mistake; as the Christians knights poured into the narrow streets of Mansourah they became sitting targets for their enemies, who hurled pieces of furniture, heavy jars of wine or oil, and anything else which came to hand upon their heads, while others attacked them in the confined space of the town's narrow alleys, where their horses bucked and reared and snorted with fear and they had no room to manoeuvre. Only five of the two hundred and ninety Templar Knights survived; William of Salisbury and almost all his English followers were killed; Robert of Artois and his closest companions shut themselves up in a house, which they defended with courage and ferocity, but the odds against them were too great, and they were overwhelmed and massacred to a man.

News of this *débacle* in the streets of Mansourah was brought to Louis by a wounded survivor of the battle there, Count Peter of Brittany, in time for the King to draw up his men on the banks of the Bahr as-Saghir in readiness to meet the inevitable Moslem counter-attack, which was not long in coming; the Mameluks charged under cover of a volley of arrows, which killed or wounded a good many Frenchmen, but they were held, and Louis ordered a counter-attack by the heavy Christian cavalry. The battle ebbed and flowed all day, and no one had much idea of who was winning and who losing. John of Joinville, who fought in it, has left a description of the fighting as vivid as a series of old sepia-coloured photographs:

Frederick of Loupey had a lance-thrust between his shoulders, which made so large a wound that the blood poured from his body as if from a bung-hole in a barrel. A blow from one of the enemy's swords landed in the middle of Érard of Siverey's face, cutting through his nose so that it was left dangling over his lips. At that moment the thought of St James came into my mind, and I prayed to him...[the Moslems were]...slashing and striking [the Christians] with swords and maces, and gradually forcing them...back upon the river. The rout there was so complete that many of our own people tried to swim across the river to join the Duke of Burgundy, but they were unable to do so, for their horses were very tired, and they had become very hot. So, as we were coming downstream towards them, we saw the river strewn with lances and shields, and full of men and horses drowning in the water...Riding straight towards us, as we were holding the little bridge, came Count Peter of Brittany with a sword cut across his face from which blood ran down to his mouth. He was mounted on a very handsome pony, but he had thrown its reins over the pommel of his saddle, which he was gripping with both hands, for fear that his men, who were following him too close for comfort, might jostle him out of position as they crossed the narrow bridge. It would seem that he had a very poor opinion of them, for as he spat blood out of his mouth he kept exclaiming, 'Good Lord, did you ever see such scum!'

At the end of the day, both sides claimed the victory; the Egyptians, who retired in good order into Mansourah, claimed to have won by inflicting heavy losses on their enemies and preventing them from capturing the city, while the Crusaders considered that they were the victors, for they had killed Fakhr ad-Din and many of his men, destroyed their camp and won a foothold across the Bahr as-Saghir. But time was on the side of the Egyptians, and as the weeks passed it became clearer and clearer that, even if the Crusaders had not lost the battle of Mansourah, they were in danger of losing the war. The long-awaited revolution against the petticoat government of the Sultana in Cairo, which the Crusaders had both expected and anticipated, did not materialise; and by the end of February the late Sultan's son and heir, a young man named Turanshah, who had been eight hundred miles away acting as his Viceroy in the Jezireh at the time of his father's death, turned up in the Egyptian camp, having been proclaimed Sultan without falling out with his step-mother, Shajar ad-Durr.

His arrival spurred the Egyptians into activity, and a blockade of the lower reaches of the Nile was quickly organised. Most of the boats bringing supplies to Louis' camp were either destroyed or captured and, although a few continued to get through, food began to get scarce. In March a convoy of over thirty boats was captured; not one got away, and it became obvious that, if the Crusaders stayed where they were, they would starve. Indeed, there was already something very like a famine in the camp, and it was soon followed by outbreaks of typhoid and dysentery. In April, Louis was forced to admit defeat, and the retreat from Mansourah began. As soon as the Moslems saw their enemies leaving the camp below the city walls, they set out in pursuit. For the Crusaders it was a nightmare journey; most of them were either too tired or too sick to fight, and although Louis distinguished himself in command of the rearguard, which was the post of greatest danger, after the first day's march he fell so ill that on the morrow he could hardly stand. There was only one course open to those who took command in his place, and they surrendered.

With King Louis and the entire crusading army his prisoners, it is not surprising that the young Sultan Turanshah was elated by his victory. Indeed, he had so many prisoners that he did not know what to do with them; feeding such a host of captives was an embarrassment. He solved the problem of their numbers by the simple expedient of having three hundred beheaded each day; but although the King himself and the other nobles were regularly threatened with death unless they agreed to various demands, Turanshah was careful to execute only men of no importance, while preserving all those who might one day be ransomed for large sums of money. But he was not a tactful young man, and his days of triumph were short-lived; he offended Shajar ad-Durr, and he antagonised the Mameluks by treating them with a casual arrogance to which his father Ayub had never dreamed of subjecting them. Such behaviour was both foolish and dangerous, and when he also began to put some of his friends from the Jezireh into lucrative posts which the Mameluks had always thought of as being reserved for members of their own *élite* corps, he virtually sealed his own fate; they decided to get rid of him. He was murdered with great brutality after a banquet, and his mutilated body was thrown contemptuously into the mud by the side of the Nile as if it were of no more consequence than the corpse of a dog. A prime mover in Turanshah's murder was a senior Mameluk of Turkish origin named Rukn ad-Din Baibars Bundukdari, of whom the Crusaders were destined to hear a great deal more.

The murder of the Sultan, the last of Saladin's descendants to rule Egypt, made little difference to the captive Franks. A senior Mameluk took Turanshah's place, covering his naked usurpation of power in a cloak of legitimacy by marrying the redoubtable Shajar ad-Durr, and the Christians had to continue negotiations for their release with a new set of gaolers. They were in no position to dictate conditions, but they did hold one trump card: Damietta had not surrendered but was still in the hands of the garrison left there by Louis when the army had marched to Mansourah. The King's wife, Queen Margaret, had been left there too, for she was pregnant; and three days after the news of her husband's surrender had reached the city she had given birth to a baby boy. She was assisted in her labour only by an ancient knight, who, according to John of Joinville, was 'not less than eighty years old or perhaps more, and every time she screamed, he held her hands and said, "Madame, don't be afraid like this. I am with you." ' As soon as she had been safely delivered of her son with the help of this somewhat improbable midwife, she was told that the men of the garrison, led by the Pisans and the Genoese, were preparing to save themselves by flight while there was still time; sending for their leaders she pleaded with them to stay, offering to feed them all at her own expense if they agreed, and the combination of her courage and her generosity was sufficient to make them change their minds. Without her, the city would have been lost; as it was, King Louis at least had Damietta with which to bargain with the new Mameluk rulers of Egypt.

It was all that he had, however, and his enemies knew it. They exploited their advantage by every means in their power, keeping up a barrage of threats against Louis' life and those of their other captives. On one occasion some of them burst into the galley where the King and some of his leading nobles, including John of Joinville, were imprisoned; they had naked swords in their hands, they carried Danish battle axes on their shoulders, and they talked loudly of decapitating them all. John of Joinville was so unashamedly frightened that he fell to his knees, crossing himself and preparing to die, while the Constable of Cyprus, Guy of Ibelin, knelt beside him and made confession of his sins. John recalled how he had said to the terrified Constable, 'I absolve you with such power as God has granted me.' But Louis was not the man to be intimidated by such a charade, and the Mameluks were no more willing to lose the ransom money which they hoped to get for their valuable prisoners than Turanshah had been, so no one died. When the threat had passed, John of Joinville found that he could not remember a word of the Constable's hurried confession.

Eventually, a bargain was struck; Louis promised to pay the enormous ransom of 400,000 *livres tournois* for himself and his nobles and to surrender Damietta on condition that all captive Crusaders were released. He was urged to guarantee the treaty by promising to renounce his Christian faith if he failed to keep his side of the bargain, but he flatly refused to make such a promise, and his courage and integrity deeply impressed his captors. In fact, they came to admire his nobility of character and firmness of purpose so much that at one time they even talked of inviting him to become Sultan of Egypt, and it seems that the suggestion was not made entirely in jest; certainly Louis himself took it seriously enough to discuss it with John of Joinville, who advised him to refuse the offer if it was made, while the King was inclined to accept it. In the event, the offer was not made, and the only people who did not keep their side of the bargain were the Moslems. They had promised not to harm any Christians left behind in Damietta when the city was surrendered to them, yet the Mameluks massacred some Franks who were too sick to be moved when everyone else departed.

As soon as he was released, Louis returned to Acre, where he announced his decision to stay in Outremer, despite urgent pleas from his mother in France that he should come home. Although he attributed the disastrous defeat of his Crusade against Egypt to God's gracious desire to teach him humility, he was very conscious of its cost; many thousands of lives had been lost, while Outremer had been rendered almost defenceless, and his conscience would not allow him to desert it in its hour of need. In fact, its need was less desperate than might have been expected, for the revolution by the Mameluks in Egypt and the murder of the Sultan Turanshah, Saladin's grandson, had not been well received by other members of the Ayubid dynasty, who still ruled in Damascus and elsewhere. They declared war on the murderers of their kinsman, plunging the Moslem world back into a chaos of divisions and conflicting ambitions. Louis was statesman enough to take advantage of these quarrels between his enemies, who vied with one another for his support, and far-sighted enough to see that the future lay with Egypt; as a result, he eventually made an alliance with his old adversaries, the Mameluks, in return for which all remaining Frankish prisoners were released and Louis was allowed to forget half of the enormous ransom he had promised to pay.

After four years as the undisputed ruler of Outremer, during which time he repaired the fortifications of Acre, Haifa, Caesarea and Jaffa, and made a close alliance with the Assassins, while still trying to forge links with the Mongols, Louis was forced by events at home to return to France. He sailed from Acre on 24 April 1254, and after a journey beset by dangers of one kind and another he reached France safely in July; but the Holy Land was in his blood, and he never forgot it. Each year he sent some money to maintain a small body of French troops there, and he dreamed of returning on another Crusade; but troubles at home made it impossible until it was too late. In 1267, when Louis was fifty-four years of age and failing in health, at last he felt free enough to prepare for another eastern adventure. Preparations for it took a long time, however, and he was not ready to sail until 1270. What would have happened if he had reached Outremer will never be known, for he was persuaded by one of his brothers, Charles of Anjou, to sail against the Emir of Tunis before proceeding to the Holy Land. Charles was a fiercely ambitious man with political designs upon the Hohenstaufen domains in southern Italy and Sicily, and he was at war with the Emir of Tunis as one stage in furthering his Mediterranean plans. He persuaded Louis that the Tunisian ruler was ripe for conversion to the Christian faith, and that a show of force would probably be enough to win an ally of supreme importance in the continuing struggle between Christians and Islam. Against the advice of friends like John of Joinville, Louis allowed himself to be persuaded. He sailed from Aigues-Mortes with a large army on 1 July, and dropped anchor near the site of the old city of Carthage eighteen days later at the height of the African summer, in unbearable heat. Disease spread through the Christian fleet like wildfire, and when the Count of Anjou arrived a week later, Louis was dead. It is said that, as he died, his last words were, 'Jerusalem, Jerusalem!'

XXI

♣♣♣

A Mirage of Great Bastions

Another excursion from Haifa is to Acre, seen across the bay
like a far-away mirage of great bastions.

Nagel's *Guide to Israel*

With the coming of the Mameluks to power in Egypt, the days of the
Franks in the Holy Land were numbered. The castles and fortified cities,
which had been built at an enormous cost of dedication, energy and blood,
were soon to enter their final destiny and become the mirage of a romantic
past for the enjoyment of tourists. At the time, however, when Louis
sailed away from Acre in the spring of 1254, the idea that a palace revolution in Cairo by a bunch of slaves could possibly have so disastrous an
effect on the fortunes of the Christians in Outremer would have been
rejected as absurd. Had they not survived Saladin, and countless other
disasters in the past?

But the Mameluks were more ruthless than Saladin; indeed, their
whole training was designed to make them so. In origin they were Turkish
slaves, who were bought as children and brought up to be soldiers, very
much as, later, the Janissaries were to be trained from childhood for the
same purpose by the Ottoman Sultans. They grew to manhood knowing
no family ties and having no feelings of patriotism, but entirely dedicated
to the service of their master, with whose fortunes their own were
intimately linked; if he prospered, they basked in his reflected glory, and

he rewarded them with riches and power; if he was worsted by his enemies, they shared in his downfall or eclipse. When they were old enough to fight, many of them were given their freedom, but this made little difference to them; there was little if any social stigma attached to slavery, and by the time that they became free men their training and circumstances had already bound them more securely to their master than any legal obligation could possibly have done. They were his men: a personal bodyguard upon whose loyalty he could entirely rely, especially if he treated them well. But inevitably, as their power grew, so the danger of their becoming a law unto themselves, like the Roman Praetorian Guard before them, grew too. All was well while the Moslem army was commanded by a majority of Kurdish officers; but as the years passed the Sultans came to rely more and more upon their Turkish troops, who became indispensable to them, and, as a *corps d'élite*, the Mameluks soon realised that they and not the Sultans wielded the power, a fact which the young Sultan Turanshah discovered too late when he was foolish enough to offend them. His place was taken by a man named Izz ad-Din Aibek, a senior Mameluk, and with his fellow Mameluks behind him no one had the power to challenge his seizure of the Sultanate. Fortunately for the Christians of Outremer he was not a very aggressive or a particularly formidable man. But ten years after the murder of Turanshah another Mameluk, who had taken a leading part in that killing, Rukn ad-Din Baibars Bundukdari, became Sultan, and Baibars was very formidable indeed.

Almost more threatening to the survival of the Christians of Outremer was the change which had imperceptibly come over the Franks themselves. Both they and their society were different from those of the earlier days of the Crusader kingdoms. It has been suggested that the failure of the Crusade led by St Louis was responsible for a loss of self-confidence amongst the Christians of both East and West. Whereas it had always been possible to put down their past failures to the wrath of God incurred by their sins, Louis was so patently a good man that it was impossible to explain his failure in Egypt in this way; the alternative was to conclude that God was no longer on the Crusaders' side. Whether people thought like this or not, certainly enthusiasm for making war on the Moslems was more difficult to arouse at this time than it had been in the past, although their bellicosity was in no way diminished, for they still spent most of their time fighting; but now they seemed to prefer fighting each other to waging war on Islam. Almost as soon as Louis had sailed for home, a bitter little civil war had broken out in Outremer over the ownership of a monastery dedicated to St Sabas, which stood on a hill between the Venetian and the Genoese quarters of Acre. The Pisans took sides with the Venetians, and so did the Templars, the southern French, and the powerful Ibelin family; while the Hospitallers and one or two of the most powerful nobles in the land supported the Genoese. There were bloody battles in the streets of Acre, battles at sea between the rival Italian fleets, and battles for the few cities remaining in Frankish hands in the rump of what used to be Outremer.

It was insane, but no one was strong enough to stop it, for there was no central government worthy of the name. Shortly after the departure of St Louis, the Emperor Frederick's son, who had been the nominal King of Jerusalem since Frederick's death, died; his two-year-old son duly became head of the house of Hohenstaufen, and was acclaimed as King Conrad III of Jerusalem in his father's place. But the infant King did not take physical possession of his new realm; he remained at home in his Italian kingdom tended by his nurses, and Outremer was left without a head. The nobles did their best to rule the country, but by this time they wielded little real power and were unable to control the various tightly organised factions which vied with one another for political pre-eminence. Chief amongst these were the men of the various Italian city states, who were constantly at one another's throats. They controlled the country's commerce by controlling the seas with their fleets; and they fought one another for control of the trade between western Europe and the countries of the eastern Mediterranean, Christian or Moslem, regardless of the fortunes of their fellow Christians in Outremer. The only other groups with anything like the same power as the Venetians, the Genoese and the Pisans were the Military Orders, which hated one another with almost as much venom as did the Italians. Like the Italians, too, they were rivals, they were rich, they were militarily stronger than any individual noble or noble family, and they were completely ruthless when it came to defending their own selfish interests. It was only when these were threatened by the struggle for power which was developing between the Mongols in the north and the Mameluks in the south that the Franks stopped fighting one another in order to avoid being crushed between the two.

When Louis left Outremer in 1254, the Mongols were ruled by a man whose mother was a devout Nestorian Christian; his name was Mongka, and he himself married a Christian girl. He had three brothers, and the huge Mongol Empire was divided between them, Persia falling to the lot of the third brother, Hulagu, who also married a Christian. The Franks were understandably delighted to hear how favourably the Mongol government looked on Christianity, although they were somewhat startled to discover how different were the manners of the Mongol Christians from those of their brothers and sisters in Christ in the West. Devout Christian though she may have been, the Great Khan's mother apparently did not consider it unseemly to return from High Mass one Sunday morning so hopelessly drunk that she could hardly stand up: a spectacle which not unnaturally astonished William of Rubruck, a Dominican monk who had been sent to her son's court as ambassador by King Louis. But the Franks were happy enough to overlook the Mongols' peculiar ideas of decorum as long as they continued to destroy one Moslem power after another, as they had been doing ever since the days of Jenghiz Khan. Indeed, in 1254 the Franks of Antioch made an alliance with them, as the Christian Armenians had before them.

The alliance was directed against the Moslems, and the wisdom of it seemed to be proved as the Franks watched Hulagu, the Great Khan's brother and Ilkhan of Persia, at the head of an enormous army of Mongols, first destroy the old Moslem sect of Assassins and then move on to capture Baghdad and massacre eighty thousand of the city's inhabitants; only the Christians, huddled for safety in their churches, were spared. Time had not softened the ferocity of the Mongols, and Hulagu himself seems to have been as bereft of compassion and kindness as the rest of his race. He was an unattractive man who suffered from epileptic fits, but he had some pretensions to learning and a certain taste for philosophy, even if this academic bent did nothing to deter him from ordering his troops to do terrible things.

After the massacre of the citizens of Baghdad, the virtual destruction of the Abbasid Caliphate, and the murder of the Caliph, Hulagu moved on westwards against the terrified Moslems of Syria, who did their best to avert his wrath by sending envoys to his camp with orders to promise almost anything that was demanded of them. Those who stood in his way were treated with calculated and almost incredible brutality; the ruler of one city, who was foolish enough not to surrender to him, was forced to eat flesh cut from his own body until he died. Aleppo was Hulagu's first objective, and although it was defended with courage and determination, it held out for less than a week before falling to the attackers; once again the citizens were massacred almost to a man, the

Christians alone being exempt from the slaughter. Damascus was the next to succumb, and it did so without a struggle, although a few brave souls defended the citadel. The majority of the Damascenes were too terrified of the consequences of resistance to fight for their city, and the gates were thrown open for Hulagu and his allies, the Princes of Antioch and Armenia, who had by this time joined his triumphal advance. The price they paid for sharing in the Mongol's victory, however, was to become in effect his vassals. In order to please its Greek inhabitants, whose importance the Ilkhan knew well, the Prince of Antioch was ordered to replace the Latin archbishop of Antioch with a Greek Patriarch.

While the Franks in Antioch and northern Syria made common cause with the Mongols, some of the Franks in Acre were less pleased by their coming. The Venetians in particular enjoyed a near-monopoly of trade with Egypt, through which much of the far-eastern trade with Europe flowed by way of Venice; the last thing they wanted was for that trade to be diverted northwards along the caravan routes to the Black Sea ports controlled by the Byzantines, with whom the Genoese were on much better terms than they were themselves. There were others as well as the Venetians who were unhappy when they heard of the triumphant progress of the Mongols; many Franks who had no commercial interests to defend did not relish the prospect of becoming vassals of the Great Khan. For years they had learned to live side by side with their Moslem neighbours in a well understood condition of armed hostility; sometimes they were at war with them, and at other times a truce was observed by both sides. Life under such conditions had become so normal that everyone knew just where he stood, whether at war or not; but no one knew what life would be like if the Mongols were to destroy the last stronghold of Islam in Egypt, a prospect which began to look increasingly probable as Hulagu advanced southwards, and the Franks feared that the change might be for the worse.

Meanwhile there had been changes in Egypt too; the first Mameluk Sultan Aibek had been foolish enough to quarrel with his wife Shajar ad-Durr, a highly dangerous thing to do, as he had discovered soon enough, for on her orders he had been murdered by one of his own eunuchs while he was in his bath. But for once the lady had over-reached herself; some of Aibek's fellow Mameluks were so incensed by his death that they rose in revolt against the Sultana. A struggle had followed in which the rebels had proved too strong for Shajar ad-Durr, and in the early summer of 1257 she was beaten to death. Aibek's teenage son was made Sultan, but he proved so ineffective that he was replaced by another Mameluk, Said ad-Din Qutuz, who came to power just before the clash between the Mongols and the Egyptians could no longer be avoided. A Mongolian envoy came to Cairo to demand the submission of the Egyptians, and this was a message to which any Mameluk could have but one reply; Qutuz murdered the Mongol ambassador, and prepared for war.

The ifs and ans of history are dangerous, but the temptation to wonder what might have happened, had not an unexpected event changed the balance of power between the two sides at this particular moment, is irresistible; for after Hulagu had issued his challenge to the Mameluks, news reached him of the death of his brother, the Great Khan Mongka, and of a power struggle in Asia for the succession. He felt obliged to march eastwards with a large part of his army, to defend the frontier of his Ilkhanate against a possible attack by one of the contenders for Mongka's place. If Mongka had not died just at this moment, Hulagu would have met the Mameluks with his entire army, and the issue could hardly have been in doubt; he would have won, destroying the last remaining bastion of Moslem power in the East. The history of the world might have been very different as a result. As it was, however, the Egyptians who marched north into Syria outnumbered the depleted Mongol army and were a good deal stronger than their enemies. Moreover, the Mameluks moved with such speed after murdering the Mongol envoy that Hulagu's men were taken by surprise, and one of their outposts at Gaza was overwhelmed and destroyed by the Egyptian vanguard under the command of Baibars. In the absence of Hulagu with the main body of the army in Persia, the Mongols were commanded by a general named Kitbuqa, who marched south down the Jordan valley to meet the Egyptians moving north up the coastal road. An Egyptian ambassador was sent ahead to Acre to ask permission to pass through Frankish territory, and also to invite the Franks to join them in the coming battle against the Mongols. Some of the hastily assembled lords of the Franks were in favour of accepting the invitation on the principle that the devil you know is better than the devil you don't, but the Grand Master of the Teutonic Knights and others did not favour the idea; they advised caution and, in the end, the Egyptians were allowed free passage through the country but were given no military support. The Sultan Qutuz and his army spent a few days under canvas in the country just outside Acre, and he and some of the senior Mameluks were invited into the city, where they were treated as honoured guests. Baibars was one of them, and he noticed how easily the place might be captured, if it were to be attacked unexpectedly; but although he suggested to the Sultan that there was no time like the present, Qutuz refused to be tempted, and Acre was left inviolate.

On 3 September 1260 the two armies eventually met at Ain Jalud. It was in Moslem country, and the local people had told the Egyptians that the Mongols were approaching in time for Qutuz to lay his plans with care; since his army was the larger of the two, he had the double advantage of superiority in numbers and surprise, and he was not the man to throw them away. He hid the main body of his troops in the hilly country round the Pools of Goliath, where the Franks had successfully defied Saladin four years before the battle of the Horns of Hattin, and he ordered Baibars to take the vanguard out to meet the approaching Mongols and to lure them into the trap. Kitbuqa, who does not seem to have sent scouts ahead of him or to have had any idea that he was about to encounter the enemy, was duly deceived by the sight of Baibars and his men, whom he charged with great dash and *élan*; Baibars duly retreated in well-feigned panic into the hills with the Mongols in hot pursuit, and led them neatly into the ambush. As usual, the Mongols fought with great courage and ferocity, but they had no chance of winning the battle; a few fought their way out to safety, but the great majority were killed, while Kitbuqa was captured after his horse had been killed under him. Dragged captive before the victorious Sultan, Qutuz chose to mock and insult him. Courageously, the Mongol replied that the Mameluks' triumph would be short-lived; they would be crushed like vermin, for only vermin murdered their masters as the Mameluks did, while he was at least a man of honour. Furious, Qutuz ordered a guard to strike off his head. It is difficult to love the Mameluks.

Kitbuqa's posthumous revenge was not long in coming. He had taunted Qutuz with the treacherous record of the Mameluks, and less than two months after his death the Mameluk Sultan was himself murdered by one of them. As a result of his victory at Ain Jalud, the whole of Syria had fallen into Qutuz' hands, and various highly desirable government posts became his to dispose of. Baibars asked to be made governor of Aleppo, but by this time Qutuz had begun to distrust him; he was becoming too powerful for the Sultan's liking, and he roughly refused to grant his request. Baibars said nothing, but a few days later, when the army was encamped on the edge of the Nile Delta, he accompanied

Qutuz as he went out for a morning's hunting with a few colleagues. When the little party was well away from the camp, one of them approached the Sultan and, as if he were about to ask a favour, took his hand to kiss it; but instead of doing so, he held it firmly, while Baibars rode up behind Qutuz and stabbed him in the back. The little party of murderers then galloped back to the Egyptian camp and announced the death of Qutuz, Baibars claiming the honour of killing him. Whereupon, as if to prove how right Kitbuqa had been in his estimate of Mameluk morality, he was unanimously acclaimed as Sultan.

His seizure of power was bad news for the Franks; he hated them for siding with the Mongols, as they had in Antioch, and he had seen their weakness when he was their guest at Acre; so that it was not long before he announced his intention of driving them into the sea. Physically, he was an enormous man, dark-skinned, red-haired, with one blue eye and one white one, which had been blinded and occluded by a scar. It is said that when he was first offered for sale as a young slave in Syria, no one would buy him because he looked so coarse and boorish, and he would have remained unsold if a senior Mameluk had not bought him; but if the story is true, his appearance belied him, for although he was indeed coarse, he was also highly intelligent. Indeed, he was a brilliant statesman and an equally gifted soldier, and the fact that he was totally devoid of morals made him even more formidably dangerous. As it was, he was completely unscrupulous, not hesitating for a moment to resort to murder, treachery or perjury, when it suited him.

At first the Franks had high hopes that Baibars would prove to be grateful for their help before the battle of Ain Jalud; but when they tried to negotiate the return of some Christian prisoners still in Egyptian hands, he bluntly refused. They persisted, however, and shortly after Christmas in 1263 a man named John of Jaffa, who seems to have got on well with the new Sultan, succeeded in arranging the release of the prisoners in exchange for some Moslems held captive in Outremer. It was something of a diplomatic triumph, and conceivably it might have ushered in a new era of co-operation with Baibars, but the chance was thrown away by the two great Military Orders for purely selfish reasons. Both the Templars and the Hospitallers refused to release the Moslems in their possession, because some of them were skilled craftsmen and therefore valuable to them; and nothing anybody said about the common good made the smallest difference to their decision. Even Baibars was shocked; but he did not allow this rare attack of moral indignation on his part to affect the speed of his response. He told John of Jaffa to go home, and he invaded Frankish territory. Having sacked Nazareth, he marched on Acre, where there was a battle below the walls in which people on both sides were killed and the suburbs of the city were destroyed; satisfied for the time being, he then retired.

Fighting continued sporadically all through the year 1264, but it was mostly on a local level. Early in 1265, however, Baibars marched north with a large Egyptian army to deal with the Mongols in northern Syria, who were showing signs of renewed aggression. But unfortunately for the Franks, before he had reached them, he received news that they had been dealt with by the troops on the spot. Baibars quickly changed course, marched on Caesarea and, one morning in late February, appeared in full strength below the city walls to the total surprise of the terrified inhabitants. The citadel held out for a few days, when its defenders capitulated on being promised their freedom. Baibars razed the place to the ground, and marched on Haifa, whose people were less lucky than the citizens of Caesarea; a few escaped by boat, but the rest were slaughtered, and their city was destroyed. The Sultan did not wait to see the work of demolition completed; he marched on the greatest of all the Templar castles at Athlit and laid siege to it. It proved too strong for him. Reluctantly abandoning the siege, he turned on Arsuf, which was defended by nearly three hundred Knights of St John, who fought with their customary sublime courage; but in this instance Baibars proved the stronger, and after a third of the Hospitallers had been killed, the remainder surrendered, having been promised their freedom. They had not yet learnt how little credence should be given to the Mameluk's promises, and not one of them was freed. His next objective was Acre; but by this time his depredations had so alarmed the Christian world that King Hugh III, who had been in Cyprus when news of Baibars' devastating victories had reached him, had arrived in Acre with a Cypriot army which was numerous enough to strengthen the place greatly, and Baibars, deciding that enough was enough, returned to Egypt. He could always come back another year.

The death of the Ilkhan Hulagu in 1265 and the inevitable dynastic squabbles for the succession which followed rendered the Mongols more or less impotent for the time being and left the Franks without the support of their one potentially powerful ally against Baibars: a fact of which the Mameluk meant to take full advantage. While Hulagu's son was trying to establish himself in his father's place, the Sultan led two armies across the Sinai in the summer of 1266; with one of them he invaded Galilee, while the other marched north against the Armenians. At first, Baibars himself had little success; Acre proved too strong for him once again and, when he invested the Templar castle at Safed, it too held out against him. But by some skilful propaganda he managed to create a rift between the Syrian soldiers inside the fortress and the Knights Templar; the Syrians began to desert in such large numbers that the Knights were forced to treat with Baibars, who promised them their freedom in return for the castle. They agreed, but as soon as they had kept their side of the bargain, Baibars had every one of them beheaded. This brutal act of calculated treachery seems to have whetted his appetite for more blood, for it was followed by a campaign of sheer terror in which he set out to kill any Christians he could find, whether they happened to be Franks or native Palestinians living in the villages which had been theirs since Byzantine days. Meanwhile, in the north, the other Mameluk army, commanded by a man named Qalawun, attacked the little Armenian kingdom in Cilicia and laid it waste; having slaughtered thousands of its citizens, Qalawun retired with forty thousand captives whom he intended to sell into slavery.

Two years later Baibars decided to attack Antioch. He appeared below its formidable walls in May 1268, and it took him less than a week to breach them; the massacre which followed is said to have shocked the Moslems themselves. Baibars ordered the gates to be closed, so that no one might escape, and an orgy of systematic killing followed. When the Egyptian soldiers were so tired that they could no longer summon up the strength to kill any more people, even children, the Antiochenes who had somehow survived were distributed amongst their conquerors as slaves, and the accumulated riches of centuries was divided among them as loot. When the news reached Acre, the Christians there were appalled; Antioch had been the first great city to fall to the Crusaders, apart from Edessa, and its loss after nearly two centuries of Christian rule was a shattering blow. Almost unbelievably, however, it was not shattering enough to deter the Venetians and the Genoese from fighting a miniature war for the control of the harbour at Acre; both traded extensively with Egypt, and the disasters which had recently befallen them had not yet persuaded them to unite against the common enemy in order to survive; the old crusading spirit seemed to be dead at last.

But it was not wholly dead in Europe. Louis tried to come to the aid of the Christians of Outremer, but died in front of Tunis instead. The following year, in 1271, the heir to the English throne, Prince Edward, arrived in Acre shortly after Baibars had inflicted another crushing blow on the Franks by capturing Krak des Chevaliers, the great fortress which had defied even Saladin. He brought only about a thousand men with him, but Baibars was so impressed by the news of his arrival that he retired once again to Egypt. Edward, who was a clear-headed, able and somewhat chilly man, was appalled by what he found on arrival in Outremer; for he soon discovered that the Venetians were the Sultan's main suppliers of war materials, while the Genoese were fully engaged in the Egyptian slave trade, and that neither would consider for a moment giving up their lucrative commerce with the common enemy. Indeed, such was their power in the affairs of the country that the High Court of Acre had even given them licences to trade with Egypt in whatever ways they liked. It was both ridiculous and infamous, but it was a fact.

Edward remained in Outremer for eighteen months, but he did not achieve much. However, he did succeed in persuading the Mongols to take a hand again, now that their internal troubles had been settled, and Hulagu's son, Abaga, had taken his father's place. A large force of Mongol cavalry raided northern Syria, where they defeated the Moslems defending Aleppo; but the raid was soon over, and they turned for home before meeting Baibars, who was at Damascus with the bulk of the Egyptian army. Meanwhile Edward himself led a raid into enemy territory, but he was not strong enough to do much more than prove a nuisance to the Moslems there. After a year he realised that he could do nothing without reinforcements from Europe, and he decided to seek a truce with Baibars. This suited the Sultan, who knew that he could destroy the little kingdom round Acre whenever he chose to do so; first, however, he wanted to deal with the Mongols, and peace with the Franks would give him the time he needed to cope with these much more formidable enemies. Edward's approaches were therefore well received, and to everyone's relief a truce was signed on 22 May 1272; it was to last eleven years. But Baibars had no intention of allowing the English Prince to return home and raise a new Crusade, if he could prevent it, and he hired an Assassin to murder him. Disguised as a native Christian, the man asked to see Edward, and stabbed him with a poisoned dagger. Though seriously wounded, the Prince did not die; he was ill for months, during which time Baibars hastened to deny any complicity in the crime and to congratulate Edward on his escape and, eventually, his recovery. He sailed for home on 22 September, only to find on arrival that his father had died, and that he was the King of England.

Five years later, in 1277, Baibars attacked the Mongols and their clients, the Seljuk Turks of Cilicia. At first he carried all before him; but his success was his undoing, for Abaga was sufficiently alarmed to march against him with a large Mongol army, and he was forced to retreat. By July he was dead. It was rumoured that he had died of drinking some poisoned *kumiz*, the highly intoxicating fermented mare's milk beloved of both Turks and Mongols, which he himself had had prepared for an enemy and which he had drunk by mistake. But however he may have died, it is difficult not to conclude that his death left the world a marginally better place; for although no one has ever been able to deny that he was immensely able and talented, even his admirers have had to admit that he was an evil man.

Although his death was extremely welcome to the Franks, it made little difference to their fate, for he was succeeded by Qalawun, who was just as determined to eliminate them from Palestine as Baibars had been. Such a prospect should have frightened the Franks into some sort of unity, but it did not do so; instead, another civil war broke out which tore the little country in half, and left it bleeding and weakened by self-inflicted wounds. Bohemund VII, the titular Prince of Antioch and the last of a great house, quarrelled with some of his cousins of the Embriaco family over who should marry a local heiress. The Hospitallers took sides with Bohemund, while inevitably the Templars fought alongside the Embriacos, largely out of hatred for their rivals of the Hospital. Each side did terrible things to the other, until in the end Bohemund proved the stronger, and his enemies were forced to surrender to him, which they did on being promised their lives. But as soon as the surrender was complete, Bohemund broke his word, killing the majority of his helpless captives, and burying his three Embriaco cousins up to their necks in a ditch, where he left them to die of thirst and starvation.

Even Bohemund's friends were shocked by this act of needless brutality, and his enemies were appalled; the bitterness which divided the little kingdom was exacerbated, and the last chance of reconciling the warring factions, while a little time remained, was thrown away. The last chance of rescue by the Mongols had been missed too; for when the Ilkhan Abaga had sent ambassadors to Acre to propose a military alliance against the Mameluks, the Franks had, with almost incredible stupidity, made a treaty of peace with Qalawun instead; only the Hospitallers had refused to be bound by it. Thus when the Mongols invaded Syria in 1281 in the hope of destroying the last great Moslem power east of Morocco, only a handful of Hospitallers came to their aid as they marched south to meet Qalawun. He was waiting for them just outside the city of Homs. In the battle which followed, the Knights of St John, few as they were, routed the left wing of Qalawun's army, and chased them all the way back to their camp; but things went less well for their Mongol allies, who were forced to retreat. Qalawun had lost too many men to take advantage of his victory, and the battle decided nothing. It is impossible to be sure what would have happened if all the Franks had been engaged instead of only a handful of Hospitallers; but it is difficult not to believe that their additional strength would have made all the difference, and that Qalawun might well have been destroyed.

Four years later, in 1285, Qalawun decided to deal once and for all with the Hospitallers, and he laid siege to their northern stronghold, the great castle at Marqab. It held out for weeks, even though it was defended by no more than twenty-five knights aided by local Christian mercenaries; but in the end some Egyptian engineers managed to drive a mine deep beneath its battlements, and the fate of the castle was sealed. When one of its principal bastions collapsed, the Knights agreed to abandon it in return for their freedom. They rode out on horseback fully armed, and the rest of the garrison marched out behind them, while the Egyptian soldiers stood by silently and watched them go. To modern ears, it sounds rather noble and romantic, but the loss of Marqab was a grievous one, which the Franks could ill afford, and it deeply alarmed them.

However there was little they could do about it. They badly needed reinforcements from Europe, but Europe was too busy with its own quarrels to take much interest in events in Outremer. The Franks turned, therefore, to Cyprus, offering to make the island's King, Henry II, King of Jerusalem as well, if he would come to their aid. He agreed and, on 15 August 1286, Henry was crowned in the Cathedral of Tyre. Although he was a boy of only fourteen years, his youth did not greatly trouble his new subjects; his mother had been an Ibelin, and they knew that he would be well guided by his Ibelin uncles, who were both liked and respected by most people. The Franks might have been less happy if they had known that their new monarch was an epileptic, but as yet the symptoms of his disease had not shown themselves; all they saw, when he arrived in Acre after his coronation, was a handsome boy with charming manners, and they were delighted. Despite the external threat to the very existence of the little country, for a fortnight Acre celebrated the coming of its new King, and the citizens were *en fête*; they filled the days with games and

19

tournaments, and no one dreamed of going to bed until the small hours of the morning. In the evenings they feasted and danced; the night air was filled with the sound of laughter and music, and pageants were staged so that members of the nobility might take part in their favourite historical romances. When it was over, on the advice of his uncles the new King returned to Cyprus, while his subjects were forced reluctantly to return to reality and take part in the grim and unromantic drama which was beginning to unfold around them.

Fortunately for them, the worst threat to their existence came to nothing. In 1282 Abaga, the Ilkhan of Persia had died. He was succeeded by his brother Tekudar, who had not been in power for long when he announced his conversion to Islam, took the name of Ahmed, and sent ambassadors to Cairo with orders to conclude a military alliance with Qalawun. If he had succeeded, the immediate end of Outremer and the Franks would have been certain, but he did not succeed. His own subjects, many of whom were Nestorian Christians, were so appalled by his religious *volte face* that they murdered him, and in 1284 he was succeeded by his nephew, a young man named Arghun. The new Ilkhan Arghun was not a practising Christian himself but he made it known that he favoured Christianity, and that he wanted to ally himself with the Christians against the Moslems of Egypt. He made diplomatic approaches to both the Franks of Acre and Pope Honorius IV, but with little success. A Mongol ambassador to the Emperor in Constantinople, which had been recovered by the Byzantines by this time, fared little better, although he was warmly welcomed; and when Arghun went on to approach the French and English kings, the same thing happened: he was greeted most warmly, but neither king would commit himself to joint action against Qalawun. Thus the last chance of saving Outremer was lost, and in all probability the last chance of the Mongol Empire becoming a great Nestorian Christian power in Asia was thrown away too.

In the spring of 1287 an earthquake shook much of northern Syria, and the walls of the Christian port of Lattakieh were badly damaged. Despite the fact that Qalawun was at peace with the Franks, the chance was too good to miss, and he ordered the commander of his forces in the area to attack the city. It fell with hardly a struggle, for the garrison was a small one, and the Franks farther south were unable to send help because the Genoese, with almost incredible irresponsibility, were fighting a naval war with their rivals the Pisans and the Venetians. They launched a full-scale attack on Acre, which they failed to capture, although they defeated

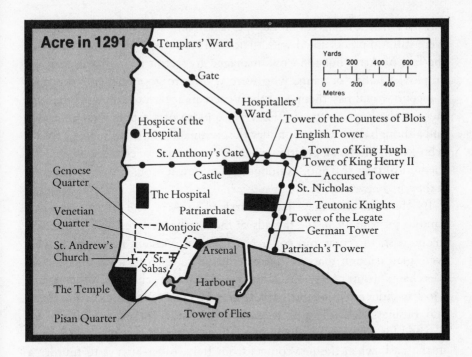

Acre in 1291

Templars' Ward
Gate
Hospitallers' Ward
Hospice of the Hospital
Tower of the Countess of Blois
English Tower
St. Anthony's Gate
Tower of King Hugh
Tower of King Henry II
Genoese Quarter
Castle
Accursed Tower
St. Nicholas
The Hospital
Venetian Quarter
Patriarchate
Teutonic Knights
Tower of the Legate
Montjoie
German Tower
St. Andrew's Church
St. Sabas
Arsenal
Patriarch's Tower
The Temple
Harbour
Pisan Quarter
Tower of Flies

Yards
0   200   400   600
0   200   400
Metres

the combined fleets of their enemies just outside the harbour. Two years later, it was the turn of Tripoli to fall to the Moslems. Its capture was brought about by a piece of equally incredible fecklessness on the part of the Venetians, who were competing with the Genoese for control of the city's commerce; rather than allow the place to fall into the hands of their rivals, they actually invited the Sultan to intervene and help them secure it for themselves. Qalawun was only too pleased to be given such a perfect excuse for breaking his truce with the city. He sent a huge army against it and, although the inhabitants defended it with great courage, they were vastly outnumbered and, on 29 April 1289, it was taken by assault. A few of the defenders escaped by sea; the rest were either killed or sold into slavery. The Sultan then ordered his men to raze the place to the ground so that it might never again be occupied by his enemies.

There could be little doubt in the minds of any of the remaining Christians in Outremer that Acre would be next on the Sultan's list, and they eagerly made peace with him, while sending urgent messages home begging their fellow Christians in the West to help them before it was too late. After some initial resistance, Qalawun agreed to another truce, which was to last for ten years, and the people of Acre sighed with relief;

but they had less success in Europe. The Kings of France and England were still too preoccupied with their own troubles to worry much about the fate of Acre, but the Pope managed to recruit a small army of un-employed Italian peasants, who were willing to go anywhere as long as someone would pay them, and the Venetians agreed to transport them to Acre at the Pope's expense. They were more of a rabble than an army, and although they were put under the command of the Bishop of Tripoli, who knew the local situation well, his authority over them was more theoretical than real and, as things turned out, it would have been better if they had never left Italy.

By the time that these Italians arrived in Acre, the citizens had had time to pick up again the threads of their ordinary lives and, as so often in the past, to renew old contacts with their Moslem neighbours, who were glad enough that the coastal cities were open to trade once again. Merchants from Aleppo, Damascus, Jerusalem and the other great Moslem cities crowded the marketplaces of Tyre, Sidon, Beirut and Acre, and business flourished; it seemed that a new era of prosperity had dawned for Christians and Moslems alike. But, as had happened so often in the past, when the newcomers from Italy, eager always to murder a Moslem or two for the love of God, found Christians hobnobbing with great crowds of Moslem merchants, they were incensed; they had come to fight Moslems, not to sit by and watch them become rich. They insulted them in the streets; they got drunk in the evenings and attacked them; and, when they had been there for about three weeks, they suddenly ran riot through the city, killing everyone who looked like a Moslem. The men and women of Acre were horrified, and their leaders were appalled but, apart from saving a few Moslems by hiding them in their houses, there was little they could do to stop the carnage; when it was over, some of the ringleaders were arrested and punished, but the damage was done. When Qalawun was told of the butchery, he decided that it was time to drive the Christians into the sea.

He made his preparations with care, and they could not be concealed. Rumours that he was raising a massive army in Egypt and another in Syria reached the Franks of Outremer, and someone told the Templars that these troops were going to attack them, but most of the Franks refused to believe it; the Sultan was still bound by the terms of the truce which he had made with them, and they did not think that he would go back on his word. This optimism seemed to be justified when news reached them towards the end of 1290 that Qalawun had died suddenly.

As usual, his death was followed by plotting and counter-plotting by contenders for the vacant Sultanate, and the Franks enjoyed a few months' respite until Qalawun's son, al-Ashraf Khalil, secured his inheritance by eliminating all rivals; but the lull before the storm did not last long. Overt preparations for war continued in Egypt and Syria, and the citizens of Outremer were forced to realise the imminence of an attack. Once again, urgent appeals for help were hurriedly sent to Europe, while every available fighting man was gathered in Acre in readiness for the coming battle, which no one could now doubt was impending.

So, on 5 April 1291, when al-Ashraf appeared below the walls of Acre at the head of an army so huge that eye-witnesses spoke with awe of a quarter of a million men, he found the city gates closed and its walls manned. The fortifications were formidable, but the defenders were vastly outnumbered. It is unlikely that the Sultan commanded as many troops as was thought at the time, but even so he had brought two armies with him, one from Damascus and the other from Cairo, together with a vast array of heavy siege weapons; while the entire population of Acre numbered no more than about forty thousand people including women and children. Amongst the defenders were men from England, France and Italy, and almost the whole strength of the three great Military Orders, the Templars, the Hospitallers and the Teutonic Knights, was mustered there. The Genoese were absent, for they had concluded a separate peace treaty with the Sultan. The Christians had only one advantage over their enemies; they commanded the sea, and food was brought to them regularly from Cyprus. Even so it was necessary to be as economical in the use of both food and water as possible; and so each time a ship returned empty to Cyprus, some of the women and children of Acre were put aboard and taken to the island and safety.

As always, the Christians fought with great bravery. The nature of the crisis was so desperate that they forgot their own quarrels at last to unite against the common foe; but courage alone was not enough to stop al-Ashraf's vast army of engineers from both battering and undermining the city's walls and towers. From the moment that the siege began, on 6 April, the fortifications of Acre were subjected to an incessant and devastating bombardment; great mangonels hurled new-fangled devices consisting of stone or pottery jars filled with explosive at the walls, while archers kept up a deadly attack on their defenders, shooting clouds of arrows at them and filling the air with the thin, high-pitched whistle of their flight feathers and the hearts of the stoutest Christians with the fear of sudden death descending from the sky. The engineers, of whom there seemed to be swarms, began to sap and mine the towers which formed strong points at intervals along the outer wall of the city: the Towers of King Hugh, King Henry II, and St Nicholas, the English Tower, the Tower of the Countess of Blois, the Tower of the Papal Legate down by the sea near the harbour, and the Patriarch's Tower beside it to give it covering fire; the German Tower and the Accursed Tower on the inner wall could not be attacked until the outer wall had been breached, and that was not very long in happening. Despite the fact that the Franks hit back at their enemies with some success, bombarding their camp with missiles hurled by a great catapult mounted on board one of their ships, and attacking them when they were asleep in their tents in a series of daring raids, after a month the walls of the city had been so weakened that they began to crumble and collapse, and so did the great Towers one after another.

On Friday, 18 May, al-Ashraf ordered a general assault upon the city So long after the event, it is difficult to recreate in the imagination what it must have been like to stand on the walls of Acre that morning as the dawn was splintered by the din of the Moslem host as it advanced to the attack. The air would have been full of the blaring of trumpets, the neighing of horses, the insistent beat of drummers mounted on camels urging their fellow countrymen on to death or glory, the battle cries of Nubians, Egyptians, Turks, Kurds, Syrians and Bedouin tribesmen, the crying of Imams and dervishes in prayer for the destruction of the impious enemies of God, the terrible swishing of arrows, the crash of exploding missiles, the shrieks of the wounded and the rattle of men dying. What did all these sounds do to the hearts and minds and adrenalin glands of the men from Kent, Provence, Venice and Pisa as they stood to their posts and buckled on their armour?

The outer wall had already been so badly damaged that it was to all intents and purposes indefensible, and it fell early in the day. This freed the Christians to concentrate their efforts on preventing the enemy from breaching the inner wall, but al-Ashraf's men were so numerous that they attacked along its whole length, thus forcing the defenders to spread out from one end to the other. Even so, it became clear that the Moslems were making special efforts to carry the Accursed Tower, sending wave upon wave of *élite* troops led by senior officers in white turbans against it, regardless of the casualties inflicted on them. So fierce and incessant was their attack that the defenders suffered badly; as men were killed or wounded, others took their places only to become casualties in their turn, and it looked as though the battle for the city would be won or lost in the fighting around the Accursed Tower. The Templars and the Hospitallers came to the aid of the defenders, fighting shoulder to shoulder as though they were blood-brothers rather than bitter rivals, but even with their help the Tower was lost. The Grand Masters of the two Orders immediately led a furious counter-attack, but although the knights fought with the kind of selfless and exalted courage which was always characteristic of them at their best, they were greatly outnumbered and could make no headway. William of Beaujeu, Grand Master of the Temple, was killed, and John of Villiers, Grand Master of the Hospital, was badly wounded, while the knights suffered heavily; and in the end they were driven back.

The loss of the Accursed Tower sealed the fate of Acre. The Moslems spread out from it along the inner wall of the city, and although they were held to the north, they carried the Gate of St Nicholas to the south, and their troops poured in and began to invade the streets, fighting their way through the city's labyrinth of alleys and squares. Those Christians who could do so made their way to the harbour in order to escape by sea while there was still time, but there were not enough ships to evacuate everyone from the doomed city, and something very like panic gripped the people on the quay. Many women and children had already left the place, but others had stayed, and now they fought with exhausted soldiers and frightened priests for places in the rowing boats and little yachts which were ferrying people from the quay to the waiting galleys off-shore. Some of these small craft became so over-loaded that they capsized and sank, drowning their passengers, while the masters of others exploited the law of supply and demand to good effect as they asked and received enormous sums of money from those who could afford to purchase their lives by agreeing to pay the extortionate fares demanded of them. A Spanish Templar, who had fought with exemplary courage during the battle for the city, made a fortune by blackmailing noble women into giving him their jewels and other valuable possessions in return for a passage to safety in his galley. Those who either could not or would not pay a similar price were left behind to be slaughtered by the conquerors, or sold as slaves in the markets of the Islamic world.

The other Frankish cities soon suffered the same fate as that of Acre. Tyre, which twice successfully defied Saladin, fell without a struggle. Sidon was defended for a time by a small group of Templars; but the odds against them were absurdly large, and eventually they sailed away from the place to join some other members of their Order in the castle at Tortosa. Beirut was the next to succumb, and Haifa fell a few days later. With the rest of the mainland gone, the Templars were not numerous enough to defend all three of the isolated castles remaining in their possession; they abandoned Tortosa and Athlit in order to concentrate on defending the fortified island of Ruad, which they managed to hold against all attacks in splendid if useless defiance of the victorious Moslems, until they were forced by the persecution of their own Order at home in France to abandon even that last, tiny, symbolic toe-hold off the coast of what had once been Outremer. Meanwhile, al-Ashraf was so determined to prevent the Christians from ever returning that he gave orders that the land should be laid waste. Orchards and vineyards were cut down, irrigation ditches destroyed, villages razed to the ground and towns dismantled until they were fit only to be the homes of a few ragged peasants and their mangy dogs.

But it is impossible to erase all traces of a civilisation and its people; and if the Sultan succeeded in discouraging the return of the Franks to the Holy Land for which they had fought so long and so hard, he failed to efface the marks that they had made on it during two hundred years of occupation. Many of their castles still stand on their rocky pinnacles as monuments to the splendour of their military architecture; and churches like that of the Holy Sepulchre in Jerusalem and the Cathedral at Tortosa are as splendid as any Gothic buildings in the West. But perhaps the thing which most aptly sums up both the fate and the faith of the Crusaders of Outremer is an inscribed stone in the wall of a building at Acre. Today it is a mosque, the Djami er-Ramel, but it was once a Christian church, and at some unknown date a Crusader, whose name has not been recorded, paid a stone mason to carve an exhortation on one of its stones. To the Moslems who pray there today the Latin words mean nothing, and few tourists from the West understand them; yet there they stand, a mute memorial to the way of life and death of the man who caused them to be cut in the stone and to those of many thousands of others like him: 'To men who pass along this street, I beg you pray for my soul.'

Select Bibliography

Select Bibliography

It is customary to include a bibliography in any book of history, but a history of the Crusades must cover the records of so many nations during the course of over two hundred years that any bibliography, if it is to be even remotely adequate, must necessarily be very extensive; one modern history of the period includes a list of reading matter covering forty-six pages. Since any such thing would be wholly inappropriate here, no attempt has been made to compile a bibliography worthy of the name; but since, too, some people may be interested in reading more about the Crusades, the titles of a few easily obtainable books on the subject are listed and briefly described below. Although one or two of them were originally published in German or French, all are available in English, and some of them have bibliographies of their own for the attention of those who may be interested.

RUNCIMAN, STEVEN. *A History of the Crusades*, 3 vols. Cambridge, 1968. The best comprehensive modern history of the period. Its length should daunt no one, for it is never dull.

MAYER, HANS EBERHARD. *The Crusades*. Oxford, 1972. Another good general history of the period, but much shorter than Runciman's.

PRAWER, JOSHUA. *The Latin Kingdom of Jerusalem*. London, 1972. A social history of the principal Crusader kingdom in Outremer, its institutions, and its various ethnic groups.

SMAIL, R. C. *The Crusaders in Syria and the Holy Land*. London, 1973. Another social history of the kingdoms of Outremer with particular attention to the arts of the period.

SMAIL, R. C. *Crusading Warfare 1097–1193*. Cambridge, 1956. A study, as the title suggests, of the Crusaders' armies and their methods of waging war.

BOASE, T. S. R. *Castles and Churches of the Crusader Kingdom*. Oxford, 1967. The best short study of the architectural achievements of the Crusaders, well illustrated by maps, drawings and photographs, many in colour.

JOINVILLE AND VILLEHARDOUIN. *Chronicles of the Crusades*. London, 1963.

Geoffrey of Villehardouin's *The Conquest of Constantinople* and John of Joinville's *Life of St Louis*, contemporary records respectively of the Fourth Crusade and of Louis IX's Crusade against Egypt, translated into English and available in Penguin Classics.

SOUTHERN, R. W. *The Making of the Middle Ages*. London, 1953. Perhaps the best account of the general social, religious and intellectual background to the Crusades.

EVANS, JOAN. *Life in Medieval France*. London, 1925. A more localised account of the background to the Crusades in France, the principal crusading nation.

OSTROGORSKY, GEORGE. *History of the Byzantine State*. Oxford, 1968. The best one-volume history of Byzantium.

VASILIEV, A. A. *History of the Byzantine Empire*, 2 vols. Madison, 1952. Another excellent general history of the Byzantine Empire, the second volume of which is concerned with the period of the Crusades and their effect on Byzantine fortunes.

CAHEN, CLAUDE. *Pre-Ottoman Turkey*. London, 1968. An admirable history of a much neglected subject by an eminent French scholar and authority on all things Islamic. He describes the culture and civilisation of the Seljuk and Danishmend Turks and their relationship with their neighbours, Byzantines, Crusaders, and Mongols.

Index

Index

20